E:
with Li
Insurance

a Wolters Kluwer business

4th Edition

Glenn R. Stephens, LL.B.

CCH Canadian Limited
300-90 Sheppard Avenue East
Toronto Ontario
M2N 6X1
1 800 268 4522
www.cch.ca

Published by CCH Canadian Limited

Edited by:
Simon B. Gallimore

Library and Archives Canada Cataloging this publication
  Stephens, Glenn R., 1954–
    Estate planning with life insurance/by Glenn R. Stephens.

Includes index.
ISBN 1-55367-953-0 (4th edition)

1. Insurance, Life — Canada.   2. Estate planning — Canada.   3. Income tax — Law and Legislation — Canada.
I. CCH Canadian Limited   II. Title.

HG9010.S84   332.024'01   C2005-905680-0

Typeset by CCH Canadian Limited.
Printed in The United States of America.

DEDICATION

This book is dedicated to my wife, Deb, who enjoys being married to an author but wonders why, if this book is good enough to merit a fourth edition, the royalties have not permitted us to retire, to my son, Matt (long live Radiohead, REM (again) and Ipods with seemingly unlimited memory), to my daughter Katie (long live Camp Tawingo, the Golden Gaels, hockey of all kinds and pretty much all hockey players — especially Mats, Vinnie, Marty, Alex, and J.T.).

ACKNOWLEGEMENTS

As with the previous edition, I would like to acknowledge the significant contributions to this book made by my friend and colleague of more than twenty years, Kevin Wark, LLB. Kevin designed the Fact Finder found in Chapter 1, contributed significantly to the commentary on leveraging in Chapter 8 (part of which originated with a paper he presented at the Ontario Tax Foundation Conference in 2004), and helped in a variety of other ways.

I am also grateful for the contributions of my other PPI colleagues, including Chris Ireland, Peter Everett (*Vah! Denuone Latine loquebar? Me ineptum. Interdum modo elabitur.*), Jocelyne Gagnon, Peter Merchant, and Melanie Zimmerman. There is much to be learned from a group of this calibre and I'm hopeful that at least some of it has found its way into this edition.

I would also like to thank Federated Press and Advocis for allowing me to use material originally written for Insurance Planning and FORUM, respectively.

Finally, I would like to acknowledge and thank Knight Ed (the "E Train") for his invaluable copy editing services in the early chapters of this book. I am hopeful that he will read beyond page 36 of this edition.

PREFACE

Since the first edition of this book in 1999, periodic changes in tax laws plus my desire to revamp certain areas of the text have led to new editions. Significant changes were made in the second edition resulting from the reduction of the capital gains inclusion rate to 50% in 2000. The third edition featured a lot of new material on leveraging, charitable giving, and critical illness, plus revised material on family business succession and shareholders agreements.

The fourth edition considers relevant changes in tax and other laws that have arisen since the third edition was published in 2005. It also has a few new topics as well.

The following is a summary of some of the key new material in this edition:

- Significant changes to the taxation of dividends were introduced in 2006, and much tinkering has taken place since then. These are described in Chapter 2, although they are referred to elsewhere in the book where appropriate (especially in Chapter 6, which deals with shareholders agreements).

- Chapter 2 also contains new commentary on refundable dividend tax on hand (RDTOH) and the small business deduction, both of which are important in corporate insurance planning, and discusses the increase of the capital gains exemption to $750,000.

- Income tax changes in the area of charitable giving seem to be an annual event and each edition of the book provides an opportunity to discuss a number of new planning possibilities. Chapter 9 of this edition features new sections on gifting publicly-traded securities to charity (and related life insurance opportunities). It also deals with an important change in CRA policy, announced in 2007, allowing a charitable receipt for the fair market value of a donated life insurance policy.

- Chapter 4 has a new section on the increasingly common and attractive strategy of having an individual sell an insurance policy to his or her corporation for fair market value.

- Chapter 5 contains some new and some revised commentary on estate freezes, and on the use of corporate-owned life insurance to redeem shares in a family business succession context.

- Chapter 6 has a new section dealing with buy-sell agreements for partnerships, with a special emphasis on partnerships with corporate partners (a business structure that is becoming more popular). Chapter 6 also has some new buy/sell related case studies, as does Chapter 12, which discusses disability buyouts.

- The federal *Bankruptcy and Insolvency Act* has been amended to provide more equality in the area of creditor protection for registered plans. This is discussed in Chapter 11.

Numerous other smaller changes and additions have been made throughout the various chapters.

The book is primarily intended for those who sell insurance products to business owners, executives and other high net worth individuals. As with the previous editions, throughout this book I will use the terms "insurance professional", "insurance advisor", "agent" or "broker" to describe the individual involved in selling insurance to the client. These different terms are intended to be synonymous.

By necessity, this book will contain a lot of income tax related material. It is not, however, intended be an income tax or estate planning text. The income tax information provided is intended to be of sufficient detail that it will help the insurance advisor understand how insurance products can best be used in client situations.

Like the previous editions, this edition will contain references to relevant sections of the *Income Tax Act* (Canada), and will also identify some pertinent CRA publications. These will be found at the end of each chapter. It is hoped that these references will be helpful to those interested in a more in-depth investigation into these issues, particularly accountants and lawyers who are being asked to advise clients but may not be familiar with some of the peculiarities of the taxation of life insurance.

Inevitably, as with the earlier editions, post-publication income tax changes will render certain portions of this book out of date, but it is hoped that there will be sufficient information of a practical nature that the book will serve as a useful reference even as new legislation and case law come along.

Glenn R. Stephens, LL.B.
Toronto, Ontario
June 2008

TABLE OF CONTENTS

Chapter 1

The Role of the Insurance Professional in the Estate Planning Process

This chapter of the book has changed little throughout the first three editions, and there will be few changes in this edition as well. Most other chapters have been updated one or more times as tax and other laws have changed over the years. New chapters have been added and others enhanced as new ideas and approaches come to mind. But this chapter, which is more about process than it is about actual strategies, remains intact simply because the insurance professionals role in the process is still the same.

Canada's top insurance professionals continue to find success in the estate planning market and, like most successes, they rarely occur overnight. Significant investments of time allow the best agents not only to close existing cases but to make themselves referable for future cases. This is critical, as referrals from lawyers and accountants are the lifeblood of the most successful life insurance practices. And in most cases the professionals from each of the three disciplines (and sometimes others) are involved in

1

the process and must work together to bring it to a conclusion that meets the client's needs.

This chapter will discuss the role of the insurance agent in the various stages of the estate planning process. The process is broken down into five stages, identified as Fact-Finding, Determination of Client Objectives, Analysis and Recommendations, Implementation and, finally, Follow-Up. Many cases will break down neatly into these various stages, while others will take on a life of their own and defy any kind of categorization. Nonetheless, this analysis should provide a framework for helping the insurance professional understand his or her role at various points in an estate planning case.

1. Fact-Finding

It is impossible to make even the simplest planning recommendations, or at least to make proper ones, without first having done a thorough job of fact finding. The insurance agent's greatest talent is motivating his or her client to act. Facts provide you with the ammunition to play the role of catalyst, a role to which you are best suited. While the lawyer and accountant may provide information during this stage, the insurance advisor, hoping to build a large case, will be the main gatherer of relevant facts.

The accumulation of facts sounds like a rather benign process, but it should not be taken for granted. Clients are often unaware as to what facts may or may not be important, or may be unwilling to disclose confidential information. Insurance agents with little or no experience in affluent markets may not know what questions to ask, and missing bits of information can cause the best laid planning to founder.

(a) Hard Facts

Most experienced insurance advisors are accustomed to collecting basic "hard" data regarding their clients. These data include:

- personal investment assets and liabilities;
- real estate holdings;
- registered retirement savings plans (RRSPs) and pension plans;
- corporate assets and liabilities;
- ownership structure of the family business;
- age, citizenship and marital status of family members;
- information regarding which family members are, and which ones are not, involved in any family business; and
- details of existing life, critical illness and disability insurance coverage.

Any information relating to the client's investment assets, or to shares held in private corporations, should include an estimate of the assets' fair market value. It is this amount, less the adjusted cost base (usually called the "ACB") of the property, that may be subject to tax on the client's death. Life insurance may ultimately be a means of paying this estimated tax liability. This will be dealt with in a later chapter.

The fact-finding process should also include a review of legal and financial documentation relating to the client's affairs. These might include wills, shareholders agreements, trust agreements, marriage contracts, financial statements, net worth statements and tax returns. Ultimately, these documents can be effective sales tools for the knowledgeable advisor. Here are a few reasons why it may be worth the extra effort to gather and analyze this information:

- The more you read and can understand these documents, the more respect you will earn from the lawyers and accountants with whom you must work. These other professionals will see you more as a business advisor and less as a salesperson. This will in turn make it more likely that they will refer clients to you.

- You will be better able to explain to your clients whether their existing legal arrangements meet their current objectives.

- You may help correct misconceptions which your clients have regarding the status of their affairs. Less sophisticated clients may, for example, believe that they have a shareholders agreement when, in fact, they have nothing but an old, unsigned draft.

- Lawyers and accountants are not necessarily experts in the area of life insurance. Mistakes abound, particularly in the drafting of shareholders agreements. Many lawyers, though admittedly not all, will appreciate your commentary regarding those portions of shareholders agreements which deal with insurance issues. This type of collaboration, while not always possible, can be of great benefit to your clients. A later chapter will provide a detailed discussion of how an insurance professional should approach the analysis of a shareholders agreement.

This chapter includes an estate planning fact-finder intended to assist insurance professionals in gathering the necessary information. See the appendix at the end of the chapter.

(b) Soft Facts

Hard data alone is often insufficient as a basis for making estate planning recommendations. An estate planning blueprint prepared on the basis of pure financial information may fail because the planner did not uncover or adequately consider the soft facts. These relate primarily to the family dynamics which are so critical to estate planning, especially for business owners. Here are some crucial soft-fact questions:

- Who gets along with whom, and who does not?

- What do the parents think of their children's abilities? Does each parent feel the same way?

- What is the state of sibling rivalry in the family? Will it worsen if one or more children inherit a disproportionately large share of the estate, such as the family business?

- Whose marriage is in trouble?

- What power struggles are going on?

- Who claims to be the decision maker in the family and who really is? How does this family make decisions?

- Is this family functional? Can the various members communicate effectively with each other?

- How prepared are the parents to back away from the business while they are alive and give the children greater responsibility?

- Are the children compatible and mature enough to manage the family business when their parents are no longer involved?

No matter how brilliant an estate planning proposal might be, it will fail if the intended participants are unwilling to let it work. Knowledge of the peculiarities of a client's family will increase the chances that a successful plan can be implemented.

2. Determination of Client Objectives

The second stage of the estate planning process, although it may take place almost simultaneously with the first, is to determine what the client wishes to achieve. Again, the main driver of this process is the insurance agent, who will help the client articulate his or her objectives through ongoing meetings and discussions.

Where the client in question is the owner of a family business, these estate planning goals can themselves create a seemingly impossible task for the estate planner. Consider the following typical list of objectives that might be articulated by a business owner:

- providing adequately for survivors;
- keeping the business in the family;
- maintaining the value of the business;
- maintaining family harmony;
- minimizing tax on death; and
- providing for retirement.

The problem is that, in many cases, these objectives are mutually exclusive. For example, tax may be minimized on death by having shares of a business corporation transferred to the business owner's spouse, or to a special trust for the spouse. However, this may do nothing for family harmony if the spouse knows nothing about the business and interferes in decisions which might be better made by children or non-family management personnel who have assumed the decision-making role from the deceased business owner. Business value can also suffer in the long run if these difficulties worsen over time.

Another objective which may be difficult to achieve is providing adequately for all survivors when only some family members are to be involved in the management and ownership of the business. In other words, even though the business may have significant value, where it comprises the majority of the estate of the deceased, it cannot necessarily be relied upon to provide for all of the survivors.

The art of estate planning, for business owners especially, is to balance these various objectives and devise an estate plan that is as fair as possible to everyone and causes a minimum of resentment amongst surviving family members. The best plan is not necessarily the one that results in the greatest tax savings. And since this is an area that may require much larger doses of common sense and people skills than it does technical know-how, there is no reason why a capable insurance agent cannot play a leading role at this stage of the estate planning process.

3. Analysis and Recommendations

Once the available information has been gathered and the client's goals have been correctly identified, it is necessary to analyze the data and recommend the required planning steps. By the time this stage is reached, the client's lawyer and/or accountant will usually have become involved. In most cases, it is the accountant who will be more actively involved in charting the specific planning direction, particularly if there is significant income tax planning to be done. Lawyers may also be participants at this time, or may sit on the sidelines until there is legal work to be performed.

In the ideal situation, the insurance professional, lawyer and accountant will work as a team in analyzing the available information and recommending to the client steps which might be taken to accomplish the stated objectives. Obviously, the agent's primary role at this stage is to make the necessary recommendations regarding how much and what kind of life insurance and related products the client should be considering. Tax planning and legal advice are best left to the other professionals, although a knowledgeable agent can also make contributions in these areas.

It is at this stage that there is the greatest likelihood of conflict between the agent and the client's other advisors. Differences of opinion will frequently arise regarding matters such as the amount and kind of insurance. Accountants unfamiliar with, or unimpressed by, the attributes of universal life may, contrary to the insurance agent's recommendations, suggest term insurance to the client. On other occasions, accountants may loudly trumpet the advantages of permanent insurance. Every situation and every advisor is different. Experienced agents will learn how to work with other professionals. They must do so, or they will not succeed in the estate planning market.

During a particularly sensitive meeting in the recommendations phase of an estate planning case, a client was overheard making the following remark to his legal advisor: "My insurance agent doesn't trust my accountant because he gets paid by the hour and my accountant doesn't trust my insurance agent because he earns a commission". While there is no sure way of avoiding conflict with the client's other advisors, and while mutual suspicion amongst professionals will never disappear, there are some basic rules which insurance professionals should keep in mind when dealing with lawyers and accountants:

- If you have not worked with a client's lawyer or accountant before, make yourself known to them at any early stage. Make it clear that you do not work alone and will be relying on their help when it is needed.

- Always treat the client's other advisors with professional respect. Communicate with them regarding what you are proposing and why, even if this is just as a matter of courtesy.

- Never present an estate planning solution to the other advisors if you have not first asked them for their input. The team concept requires that all the professionals should have an opportunity to make recommendations. Other professionals will not accept your recommendations, no matter how valid, if it appears that you are excluding them from the planning process. Remember that on most occasions your suggestions will either proceed or be dismissed on the basis of recommendations from the client's other advisors, and in particular, the accountant.

- Never assume that the other advisors know anything about life insurance. In many cases, your client's lawyer and accountant will be looking to you for all of the insurance details, even to the point of asking for your views on the drafting of clauses in a shareholders agreement which deals with life insurance. The majority of lawyers and accountants will understand their own limitations and seek your advice regarding unfamiliar insurance concepts. Other lawyers and accountants, unfortunately, assume that their expertise knows no limits and this can frequently become the greatest obstacle to solving problems.

- Never assume that the client's advisors do not know anything about life insurance. The last thing you want to do is offend another professional by appearing condescending or by patronizing them. Try to determine, in a diplomatic way, the level of the other advisors' insurance expertise if you have not previously worked with them.

Clearly every case and every agent is different, and what works in one situation may not work in another. As a rule, however, good relationships with other professional advisors are critical if an agent is to be successful in the business insurance market, because it is typically these relationships which make an agent referable. A successfully implemented estate plan can benefit the client and can be lucrative for the professionals involved. Properly handled, it is a classic "win-win" situation.

4. Implementation

The implementation stage normally involves the preparation of documents by the client's lawyer to put into place the plan authorized by the client. These documents might include any one or more of wills, powers of attorney, trust agreements, shareholder agreements and miscellaneous corporate documents.

While the lawyer will be the most involved professional at this point, the agent's participation will continue. Most importantly, it is hoped, there will be insurance applications to be processed. Attention to detail is critical in the preparation of documents and the placing of the life insurance. For example, if the case involves the funding of a shareholders agreement with life insurance, the insurance professional should ensure that the ownership and beneficiary designations under the relevant insurance policies are consistent with the agreement. Believe it or not, there have been numerous situations where ownership of the policies has been inconsistent with what was anticipated under the shareholders agreement. This is usually the result of a communication breakdown between lawyer and insurance agent.

As noted previously, lawyers and accountants frequently have limited insurance knowledge and may even assume that the agent is handling all relevant details regarding the insurance policies. Communication among the various professionals is essential to ensure that the insurance is properly placed and that silly, but costly, mistakes are avoided.

Once implementation is complete, lawyers and accountants are trained to report to their clients on the various transactions. These reports typically provide a summary of the steps which were taken and an overview of relevant legal and tax issues involved in the plan. Insurance professionals should provide a similar written report on insurance matters. This serves several useful purposes. First of all, it will summarize the many considerations which were relevant in deciding what type of life insurance to acquire, how much coverage was needed, and which insurer(s) would be used. Second, this letter should make it clear that the agent's professional obligation is limited to arranging for the most appropriate insurance coverage for the client. It should indicate that the client must rely on the other professionals for the legal and tax effectiveness of the estate plan. This will provide some legal protection to the agent in the event that issues of professional negligence arise at a later date.

5. Follow-Up

Insurance professionals are uniquely suited to being the catalyst that starts the estate planning process. Lawyers and accountants are rarely as proactive in guiding their clients' affairs. Similarly, because estate planning can be an ongoing process, it is usually the agent's role to review and follow-up periodically in order to ensure that the estate plan still represents the client's objectives. For example, share values may change, leading to greater insurance needs. Similarly, the estate plan can be affected by economic and business cycles, marriage breakdowns, family members entering or leaving the business, and legislative changes. Constant monitoring is essential and a good insurance agent will make it his or her business to perform this function.

Estate Planning Factfinder
Personal Data

Date: _____

Client

Name: _____ Date of Birth: _____ Sex: ❏ Male ❏ Female

Home Address: _____

Telephone: Res: _____ Bus: _____ Fax: _____

Email : _____ Smoker: ❏ Yes ❏ No

Are you a Canadian Resident? ❏ Yes ❏ No _____

Occupation: _____

Business Address: _____

Are you married? ❏ Yes ❏ No

Where were you married? _____ When? _____

Is there a marriage contract? ❏ Yes ❏ No
Have you been married previously? ❏ Yes ❏ No
  If yes, any support obligations? ❏ Yes ❏ No Amount: _____

Spouse

Name: _____ Date of Birth: _____ Sex: ❏ Male ❏ Female

Home Address: _____

Telephone: Res: _____ Bus: _____ Fax: _____

Email : _____ Smoker: ❏ Yes ❏ No

Canadian Resident? ❏ Yes ❏ No _____

Occupation: _____

Business Address: _____

_____

Children

Name	Sex	Married/Single	Date of Birth	Comments (Please indicate residency if other than Canadian)

Grandchildren

Name	Parents Name	Sex	Date of Birth	Comments (Please indicate residency if other than Canadian)

Are any of your children/grandchildren adopted?   ❏ Yes   ❏ No

    Is adoption complete?   ❏ Yes   ❏ No

    Name: _____

Do you have any other dependants?   ❏ Yes   ❏ No

    Name: _____

Do any of your children/grandchildren have special needs?   ❏ Yes   ❏ No

Please describe: _____

BALANCE SHEET AS AT _____
Liquid Assets

	Description/Comments/ Purchase Date	Client	Spouse	Jointly	ACB/UCC
			Current Fair Market Value		
Bank Accounts					
Bonds (other than private company)					
Stock Portfolio					
Savings Plans or Certificates					
Mutual Funds					
Segregated Funds					
Notes Receivable					
Life Insurance, Cash Values (from Appendix A)					
RRSP's (from Appendix B)					
Commutable Annuities, RRIFs					
Other					
TOTAL LIQUID ASSETS					

Non-Liquid Assets

	Description/Comments/ Purchase Date	Client	Spouse	Jointly	ACB/UCC
			Current Fair Market Value		
Residence	_____	____	____	____	____
Cottage	_____	____	____	____	____
Other Real Estate	_____	____	____	____	____
Business Interests	_____	____	____	____	____
Personal and Household Effects	_____	____	____	____	____
Automobiles, Boats, etc.	_____	____	____	____	____
	_____	____	____	____	____
Notes from Family Members	_____	____	____	____	
Collectors Items	_____	____	____	____	____
Mortgages	_____	____	____	____	
Non-Commutable Annuities	_____	____	____	____	
DPSP, RPP	_____	____	____	____	
Other Non-Liquid Assets	_____	____	____	____	____
TOTAL NON-LIQUID ASSETS		____	____	____	

Appendix 1

Liabilities

	Description/Comments	Client	Spouse	Jointly
Bank Loans (Life Insured ❑ Yes ❑ No)	_____	_____	_____	_____
Life Insurance Policy Loans	_____	_____	_____	_____
Mortgages (Indicate property concerned)	_____	_____	_____	_____
Credit Cards	_____	_____	_____	_____
Loans from Family Members	_____	_____	_____	_____
Other Indebtedness	_____	_____	_____	_____
TOTAL LIABILITIES		=====	=====	=====
Net Worth (Total Assets - Total Liabilities)		▬▬▬	▬▬▬	▬▬▬

Additional Notes _____

CURRENT SOURCES OF INCOME

	Description/Comments	Client	Spouse	Jointly
Employment	_____	_____	_____	
Dividends	_____	_____	_____	_____
Interest	_____	_____	_____	_____
Rent	_____	_____	_____	_____
Annuities	_____	_____	_____	_____
RRSPs/RRIFs	_____	_____	_____	
Pension Plans	_____	_____	_____	
CPP/QPP/OAS	_____	_____	_____	
Other	_____	_____	_____	_____
TOTAL INCOME		▬▬▬	▬▬▬	▬▬▬

Appendix 1

ESTATE DISTRIBUTION

Do you have a will?   ❑ Yes   ❑ No
Who prepared your will?
Last reviewed (Date)   _____
                                                        _____

Does your spouse have a will?   ❑ Yes   ❑ No
Who prepared your spouse's will?
Last reviewed (Date)   _____
                                                        _____

Have you appointed a guardian for minor children?   ❑ Yes   ❑ No   ❑ N/A

Name and address of guardian: _____

Who is/are the executor(s) of your will?   Name: _____
                                                        _____
                                                        _____

Is your executor knowledgeable about   Your family's needs?   ❑ Yes ❑ No
                                                        Investments?   ❑ Yes ❑ No
                                                        Running a business?   ❑ Yes ❑ No
                                                        Tax and trust laws?   ❑ Yes ❑ No
Where do you keep your will?   _____

Can I get a copy of you and your spouse's will?   ❑ Yes   ❑ No

Do you have a power of attorney?   ❑ Yes   ❑ No
Your spouse?   ❑ Yes   ❑ No

Do you have a power of attorney
for personal care (living will?)   ❑ Yes   ❑ No

Who prepared your power of attorney?   _____

Last reviewed?   (Date)   _____

Can I get a copy of your and
your spouse's power of attorney?   ❑ Yes   ❑ No

WILL PLANNING
(If no current will or will needs revision)

On you predeceasing your spouse :

How much income will your spouse/family require to $ _____
maintain his/her/their standard of living?

Do you want this income indexed?   ❑ Yes   ❑ No
                                                            If Yes, at what rate? _____

What is a reasonable rate of interest that could be earned on
invested capital?
                                                            _____ %

Specific bequests at death: ❑ Yes   ❑ No
    What property: _____
    To whom: _____

❑ Other (explain)   _____
Disposition of residue (other than business interests)   _____

❑ Bequests to children $ _____   or   _____ %   At age _____

❑ Immediate to spouse $ _____   or   _____ %   Absolutely

❑ In trust solely for benefit of spouse   Explain: _____

❑ In trust with income only to spouse

❑ With capital to children at spouse's death

❑ Other distributions as follows: _____

Disposition of business interests:

❑ To be liquidated and included as part of residue   Estimated liquidation value $ _____

❑ Business to be retained?   ❑ Yes   ❑ No
    Who will continue the business?   _____
    Who will receive the business?   _____

OTHER

Where do you keep your life insurance policies? _____

At which banks do you maintain your accounts? _____

Do you have a safety deposit box? ❏ Yes ❏ No
                                    If Yes, where? _____

Who is your Accountant?   Name: _____
                                    Firm: _____
                                    Phone No. _____

Who is your Lawyer?   Name: _____
                                    Firm: _____
                                    Phone No. _____

Who is your Investment Advisor?   Name: _____
                                    Firm: _____
                                    Phone No. _____

May I have the permission to consult any of these advisors if
necessary?   ❏ Yes ❏ No

May I have the permission to consult any life insurance
companies regarding your present insurance? ❏ Yes ❏ No

Do you anticipate receiving any gifts or inheritances? ❏ Yes ❏ No
    From Whom?   _____
    When?   _____
    Approximate amount? $ _____

BUSINESS INTERESTS

Is this business operated as a:
- ❏ Sole Proprietorship
- ❏ Partnership
- ❏ Incorporated Company (fiscal year end _____)

When was the business formed or incorporated?_____

Firm name: _____

Description of business: _____

Partner/Shareholder	Address	Age	Sex	Smoking Status	How Active

	Common	Preferred
Number of issued shares	_____	_____
Number of shares held by you	_____	_____
Number of shares held by others:		
Name: _____	_____	_____
Name: _____	_____	_____
Name: _____	_____	_____

What is the total fair market value of the business? $ _____

What was the approximate value of your business on the later of
V-Day (December 1971) and the day you acquired your interest? $ _____

Can I obtain a copy of your financial statements for the last 3 years?   ❏ Yes   ❏ No

Does your firm have any individuals whose contributions
seriously affect the profits of the business?   ❏ Yes   ❏ No
If Yes, who?

Name	Age	Smoker	Position	Salary
_____	___	___	_____	___
_____	___	___	_____	___
_____	___	___	_____	___

What group benefits does your firm provide?
- ❏ Group Life   ❏ Weekly Income   ❏ L.T.D.   ❏ Major Medical   ❏ Dental
- ❏ Pension Plan   ❏ Other

Are there different benefit levels for various employee classes?   ❏ Yes   ❏ No

Does your firm have a:
- ❏ Deferred Profit Sharing Plan   ❏ Group RRSP   ❏ Non-Registered Pension Plan
- ❏ Retirement Comp. Arrangement

Number of employees in the company   _____

BUSINESS CONTINUATION

Do you have a buy-sell agreement?	❑ Yes	❑ No
If Yes, can I get a copy of your buy-sell agreement?	❑ Yes	❑ No
If No, are there any succession plans in place?	❑ Yes	❑ No

If Yes, please describe: _____

If Yes, how is the price determined in the agreement? _____

Is this agreement fully funded with life insurance?   ❑ Yes   ❑ No

What arrangements have you made for the continuation of your business
operation in the event of your retirement or disability? _____
_____

If business is a partnership:

Name: _____   Capital Account: _____
Name: _____   Capital Account: _____
Name: _____   Capital Account: _____

If business is incorporated:

Does the corporation qualify for the small business deduction?   ❑ Yes ❑ No

Do the shares qualify for the enhanced capital gains exemption?   ❑ Yes ❑ No

Amount of exemption claimed by client? $ _____

What is the balance of your cumulative net investment losses? $ _____
What is the balance of the RDTOH account? $ _____

What is the balance of the capital dividend account? $ _____

Estimated annual growth rate of company   _____ %

STRUCTURE OF OWNERSHIP
(Diagram)

APPENDIX A
LIFE INSURANCE AND GROUP PLANS
(Include business coverage and group life)

	Company	Plan	Face Amount	Riders	Cash Value	Owner	Beneficiary
On Self							
On Business Associates							
On Spouse's Life							
On Children							
Please mark with an asterisk any insurance policies assigned as collateral for bank financing.							
Disability Insurance							
Critical Illness Insurance							
Long Term Care							

APPENDIX B
Registered Investments

Fixed Income:

Issuer	Original Deposit	Current Value	Interest Rate	Maturity Date	Spousal	Beneficiary

Equity Based:

Issuer	Original Deposit	Current Value	Current #Units	Current Unit Value	Spousal	Beneficiary

RETIREMENT PLANS

When do you plan to retire?   Age: _____

What level of income will you require? $ _____

Do you want this income indexed for inflation?   ❑ Yes   ❑ No   If Yes, at what rate? _____%

How much income will your spouse require if you predecease him/her? $ _____

Sources/amounts of retirement income   RRSPs $ _____

     Pension Plans $ _____

     Government Benefits $ _____

     Non-Registered Funds $ _____

APPENDIX C
Non-Registered Investments

Fixed Income:

Issuer	Original Deposit	Current Value	Interest Rate	Maturity Date	Beneficiary

Equity Based:

Issuer	Original Deposit	Current Value	Current # of Units	Maturity Date	Beneficiary

Appendix 1

Estate Planning Objectives
(1 is Low, 10 is High)

Financial	Rating
1. Maximizing retirement income	——
2. Maximizing estate values	——
3. Minimizing probate fees	——
4. Minimizing taxes while alive	——
5. Minimizing taxes to beneficiaries	——

Family

1. Providing income to spouse and dependents	——
2. Updating/completing wills	——
3. Updating/completing Powers of Attorney	——
4. Establishing a family trust	——
5. Funding costs related to illness or hospitalization	——

Disposition of Estate

1. Establishing trusts for dependent children/grandchildren	——
2. Making a gift to charities	——
3. Appointing guardians for minor children	——
4. Successful transfer of business interests	——
5. Taking care of special needs dependents	——

OTHER NOTES

_____
_____
_____
_____
_____
_____
_____
_____
_____
_____
_____
_____
_____
_____
_____
_____
_____
_____
_____
_____
_____
_____
_____
_____
_____
_____
_____
_____
_____
_____
_____
_____
_____
_____
_____
_____
_____
_____

Chapter 2

Taxation Overview

1. Introduction: Some Income Tax Basics

Sophisticated life insurance and estate planning strategies invariably have a significant income tax component. Given the nature of this book, a discussion of many complex tax rules is unavoidable, although there is no pretense that this is a comprehensive text on Canadian income tax law, or even on the taxation of life insurance itself (regarding which many excellent books and other references are available).

However, this chapter of the new edition will provide some additional information on a few income tax issues relevant to our subject. The purpose is to provide background information on certain income tax essentials that frequently play a role in life insurance planning in the corporate market. Some of this information appeared in other chapters in previous editions, and some is included in this book for the first time.

2. Taxation of Dividends

Most insurance advisors understand that taxable dividends received by an individual are subject to a lower rate of tax than other income, such as interest or employment income. This lower rate is available because of the dividend tax credit, which individual shareholders receive in recognition of the fact that dividends represent a distribution of income that has already been taxed at the corporate level. The dividend tax credit is representative of one of the underlying principles of Canadian tax law, that income earned directly by an individual should attract no more or less tax than if it is first earned by a corporation and subsequently distributed to the individual as a dividend. This is called the theory of "integration". The dividend tax credit is a function of the integration theory. So is the concept of refundable dividend tax on hand ("RDTOH"), discussed below, and the capital dividend account, which is an essential part of tax planning strategies featured throughout the book. All are central features of this system, and all have a role to play in insurance planning.

Significant changes to the taxation of dividends were introduced in 2006. The concept of "eligible dividends" was introduced as part of the government's decision to deal with perceived inequalities between the taxation of corporations and income trusts. Under these changes, corporations will be able to pay dividends that benefit from a lower rate of federal tax if they originate from corporate business income that was ineligible for the small business deduction. (The latter deduction, which is discussed in greater detail below, allows corporations to pay a lower rate of tax on a specified level of active business income.)

The focal point of the new dividend taxation regime is the general rate income pool ("GRIP"), which will reflect a private corporation's after-tax income that was taxed at the general corporate rate (which in 2008 is in the range of approximately 30%–35% depending on the province, and trending downward in future years). Added to the GRIP balance will be eligible dividends received from other corporations, less eligible dividends previously paid. Investment income and income that qualifies for the small business tax rate is excluded from a corporation's GRIP.

A corporation can pay eligible dividends to the extent it has a positive balance in its GRIP at the end of the taxation year. It can elect to pay eligible dividends before paying non-eligible dividends and can select which shareholders can receive eligible dividends, although shareholders owning the same class of shares must be treated equally.

The net effect of these changes depends upon the province. Most but not all provinces have elected to harmonize their rules with the federal changes. Here are a few examples of 2008 tax rates in various provinces of eligible and ineligible dividends. To put it mildly, they are not consistent.

PROVINCE	INELIGIBLE DIVIDENDS	ELIGIBLE DIVIDENDS
Quebec	36.35	29.69
Ontario	31.34	23.96
Alberta	26.46	16.00
British Columbia	31.58	18.47

Interestingly, because of changes to the dividend gross-up and tax credit mechanism in the 2008 federal Budget, the eligible dividend tax rates will start to increase beginning in 2010 in most provinces. This, of course, assumes that no other changes are announced in the interim, which seems unlikely.

The new dividend taxation rules will affect many planning strategies for owners of private corporations. Most prominently, it will have an impact on the time-honoured strategy of paying bonuses to owner/managers in order to reduce corporate income to the level eligible for the small business deduction. For business owners who do not require a current distribution of corporate income for personal living expenses, it may be more attractive to retain income in the corporation and pay it out as an eligible dividend in future years. Strategies will vary from province to province and client to client.

These new rules will also have an impact on strategies for the purchase and sale of shares on death. This will be addressed in Chapter 6.

Prior to the introduction of the eligible dividend rules, there was a clear preference to realize corporate value as a capital gain, particularly if the shareholder could utilize the capital gains exemption. However, in harmonizing provinces the tax differential between capital gains and eligible dividends will be greatly reduced (and in some provinces will disappear), thereby leaving the owner/manager somewhat indifferent between these two types of income.

3. Refundable Dividend Tax on Hand ("RDTOH")

The RDTOH mechanism is used to integrate investment income earned by a corporation and distributed as a taxable dividend to the shareholder. The tax rate payable by corporations on investment income is significantly higher than the rate paid on business income, and generally higher than the top marginal rate for individuals. Typical rates are in the 45%–49% range, but an RDTOH credit of 26.67% is available and may be refunded to the corporation on the basis of $1 for every $3 of taxable dividend paid. These dividends are ineligible, as they do not originate with corporate business earnings. Therefore, they do not qualify for the lower tax rates introduced in 2006.

The following example, using Ontario tax rates, may be instructive:

Interest income earned in corporation	1,000
Corporate tax (48.67%)	(487)
RDTOH (1,000 × 26.67%)*	267
Available for dividend	**780**
Tax payable by:	
Corporation (487 − 267)	220
Individual (780 × 31.34%)	244
Total individual and corporate tax	**464**
Tax at top marginal rate if interest received directly by individual	**464****

* RDTOH is refunded at the rate of $1 for every $3 of taxable dividend paid to the shareholder. The example assumes that the refund itself is included in the dividend.

** Combined personal and corporate tax is the same as the tax that would have been paid if the interest had been earned directly by the individual. Results will vary by province.

4. Small Business Deduction

Canadian-controlled private corporations are eligible for the small business deduction, which currently provides a special low rate of tax on the first $400,000 of business income earned each year. The low rate does not apply to investment or other income. Each province also has its own small business deduction. The income threshold in most provinces is also $400,000 although there is some variation. The combined federal/provincial tax rate on small business income is in the range of 14%–16%. As already discussed, income in excess of the threshold is typically taxed at approximately 30%–35% and may also be distributed as an eligible dividend to shareholders.

5. The $750,000 Capital Gains Exemption

This exemption, which applies to shares of qualifying small business corporations and for certain fishing and farm properties, was introduced in 1985. At the same time, a $100,000 capital gains exemption for all other property was enacted. Almost immediately, tax advisors and their clients began predicting the inevitable demise of these exemptions. To date, given the phase out of the $100,000 exemption in 1994, these predictions have only been partially correct. In fact, it appears that the capital gains exemption for small business has become a permanent fixture, as the amount of the exemption increased in 2007 to $750,000 from its original level of $500,000.

The elimination of this exemption would inevitably create political problems for the government with the small business, farming and fishing communities. Additionally, with the recent decline in income tax rates and the reduction of the capital gains inclusion rate to 50%, there is less monetary incentive than in previous years for the Department of Finance to repeal these provisions.

This section will review the major rules relating to the $750,000 capital gains exemption for small business corporation shares (for simplicity, this will simply be referred to as the "exemption"). The impact of corporate-owned life insurance on the exemption will be addressed, as will tax planning strategies designed to maximize access to the exemption.

(a) Basic Rules

The following is a summary of some of the key rules relating to the exemption:

- The exemption is available only to individual taxpayers who own shares of qualifying small business corporations. It is not available, for example, where a holding company realizes a capital gain on the sale of shares of an operating company.

- The exemption is provided on a lifetime basis per individual. If a portion of the exemption is used at a certain time, it reduces the amount of exemption available on a future disposition of qualifying shares. The $750,000 lifetime limit is also reduced by any portion of the above noted $100,000 exemption used by the taxpayer prior to the abolition of that exemption.

- At the time the gain is realized, the shares in question must be those of a qualifying small business corporation. In the CRA's view, this means that at that time, 90% of the fair market value of the assets of the corporation must be used principally in an active business carried on primarily in Canada. Throughout the 24 months prior to the realization of the gain, 50% of the fair market value of the assets must have been so used.

- Where an individual owns shares of a holding company, which in turn owns shares of an operating company, the shares of the holding company may qualify for the exemption. Essentially, the rules provide for the assets of the two corporations to be analyzed on a consolidated basis. In other words, the combined assets of the two must meet the above tests.

(b) Assessing Eligibility for the Exemption

The determination of whether shares of a corporation qualify for the exemption requires a careful financial review covering at least a 24-month period. In most cases, the corporation's accountant will be in the best position to do this analysis.

In order to take a preliminary look at this issue, it may be helpful to review the corporation's recent financial statements. While they will not contain all the information needed to determine the availability of the exemption, they will generally disclose the existence of non-active business assets (the most common of which is cash and other liquid investments) that could prevent the exemption from being available.

It is also important to keep in mind certain items that are not disclosed on the financial statements. For example, goodwill is usually a critical part of business value but generally is not found on financial statements. Financial statements may also show certain assets at their historical cost rather than their current fair market value.

For the above reasons, while financial statements will contain useful information, they should be viewed with caution when used for the above analysis.

(c) The Impact of Corporate-Owned Life Insurance

Corporate-owned life insurance is not an active business asset. Therefore, the exemption may not be available if the fair market value of corporate insurance policies, when combined with the value of other passive assets, is more than 10% of the total.

The Act contains certain rules regarding the valuation of corporate-owned life insurance for the purposes of the exemption. The key features of these rules are as follows:

- Prior to the shareholder's death, the fair market value of a corporate-owned policy on his or her life will be its cash surrender value. The wording could be interpreted to include multi-life policies, joint first-to-die and joint second-to-die policies under which the shareholder was one of the insured parties.

- After the shareholder's death and the payment of the proceeds, the policy will continue to be valued at its cash surrender value as long as the proceeds are used to fund the redemption or purchase of the deceased's shares within 24 months of death (or such later date as may be allowed by the Minister upon the written application of the corporation).

In light of the above, it is usually advisable to ensure that life insurance with cash values is not held within operating companies. See additional discussion on this issue in Chapter 4.

(d) Purification and Related Strategies

Passive assets such as cash (over and above that required for day-to-day business operations), marketable securities and the cash surrender value of life insurance policies can often exceed 10% of a corporation's total asset value. In that case, the shares of the corporation will not qualify for the exemption. These passive assets can often be removed from the corporation using a strategy known as purification. In essence, purification implies the transfer of the passive assets to a separate corporation controlled by the same shareholder. Depending on the nature of the assets, this can generally be done on a tax-deferred basis.

Occasionally, purification can be achieved by transferring passive assets of an operating company ("Opco") to its holding company ("Holdco") as a tax-free intercorporate dividend. However, little is achieved if Holdco owns all of the Opco shares because, as previously described, the assets of the two corporations are viewed on a consolidated basis. A couple of alternatives may be considered:

- The corporate structure can be organized in a way that allows the individual shareholder to hold a given percentage of the Opco shares, with the balance being held by Holdco. Once Opco is purified, the Opco shares owned by the individual shareholders are those that will ultimately qualify for the exemption.

- Alternatively, the passive assets can be transferred to a separate company ("Newco") controlled by the individual shareholder. In that case, Newco and Opco would be sister corporations controlled by the same person, with Newco holding the passive assets and Opco holding the active business assets.

Complications can arise where a life insurance policy must be transferred to another corporation as part of a purification strategy. If the policy's cash surrender value exceeds its adjusted cost basis, the excess will be taxable to the transferring corporation. This is in contrast to most types of assets, which can be transferred on a tax-deferred basis. This further emphasizes the need to hold permanent insurance policies outside of operating companies. See Chapter 4 for further commentary on this issue.

(e) Capital Gains Crystallization

There are certain methods that can be used to trigger, or "crystallize", capital gains without actually selling shares to a third party. This is discussed in greater detail in the discussion in Chapter 5 dealing with estate freezes.

Overview of Life Insurance Taxation

6. The Changing Role of Life Insurance

The central purpose of life insurance has not changed over the past 100 or so years that it has been available in Canada. People purchase insurance because funds will be required on their deaths to deal with various needs which inevitably arise at that time.

This is not to say that those needs are the same as they always were. At one time, insurance was purchased almost exclusively by family breadwinners to provide funds to pay off personal debts and funeral expenses, and to provide a financial cushion to their beneficiaries. This is still true in many, if not most, cases, but other kinds of needs have arisen over the years for which insurance is now required: the payment of capital gains tax; probate fees and charitable bequests; and a myriad of needs relating to business owners, such as funding the purchase of shares under shareholders agreements, "key person" insurance, and collateral insurance to cover bank loans. Therefore, while the increasing complexity of our economy and our tax system has created wider uses for life insurance, its primary purpose remains the same — to provide cash on death.

However, spurred on by significant product developments in the past twenty or so years, life insurance has evolved into a versatile financial instrument which can provide significant benefits both during lifetime and on death. Beyond simply providing liquidity on death, it has become a sophisticated financial and tax planning tool.

The focus of this book is on the use of life insurance as an estate planning tool. In other words, the majority of the discussion relates to the use of death benefits. However, as life insurance continues to be used more frequently as a financial tool during lifetime, the taxation of policy transactions while the insured person is alive is an essential ingredient to understanding how insurance might fit into a client's overall planning. After a brief discussion of recent product developments, this chapter provides an introduction to the major concepts involved in the taxation of policyholders.

7. Product Developments

Most insurance companies offer a (sometimes bewildering) variety of term and permanent life insurance products. Many, like five- and ten-year term and participating whole life insurance, have been available for decades, although whole life is much less prominent in the market than it used to be. Others, like Term to 100 and universal life, have been added more recently. New features, such as sickness and disability insurance benefits, and preferred insurance rates, continue to be added to life insurance policies.

Critical illness insurance is an even newer product that has grown significantly in popularity in recent years. It is not subject to the same taxation rules as life insurance policies and is dealt with separately in this book (see Chapter 12).

Life insurance products which provide benefits during lifetime are typically those with cash values (i.e., policy reserves that can be accessed in a variety of ways by the policyholder during lifetime). Participating whole life and universal life are the most common examples of these types of insurance contracts. Term to 100 policies, which typically have no cash values but are nonetheless a form of permanent insurance, can also provide benefits during lifetime, as can "minimum-funded" universal life policies. Insurance-backed accumulation and leveraging strategies are considered in Chapter 8.

Before considering taxation issues relating to life insurance in Canada, this section will briefly review the product features of participating whole life and universal life plans. For the sake of discussion, most of the planning ideas discussed in this book will assume that a universal life plan is being used, although many of these same applications will also work effectively with participating whole life.

Participating Whole Life

Traditional participating whole life plans require premiums to be paid for life, and have specified cash values and death benefits, all of which are guaranteed. The pricing of these policies generally takes into account three main factors: the insurer's mortality experience, the investment return and expenses. Lapse rates may also be built into the calculation.

Typically, assumptions made by the insurer are extremely conservative and are ultimately exceeded by results, which means that premiums have been higher than required to cover the insurer's risk. In these circumstances, dividends are paid by the insurer, essentially representing a refund of premiums to its participating whole life policyholders. The insurance contract usually permits the policyholder to use dividends in one or more of the following ways:

- to receive them in cash;

- to leave them on deposit in an interest-bearing account with the insurer;

- to apply them against the amount due for the next policy premium;

- to use them to purchase paid-up additions (i.e., an additional death benefit which requires no further premiums); or

- to use them to purchase small amounts of term insurance (which may ultimately be converted to paid-up additions) to be added to the basic face amount.

Because their calculation depends on a number of variables, none of which can be estimated with absolute precision, dividends under participating whole life plans are not guaranteed. Therefore, illustrations which assume that dividends will be available for the purchase of policy enhancements, such as paid-up additions, must be treated with caution (as must universal life illustrations, which assume future interest rates, as discussed below).

Participating whole life policies are still offered by many insurance companies in Canada but in general sales have been in decline for many years as universal life has become the permanent product of choice in most situations.

Universal Life

Universal life policies have their genesis in the high interest rate environment of the early 1980s. Rather than relying upon the insurer's investment expertise, as do participating whole life policyholders, clients acquiring universal life plans are credited with rates of return which are calculated on the basis of various investment accounts offered by the insurer. These accounts typically reflect external factors, such as prevailing interest rates, and can even be tied to stock market indices. Investment income earned within a universal life policy, as based upon these external factors, is credited to the policy and may be used to purchase additional coverage within the plan.

In a sense, those who acquire participating whole life plans are choosing a conservative investment route, and their rates of return depend upon the investment expertise of the insurance company. On the other hand, universal life is "self-administered" life insurance that provides a range of investment options chosen by the client. In this way, universal life plans may be more attractive to knowledgeable investors who are prepared to make ongoing investment decisions regarding their insurance policies. It follows that the potential risks and rewards of using universal life for investment purposes are greater than those of participating whole life plans. In general, the attractiveness of life insurance as a pure savings vehicle has waned in recent years, although it is as important as ever for estate planning purposes. The role of life insurance as an investment will be discussed more fully in Chapter 8.

Although competitive forces have led participating whole life to become more adaptable to policyholders' changing needs, universal life policies usually have a number of key features that make them more flexible than whole life policies, for example:

- As noted, universal life offers a much wider range of investment options, all of which are exercised by the policyholder, not the insurance company.

- Premiums can be increased, decreased or stopped (either permanently or temporarily) within reasonable limits. Where premiums are reduced or stopped, insurance charges are funded through existing policy values, although the insurance will lapse if these values are ultimately exhausted.

- Universal life plans offer different methods for paying mortality costs. Most often, life insurance charges will be level throughout the life of the contract. But many companies also provide insurance charges on a yearly renewable term (YRT) basis. Under this option, insurance charges start at a lower level but increase, sometimes dramatically, over time. To offset the impact of increasing rates, many contracts allow policyholders to switch from YRT to level insurance charges at given points in time.

- Universal life typically offers greater death benefit options, including "face plus fund value" options, which pay a death benefit equal to the face amount of the contract, plus the fund value existing at the time of death. Universal life policies that insure more than one life, such as joint life and multi-life contracts, may also permit the cash surrender value of the policies to be paid as a death benefit on the death of each insured person, even though the policy will continue in force.

- Universal life plans may offer death benefit options that increase by a specified rate each year, which is particularly convenient for clients whose needs tend to increase annually (as their exposure to capital gains tax increases, for instance).

- A key feature of universal life policies is the "unbundling" of the various charges payable by the policy owner. Mortality and administrative charges under these contracts are clearly identified and may be kept separate from the savings element of premium payments. This has introduced planning opportunities usually unavailable in other types of insurance products, including the ability to insure more than one life under a single insurance contract (a "multi-life contract"). Multi-life policies are discussed in greater detail below.

- Many universal life policies offer other types of coverage, such as critical illness, long term care and disability insurance benefits within the life insurance policy. These products can provide comprehensive life and sickness insurance protection in one contract.

8. Exempt Life Insurance Policies: Income Tax Basics

Taxation of Policy Accumulations

(a) General Rules

Life insurance policies are not subject to taxation on their accumulating cash reserves as long as they qualify as "exempt policies" within the meaning of the *Income Tax Act* (Canada) (the "Act") and the Income Tax Regulations (the "Regulations"). An insurance policy will be exempt if its cash accumulations do not exceed that of a benchmark policy known as the "exemption test policy". The attributes of the exemption test policy are outlined in overwhelming actuarial detail in the Regulations, which effectively establish the limit of tax deferral that the federal government is prepared to accept. Essentially, any policy that stays within the confines of the exemption test policy is, for tax purposes, primarily a life insurance policy, and any policy that exceeds those confines is primarily an investment vehicle.

As a practical matter, an overwhelming majority of policies sold in Canada are exempt policies. It is also comforting to note that neither taxpayers nor their advisors are responsible for determining whether or not a given policy is exempt. In fact, it is the contractual responsibility of the insurer to ensure that a policy is and remains exempt. This is particularly important because it is theoretically possible for an exempt policy to become non-exempt at any particular point in time, with onerous income tax consequences, and taxpayers cannot be expected to have the information or actuarial expertise necessary to monitor their policies in this way.

The exempt test rules are due for update and revision. One problem is a lack of consistency in how these rules are administered because, to the actuarial eye, they are capable of differing interpretations. Representative groups from the life insurance industry made a comprehensive submission to governmental authorities several years ago, but there has been little or no progress on recommended reforms. The fact is that insurance policyholder taxation is not presently a priority of the Department of Finance, despite the fact that the current rules lag significantly behind product developments. The Department's priorities could, of course, change at any time.

(b) Income Tax Consequences of Becoming Non-Exempt

It is possible for an exempt policy to become non-exempt after issue. This would normally occur because the growth in cash surrender value became too large in relation to its death benefit, perhaps because of better than anticipated investment results within the insurance policy.

If no action is taken within the grace period discussed below, a policy that becomes non-exempt will be subject to a deemed disposition, and the policyholder will be taxed on the amount by which the accumulating fund of the policy exceeds its adjusted cost basis ("ACB"). Thereafter, annual growth in the policy's cash surrender value will be subject to annual accrual taxation.

The Act provides a 60-day grace period, following the anniversary date on which the policy becomes non-exempt, for the policy to be restored to an exempt footing. This can be accomplished in one of two ways:

1. The death benefit under the policy can be increased so that it becomes sufficiently high in relation to its cash surrender value. There is an anti-avoidance rule, however, which provides that this increase cannot be greater than 8% in any year; or

2. A cash withdrawal can be made from the policy. In that case, assuming the policy's cash surrender value exceeded its ACB at that time, the prorated portion of the withdrawal would be taxable in full to the policyholder.

(c) The "Anti Dump-In" Rule

Another anti-avoidance rule is sometimes known as the "anti dump-in" rule. It applies if the accumulating fund, on the tenth or any subsequent anniversary date of the policy, exceeds 250% of the value of the accumulating fund on the third preceding anniversary date. If so, a separate exemption test policy will be deemed to have been issued in respect of that policy. In that event, because of the rapid increase in the policy's cash surrender value over a relatively short period of time, there is a likelihood that the policy will at that point become non-exempt unless corrective action is taken as described above.

The anti dump-in rule is a particular problem for a universal life policy that has been "minimum funded" for a number of years, resulting in a relatively small build-up of cash surrender value. If in later years the policy owner decided to make significant additional deposits to the plan (as most universal life policies permit), this could create a substantial growth in cash surrender value. This in turn would make it more likely that the policy would run afoul of the anti dump-in rule.

This rule can also be of concern in certain policies which insure more than one life. One such policy is a "joint second-to-die" plan which insures two lives, with the death benefit payable on the second death. Another is a multi-life policy under which two or more lives are insured, with a death benefit paid on each death. Under the former type of policy, it is possible to have the cash surrender value of the policy paid on the first death. Under the latter policy, the cash surrender value can be paid on each death (in addition to the usual death benefit).

In the above circumstances, the cash surrender value may be removed from a policy which will nonetheless be continuing in force for an indefinite period. If this occurs seven years or later after the policy issue date, a monitoring of the policy will be necessary to ensure that it does not contravene the anti dump-in rule.

Unless otherwise indicated, this book will assume that the policies being discussed are, and will remain, exempt policies for the purposes of the Act.

Calculation of Adjusted Cost Basis ("ACB")

In order to properly compare the taxation of withdrawals, policy loans and other transactions involving life insurance policies, it is necessary to have an understanding of how the ACB of a policy is calculated. As might be expected, the Act contains a complex set of rules for these purposes. The following is a non-exhaustive list of factors which either increase or decrease the ACB of an interest in a life insurance policy:

Factors that increase the ACB:

- amounts paid to acquire the policy (either premium payments or amounts paid to purchase a policy from another policyholder);

- policy gains included in income (for example, from withdrawals or policy loans as discussed below); and

- repayment of policy loans that were previously subject to tax.

Factors that decrease the ACB:

- the proceeds of disposition of an interest in a policy, including policy loans taken after March 31, 1978;

- the net cost of pure insurance of policies acquired after December 1, 1982 (discussed in greater detail below); and

- policy dividends received, net of those used for the payment of policy premiums (applicable only to participating whole life policies).

As is the case for capital property, the higher the ACB of a life insurance policy, the lower the amount of income to be realized on the disposition of an interest in the policy. Ordinarily, one would assume that as long as premiums were being paid under a policy, its ACB would continue to increase. However, the impact of the net cost of pure insurance ("NCPI") is such that this assumption can rarely be made with any degree of certainty.

In essence, the NCPI is the net amount at risk (generally the policy proceeds less its cash surrender value) multiplied by a mortality factor prescribed under the Act. This mortality factor increases each year as the life insured grows older, with the result that the NCPI erodes an increasing amount of the policy's ACB each year. In most cases, a policy's ACB will grow in the early years because the NCPI will be less than the premiums being paid. However, at some point the NCPI will start to exceed premiums, causing the ACB to reduce. The reduction of the ACB is such that, within a number of years after the policy is issued, and generally well before life expectancy, the ACB will be nil (it cannot become negative).

Taxation of Policy Dispositions

There are a variety of different transactions that can cause a disposition, or partial disposition, of an interest in a life insurance policy for tax purposes. If the proceeds of disposition exceed the ACB of the policy, the excess is taxable in full to the policyholder, even if the policy is an exempt policy. The following are the most common examples of transactions that constitute a disposition of a life insurance policy for tax purposes:

- a surrender of a policy for its cash surrender value ("CSV");

- the withdrawal of a portion of the funds from the CSV of a policy (often referred to as a partial surrender);

- the payment of a dividend under a participating whole life policy;

- a policy loan made after March 31, 1978; and

- a change of ownership from one policyholder to another.

The death of the life insured under an exempt policy is not a disposition for income tax purposes, and the proceeds payable thereunder are not subject to tax. Many permanent policies provide for a death benefit equal to the face amount plus the CSV of the policy at the time of death. These proceeds are also tax-free, as they are considered to be payments made as a consequence of death.

Certain other policies that insure two or more lives — on a joint second-to-die basis or on a multi-life basis — provide an option allowing the payment of a death benefit equal to the CSV on the first death (and on succeeding deaths, where applicable). The CRA at one point expressed concern that the payment of such proceeds did constitute a policy disposition. However, after submissions from interested groups within the insurance industry, this statement was retracted. Under current law, the payment of such proceeds does not constitute a disposition for tax purposes as long as the benefit can be considered to have been paid "as a consequence of death". Generally, a payment will be considered to have been made as a consequence of death where, at the time the policy was issued, the policyholder elected to have this feature apply. On the other hand, where the election of whether or not to receive proceeds is made at the time one of the insured parties dies, the payment may be considered to have been made as a consequence of that election, rather than because of death. In that case, the CRA might consider the payment to constitute a policy disposition.

Other specific exclusions from the definition of "disposition" include the collateral assignment of a life insurance policy as security for a loan (other than a policy loan), and the payment of a disability benefit under the policy.

(a) Full Surrender of Policy

In the case of a complete surrender of the policy, the taxable gain is the amount, if any, by which the CSV of the policy exceeds its ACB.

(b) Partial Surrender of Policy

In the case of a partial surrender or withdrawal, these amounts are prorated, which means that a taxable gain will result from a partial surrender as long as the total CSV of the policy at that time exceeds its ACB. As an example, assume that an individual owns an insurance policy with an ACB of $10,000 and CSV of $30,000. If a withdrawal of $15,000 is made, the ACB attributable to the withdrawn portion will be ($10,000 ÷ $30,000) × $15,000 = $5,000. Therefore the taxable amount of the withdrawal will be $15,000 - $5,000 = $10,000.

(c) Dividends

As noted previously, dividends are in effect a return of premiums under participating whole life policies. The payment of a dividend is a disposition under the Act and reduces the ACB of the policy. If the dividend is used to purchase additional insurance, it is added back to the ACB. No tax is payable on a policy dividend until the total dividends paid under the policy, not including those used to purchase additional insurance, exceed the ACB.

(d) Policy Loans

Under the Act, a policy loan is "an amount advanced by an insurer to a policyholder in accordance with the terms and conditions of the life insurance policy". The amount of any policy loan, less the ACB of the policy, will be taxable to the policyholder. If the amount of the loan is less than the ACB, no taxable gain will result. This is in contrast to partial surrenders, which will be taxable on a pro-rated basis if the CSV exceeds the ACB, even if the amount withdrawn is less than the ACB.

Amounts advanced by a lender other than the insurer are not policy loans, even if the life insurance policy is assigned as collateral by the borrower. Neither are commercially negotiated loans made by an insurer to a borrower where the policy is used as collateral. These are critical distinctions for comments made later in Chapter 8 of this book on the subject of leveraging.

The amount of any non-taxable loan will reduce the policy's ACB, thus increasing any taxable gain on future dispositions. In circumstances where the amount of a policy loan exceeds the ACB of the policy, the taxable amount is added to the ACB.

(e) Leveraging

It is rare for a policyholder to take a policy loan that results in taxable income being received. Instead, it is far more tax-effective to use the policy as collateral for a loan from another financial institution, or as a collateral loan from the insurance company itself. These are not included in the definition of "policy loan" referenced above. As mentioned, these and other leveraging strategies are dealt with in Chapter 8.

(f) Change of Ownership

As noted above, and absent any rules to the contrary, the transfer of ownership of a life insurance policy constitutes a disposition of the policy for an amount equal to its CSV. Certain types of transfers, however, are subject to special rules, such as those below which deal with the taxation of policy transfers between certain family members.

9. Multi-Life Policies

(a) Definition of Multi-Life Contracts

As the name implies, a multi-life contract is an insurance policy under which two or more lives are insured, and which pays a death benefit on the death of each life insured. This should not be confused with joint "first-to-die" or "last-to-die" policies which insure two or more lives but pay a death benefit only on the first or last death.

(b) Some Advantages of Multi-Life Contracts

Multi-life contracts are attractive for the following reasons:

- Under most of these policies, the proceeds payable on each death will equal the deceased's portion of the face amount, plus the entire cash surrender value of the policy immediately before the death. Therefore, on the first death, the proceeds will include the cash surrender value relating to all of the life insured parties, not just that relating to the deceased. Obviously, if each party had been insured under separate policies, only the cash surrender value relating to the deceased's policy would have been paid on his or her death. This allows access to the cash surrender value as a tax-free death benefit on the first and each succeeding death.

- In most circumstances, it will be easier to administer a multi-life contract than several single-life policies. A multi-life contract requires only one monthly or annual premium and will generate only one annual policy statement.

- Having a multi-life contract means that the client will be subject to only one policy fee, rather than several. This will usually result in significant savings over the life of the contract.

(c) Some Disadvantages of Multi-Life Contracts

While multi-life contracts have their benefits, they are not suitable for every situation. The following are some potential disadvantages of these policies:

- As noted above, the cash surrender value of a multi-life contract is paid out on each death. In these circumstances, where one or more life insured parties remain alive, additional premium payments will be required in order to keep the policy in force. This process will be repeated on each death as long as at least one insured person remains alive. It is possible to make these additional payments using some of the proceeds received on the death; however, this should not be done without considering the "anti-dump-in rule" discussed earlier in this chapter. This rule could cause the policy to become nonexempt for income tax purposes.

- Where the beneficiary of a life insurance policy is a private corporation, the amount of any proceeds, less the ACB of the policy, is credited to the corporation's capital dividend account ("CDA"). Therefore, the lower the ACB, the higher the CDA credit and the greater the ability to pay tax-free capital dividends to the shareholders. Unfortunately, in the rules concerning the calculation of a policy's ACB, the Act does not recognize the existence of multi-life contracts. This means that the ACB of a multi-life contract is, for these purposes, the aggregate of premiums paid, less the net cost of pure insurance, for all insured lives. On the first death, for example, the CDA credit will be proceeds received less the aggregate ACB of the entire policy. In most cases, this will result in a lower CDA credit than if the deceased had been insured under a single-life policy. In addition, the ACB attributable to the deceased's portion of the policy will not be eliminated and therefore may, in the future, reduce the CDA credit on a subsequent death. (This problem can be eliminated where the owner and beneficiary are two separate corporations. See the discussion of split-beneficiary designations in Chapter 4.)

- Multi-life contracts can be less flexible than single-life policies. For example, the owners of a single-life policy wishing to access the cash surrender value of a policy for retirement or other purposes may do so at any time. In a multi-life situation, however, the consent of the other insured parties may be required if any one of them wished to access the cash surrender value of the policy. It might also be necessary to have an agreement amongst the owner and the life-insured parties dealing with ownership rights and related matters pertaining to the policy.

- If a corporation is insuring several shareholders under one multi-life contract, complications may result if one of the shareholders departs the corporation and wishes to acquire his or her "piece" of the contract. While it is possible under the insurance policy to sever the portion of the contract relating to that shareholder's life, it is likely that this would be considered a partial disposition for income tax purposes. This would result in a taxable gain to the corporation if the cash surrender value of this portion of the policy exceeded the ACB. Care should also be taken in these circumstances to avoid a taxable benefit being assessed to the departing shareholder. This could occur if he or she does not pay what the CRA considers to be fair market value for this interest in the policy.

As a general rule, it appears that the main advantage of a typical multi-life policy is that it allows for savings in the policy fees charged by insurance companies. Only one policy fee is charged for a multi-life plan, whereas a group of individual policies would each be subject to separate fees. These modest savings, however, will often be outweighed by the disadvantages described above. Insurance advisors should carefully review the pros and cons of multi-life policies with their clients.

10. Taxation of Policy Transfers between Family Members

In contrast to many income tax rules, those which deal with transfers of life insurance policies between individuals, particularly spouses, parents and children, are reasonably consistent and sensible. In fact, they even present some marketing opportunities. This section will explore some of these key rules in the hopes of providing both enlightenment and earnings potential to the insurance advisor.

As a general rule, the Act provides that whenever a policyholder's interest in a life insurance policy is transferred by gift or sale to a person with whom the policyholder does not deal at arm's length, a disposition occurs. Common examples of individuals who do not deal at arm's length are siblings, parents and their children, grandparents and their grandchildren, and a husband and wife. The person transferring ownership (the "transferor") is deemed to receive proceeds equal to the CSV of the policy at that time (nil in the case of term policies). The amount by which this exceeds the ACB of the policy is taxable in full to the transferor. The CSV, in turn, represents the ACB of the policy to the new owner (the "transferee").

The above will apply in a number of circumstances, such as where a corporation transfers ownership of a policy to a shareholder, or where one individual transfers ownership to another in circumstances where the Act provides no relief from the general rule.

On the other hand, the Act does provide a rollover for certain intra-family transfers, each of which will be discussed below. In these cases, the disposition is deemed to occur at the ACB of the transferor, resulting in no taxable gain.

Transfers to Children or Grandchildren

A rollover will occur where an interest in a life insurance policy is transferred by gift to the policyholder's child, but only where a child of the policyholder or a child of the transferee is the life insured under the policy. ("Child" for these purposes includes a grandchild.) Note that a rollover is not available where the parent making the transfer is the life insured under the policy. Also note that the child must be the party whose life is insured, as opposed to being simply one of the insured parties. This generally excludes multi-life and joint life policies from this rollover, although the rollover may be available in these circumstances where the child is the only remaining life insured, i.e., where the other insured party or parties have died prior to the transfer of ownership to the child.

There are, of course, many situations under which a parent acquires insurance on the life of an infant child. This rule would allow the parent to transfer ownership of that policy to the child, at some future date, on a tax-deferred basis. This transfer could occur many years in the future, after which the child could access the accumulated value for his or her own purposes (such as post-secondary school expenses). If, for example, the child removed funds from the policy, it would constitute a partial disposition and result in taxable income. However, as long as the child is at least 18 years of age at the time, it will be taxed at the child's own tax rate, which may be zero.

Another possible marketing application is to involve a third generation in the arrangement. A 60-year-old grandparent might purchase insurance on the life of his or her 30-year-old child under which the policyholder's grandchild, or a trust for the grandchild, was the beneficiary. If the grandparent lived long enough, he or she could transfer ownership of the policy to the grandchild at some point after the grandchild reached a mature age. As described above, this would be a rollover for income tax purposes.

The grandchild (or a trust for the grandchild) could be named as contingent owner so that he or she would acquire ownership if the grandparent died while still owning the policy. The transfer of ownership on the grandparent's death would take place on a rollover basis, with the child or trust assuming the grandparent's ACB. If it was a trust which acquired the policy, any subsequent transfer of the policy from the trust to the grandchild would also be tax-deferred.

After the transfer of ownership, funds which had accumulated within the policy could be accessed by the child, if desired, for schooling or other expenses. On the death of the parent/life-insured, the child would receive the insurance proceeds free of tax.

Transfers to Spouses

The Act formerly permitted tax-deferred transfers of insurance policies from one spouse to another only in settlement of property rights arising out of their marriage. The rules have been relaxed so that a rollover is available where an interest in a policy, no matter whose life (or lives) may be insured thereunder, is transferred in the following circumstances:

- during the policyholder's lifetime to his or her spouse;

- to a former spouse in settlement of marital property rights; or

- on death to the surviving spouse.

The above rules require that both spouses be Canadian residents for income tax purposes at the time of transfer. In the case of a transfer on death, the residency test is applied immediately before the death. For these purposes, as well as for most others under the Act, "spouse" includes a common-law partner (i.e., a person of the same or opposite sex with whom the individual has resided in a conjugal relationship for at least 12 months, or with whom the individual has had a child).

In the above circumstances, it is also possible for the person making the transfer to elect that these rollover provisions not apply. In the case of a deceased spouse, the election would be made by his or her personal representative in the tax return for the year of death. Where this election is made, the spouse making the transfer would be considered to have received the CSV of the policy (with the tax consequences described above), and the recipient would have a corresponding ACB. There is no prescribed form for this election — an informal statement in the tax return will suffice.

It is difficult to conceive of many situations where this election would be an attractive alternative to the usual rollover treatment. One instance might be where the income triggered by this election would not in any event be subject to tax — for example, where the transferring spouse's income for the year was below the taxable threshold.

Attribution Rules

As demonstrated above, there are many opportunities for life insurance policies to be transferred between family members on a tax-deferred basis.

However, it is important to keep the attribution rules in mind when planning of this nature is undertaken.

These rules provide, among other things, that where a person makes a gift of property to a spouse, or to a child under the age of 18, income earned from that property will be attributed for tax purposes to the original owner. For example, an individual might decide to gift a life insurance policy to his or her spouse. Taking advantage of the rules described above, this could be accomplished on a tax-deferred basis. However, if the recipient subsequently withdrew funds from the policy's cash surrender value, or surrendered the policy for cash, any taxable income generated would be attributed to the original owner. Similar rules apply where the policy is held by, or in trust for, children under the age of 18.

11. Taxation of Policy Transfers between Corporations and Their Shareholders

The income tax rules governing the transfer of insurance policies between corporations and their shareholders present an entirely new set of complications. These will be dealt with in Chapter 4.

References

Income Tax Act (Canada)

Subsection 12.2(1) — accrual taxation of non-exempt life insurance policies

Sections 74.1–75.1 — attribution rules

Subsection 82(1) — taxable dividends

Section 110.6 — capital gains exemption

Section 121 — dividend tax credit

Section 125 — small business deduction

Subsection 129(1) — refundable dividend tax on hand (RDTOH)

Subsection 138(12) — definition of "life insurance policy"

Subsections 148(1) and (2) — taxation on disposition of life insurance policy

Subsection 148(4) — taxation on partial disposition of life insurance policy

Subsection 148(7) — non-arm's length disposition of life insurance policy

Subsection 148(8) — tax-free rollover of certain life insurance policies to a child

Subsections 148(8.1) and (8.2) — tax-free rollover of life insurance policies to a spouse

Subsection 148(9) — definitions relevant to section 148 including "adjusted cost basis", "cash surrender value", "disposition", "policy loan", "proceeds of the disposition", and "value"

Subsection 248(1) — definition of "common-law partner"

Subsections 248(1) — definition of "life insurance policy"

Income Tax Regulations

Section 306 — exempt policies (including anti dump-in rule)

Section 307 — accumulating funds

Section 308 — net cost of pure insurance

Interpretation Bulletin

IT-87R2 — Policyholders' Income from Life Insurance Policies

Chapter 3

Life Insurance and the Need for Estate Liquidity

E state planning is, in many respects, the process of preparing for the convergence of life's two most inevitable occurrences, death and taxes. It will come as no surprise to readers that the Act contains many and varied rules dealing with the taxation of a deceased taxpayer. Lawyers, accountants and financial advisors spend a great deal of time and effort trying to help their clients minimize the impact of these rules.

Insurance brokers, on the other hand, devote much effort to funding any tax liabilities which cannot be avoided, even with expert advice. Although income tax gets the most attention, liquidity in an estate may also be required for the payment of probate fees, executors' and trustees' fees, professional fees and charitable and other bequests.

This chapter will review some key issues relating to estate liquidity and how these needs can be met with life insurance.

1. Taxation of Property Held at Death

Deemed Dispositions

Unlike many countries, such as the United States, Canada does not impose estate taxes, which are levied on the value of an estate held by a deceased person. Instead, a Canadian resident is generally deemed to have disposed of his or her property for fair market value immediately before death. Thus, the deceased is taxed as if the property had been sold to an arm's length third party and realizes accrued gains or losses in the tax return filed for the year of death (this is cheerfully labeled the "terminal return"). The taxpayer's estate/beneficiaries will acquire the property at an ACB equal to fair market value.

Of course, properties with accrued gains can create significant tax burdens in the year of death, a factor which has allowed the business of many a life insurance broker to flourish. These gains can be deferred where property is transferred to a surviving spouse, or to a qualifying spouse trust, but will be realized when the spouse dies or otherwise disposes of the property (see "Transfers of Property to Spouses and Spouse Trusts" in the next section). The tax deferral available on property transferred to a spouse or spouse trust is called a "spousal rollover" and will also be discussed in greater detail below.

Taxation of Different Types of Property

Virtually all of a taxpayer's property is deemed to be disposed of immediately before death, although the income tax consequences of a disposition can vary according to the type of property in question. The following is an overview of the rules that apply to some common types of property held by a deceased taxpayer. Please remember that this analysis assumes that no spousal rollover is available.

(a) Shares of Public Corporations

Shares of a corporation (whether publicly traded or private) are considered capital property. The difference between the shares' ACB and fair market value is treated as a capital gain or loss in the year of death. The calculation is relatively straightforward and the value easy to determine by reference to the stock quotations for the last trading day before death. One-half of any capital gain is added to the deceased's income in the year of death; one-half of any capital losses are allowable.

(b) Shares of Private Corporations

Shares of private corporations are of course taxed in the same manner, but are more problematic from a planning standpoint. Frequently, a major difficulty is valuation; unlike shares of public corporations, the value of private corporation common shares cannot simply be looked up. Preferred shares with a fixed redemption amount pose fewer problems, but it is still open to the CRA to "look behind" the value of those shares to determine whether the redemption amount represent the shares' actual value. Ideally, business owners should retain the services of a valuations expert to determine (or at least estimate) share values from time to time. It can be a cumbersome and expensive process, but may be necessary if proper estate planning is to be done. A couple of other points are worthy of mention:

- In valuing shares held by a deceased shareholder, subsection 70(5.3) of the Act provides that the cash surrender value (if any) of any insurance owned by the corporation on the deceased's life will be included. The proceeds themselves do not need to be considered. This valuation rule will also apply to policies owned by the corporation on the life of a person not dealing at arm's length with the deceased (for example, close family members such as a spouse, parent, child or sibling of the deceased). However, under CRA guidelines, any insurance held by the corporation on the lives of others, such as surviving shareholders who deal at arm's length with the deceased, will be valued according to general valuation principles. The value of these policies could be greater than their cash surrender value if, for example, the life insured was uninsurable or suffering from a terminal illness. There is no apparent reason for this distinction.

- The CRA takes the position that it is not bound by share values determined under a shareholders agreement between non-arm's length parties (such as members of the same immediate family). It is questionable whether the CRA is correct in this position, but it is best to avoid having clients become a test case. There is no doubt that proper valuation is even more critical in the case of family-owned businesses.

The capital gains exemption, which was recently increased to $750,000, may be claimed in the year of death if the shares qualify. This exemption is discussed in Chapter 2.

(c) Partnership Interests

An interest (or unit) in a partnership is treated as capital property, like a share of a corporation, and is subject to a capital gain or loss on death.

(d) Mutual Funds and Segregated Funds

Most mutual and segregated funds will buy and sell investments periodically throughout the investor's lifetime, creating ongoing capital gains and losses. On the individual's death, any unrealized gains or losses will show up on the terminal return. There are features unique to segregated funds, however, which may cause unforeseen income tax consequences on the owner's death. These arise largely because there is another individual, known as the "annuitant", who is a party to any segregated fund contract. The annuitant is the person whose life is used to calculate the amount of payments if, for example, the owner elects to receive an annuity under one of the settlement options of the segregated fund contract. The owner and annuitant may or may not be the same person.

Consider the example of Mrs. Apple, who is the owner and annuitant of a segregated fund contract. She has named Mr. Apple as beneficiary of the contract in the event of her death. On Mrs. Apple's death, one would expect that, under the usual rollover provisions of the Act, the contract would pass to Mr. Apple on a tax-deferred basis. However, because Mrs. Apple was the annuitant, her death results in the termination of the segregated fund contract, and the realization of any inherent capital gains. This is in contrast to a mutual fund, which would pass from the deceased to her husband on a rollover basis.

This unusual result can be avoided through careful selection of the annuitant under a segregated fund. Some insurance companies will permit a husband and wife to be named as joint annuitants under a segregated fund so that the contract will simply continue when one of them dies. Alternatively, and more commonly, a contingent or successor annuitant can be named, which allows the contract to continue after the death of the first-named annuitant.

(e) Bonds

Certain types of bonds have a trading value which fluctuates according to current interest rates. To the extent that a bond held by a deceased taxpayer has increased or decreased in value, a capital gain or loss will be realized immediately before death.

(f) GICs, Term Deposits, Bank Accounts

Technically, these assets are deemed to be disposed of like any other. However, they do not generate any gain or loss, as they essentially represent tax-paid money. Interest earned in these accounts will, of course, be taxed in the year of death, but will be prorated between the terminal return and the tax return for the first taxation year of the estate.

(g) Real Estate (Personal)

Gains relating to a house, cottage or condominium which was the deceased's principal residence are tax-free. (Each taxpayer is entitled to only one principal residence at a time. Married couples may have only one between them.) A personal-use real estate property that does not qualify as a principal residence will generate a capital gain or loss on death. Given the value of recreational property in many areas of the country, it is not unusual to find situations where an individual's cottage has a higher inherent gain than his or her house. In that case, the cottage will qualify as the principal residence as long as the owner uses it on a regular basis. Even a couple of weeks per year will suffice. The choice of which property will be elected as principal residence does not have to be made until the property is sold, or until a deemed disposition on death.

(h) Real Estate (Investment)

Individuals frequently own real estate that is rented out to others. In many cases, depreciation (or capital cost allowance) may be claimed as a deduction against rental income. In the year of death, if the fair market value of the property exceeds its undepreciated capital cost ("UCC"), the amount of any recaptured depreciation will be taxed. If the value is less than its UCC, the difference may be claimed by the deceased taxpayer as a terminal loss and deducted against other income. A capital gain will also be realized if the value exceeds the taxpayer's original cost. In certain circumstances, the CRA will consider that a taxpayer's business is the trading of real estate, in which case gains or losses on death are fully taxable as business income, or fully deductible as business losses, as the case may be.

(i) Other Depreciable Property

Property against which capital cost allowance may be claimed is called depreciable capital property. Buildings rented out to others, as described immediately above, are in this category. Other types of depreciable property are furniture, machinery, equipment and automobiles used by a deceased individual in a business which he or she operates as a proprietorship (i.e., not through a corporation or partnership).

(j) RRIFs and RRSPs

Unless there is a surviving spouse named as beneficiary, amounts remaining in a RRIF or RRSP are fully taxed in the year of death. (This really bothers some clients, although it's hard to complain after decades of tax-deductible contributions and tax-deferred earnings.) There are some limited exceptions to these rules, primarily related to situations where there is a financially dependent or disabled child named as beneficiary.

(k) Life Insurance Policies

An exempt life insurance policy held by a deceased taxpayer on the life of another person may be subject to taxation. If its cash surrender value at that time exceeds its ACB, the excess is taxable to the deceased. As described in Chapter 2, there are exceptions if the policy is transferred to the deceased's spouse, or if the policy is transferred to the deceased's child, and a child or grandchild of the deceased is the life insured.

Role of Life Insurance

Needless to say, one of the most fundamental uses of life insurance is to provide cash to satisfy the income tax burden realized in the year of death. Insurance on the individual's life, payable to his or her estate, can provide tax-free cash for the payment of these liabilities. Where property is to be passed to a surviving spouse, insurance on both lives, payable on the second death, is an attractive option, particularly given the greatly reduced mortality charges applicable to this type of policy.

Assuming the client is insurable, life insurance is inevitably the least expensive means of funding estate liabilities. It is much more cost efficient than, for example, borrowing money, liquidating assets or self-insuring through a personally managed sinking fund. In addition, insurance has the great advantage of being paid exactly when it is needed.

Joint last-to-die insurance for estate purposes may be personally-owned or, as described later in this chapter, may be owned in a corporation. Where the insurance is to be held personally, care should be taken regarding how the ownership is structured. For example, in one case an individual owned a policy on the lives of himself and his wife. The policy owner died without a will, which delayed the transfer of the insurance policy to the surviving spouse and caused it to be caught up in the delay in the administration of the estate. Necessary policy transactions could not be taken until this cumbersome process was completed.

The above difficulties could have been avoided if the deceased had his wife named originally as contingent owner of the policy. In that case, the insurance company would have quickly transferred ownership without concern for the fact that the deceased had no will. A simple step taken when the policy was issued would have avoided significant problems.

The naming of a contingent owner is generally preferable to having the husband and wife named as joint owners of the contract, as certain insurance companies (somewhat surprisingly) do not automatically transfer ownership of a policy to the surviving joint tenant. The naming of a contingent owner seems a more readily accepted alternative.

2. Other Issues Relating to Taxation in Year of Death

Transfers of Property to Spouses and Spouse Trusts

It is common knowledge amongst financial and estate planners that if an individual leaves property to his or her surviving spouse, a "rollover" occurs for income tax purposes. This means that the deceased is deemed to have disposed of the property for its ACB, resulting in no capital gain or loss. The survivor acquires the property at that same ACB.

It is important to note that the definition of spouse for income tax purposes has been considerably expanded in recent years. It, of course, refers to a legally married spouse of the opposite sex. However, the *Income Tax Act* also includes in this definition a person who is the "common-law partner" of another (i.e., a person of the same or opposite sex who has cohabited in a conjugal relationship with that person for at least one year).

A rollover is also available where property is left to a special trust (established under the deceased's will) whose income must be paid to the surviving spouse. Income for these purposes generally means interest and dividends, as capital gains do not qualify as "income" for trust purposes. The terms of the trust may allow the spouse to receive distributions of capital at the discretion of the trustees, although this is not mandatory.

If the trust allows anyone other than the spouse to receive either income or capital during the spouse's lifetime, the trust does not qualify for rollover treatment. A trust will also be disqualified if, for example, it provides that the spouse's entitlement will end if he or she remarries, or if it attaches other conditions to the spouse's right to income or capital.

As noted, a rollover is available whether property is left outright to the spouse or to a spouse trust. Therefore, the decision as to which alternative to select is really based upon factors having nothing to do with income tax. The main advantage of a spouse trust (and probably most other trusts as well) is control. Here are three common situations where a spouse trust may be attractive from a will planning point of view:

- Some testators are concerned that, if property is left outright to the survivor, the survivor may ultimately remarry and give the property to the new husband or wife, or to children from that marriage. The spouse trust allows a testator to specify who will inherit the property on the spouse's death.

- Some types of property, such as shares of private corporations which carry on an active business, require management expertise. Where the surviving spouse has no experience or involvement in the business, it may be preferable to leave the shares in a spouse trust, whose trustees do have the ability to manage the corporation. This alternative is particularly attractive where there are children who are able to run the business and who will inherit the shares on the spouse's death. In these cases, it is often advisable to have a panel of three trustees — the spouse, one of the adult children, plus an independent third party who can provide sage, objective advice should disputes arise.

- A spouse trust may also be recommended where the spouse is extremely elderly or is suffering from mental incapacity and is unable to properly manage his or her affairs.

There are occasions where a rollover on the transfer of property to a spouse or spouse trust is not desirable. For example, a deceased taxpayer may not have fully utilized the capital gains exemption for small business shares during his or her lifetime. Alternatively, the deceased may have capital losses on certain property against which capital gains on another property could be offset. In these circumstances, the executor is permitted to elect that certain properties pass to the spouse or spouse trust at fair market value. This allows the selective triggering of capital gains, thereby maximizing the deceased's income tax benefits, and providing the recipient with a bump up in the ACB of the property.

In order to achieve maximum tax deferral, clients generally arrange to have their property left to a spouse or spouse trust. As insurance professionals know, this creates an opportunity for insurance on the lives of both husband and wife, with proceeds payable on the second death. This ensures that cash will be available on the second death when the tax liability will arise. It is also much less expensive than insurance on a single life. (See Chapter 4 for a discussion of how corporate-owned life insurance might play a role in these circumstances.)

Utilization of Losses in Year of Death

Most readers will be familiar with the general rule that taxpayers who have net capital losses in a given year can carry them back three years or forward indefinitely. These losses can only be utilized against capital gains. However, in the year of death, any capital losses carried forward, or capital losses realized in the year of death, can be used to offset other income that year. Therefore, if there are insufficient capital gains in the year of death to soak up these losses, they may be written off against other income, such as business, employment or investment income. If unutilized losses still remain, they may be applied against other income in the immediately preceding year.

Any non-capital losses, such as business or rental losses, can also be used against other income in the year of death, although this is true for any taxation year.

Losses Realized in the Estate

Capital and non-capital losses realized in the first taxation year of an estate may be carried back against income earned in the year of death. In this case, capital losses may only be applied against capital gains, not other income. In this regard, it is important to remember that the estate's first taxation year, as selected by the executor, can end any time within 365 days of death.

This rule can have a couple of useful applications. Consider the example of Enid, who in 2004 purchased 10,000 shares of Tech Monster Inc. for $1 each. At the time of her death in 2008, the shares were worth $200 each, a capital gain of $199 per share, or $1.99 million. The estate acquired the shares at an ACB of $2 million, the total fair market value of the shares at the time of death.

Within a few months of Enid's death, Tech Monster's stock price plummeted, with the result that the deceased's executors sold the shares within the estate's first taxation year for $10 each ($100,000). This was well in excess of the original purchase price to the deceased but, because the estate had an ACB of $2 million, it realized a capital loss of $1.9 million. The estate had no other income or losses in that year.

In this example, because the sale took place in the estate's first taxation year, the loss can be carried back against the capital gains realized by the deceased in the year of death. This reduces the capital gain to $90,000 ($1,990,000 - $1,900,000), mirroring the result that would have occurred had Enid lived to sell the shares herself for this amount. This rule recognizes the fact that the deemed disposition immediately before death is essentially an artificial paper gain which can be reduced if an actual disposition of the property, within the required time limit, results in a loss.

Another example of the loss carryback rule relates to the use of corporate-owned life insurance to redeem the shares of a deceased shareholder. Under a convoluted set of rules, the redemption of shares can trigger a capital loss to the estate, which can be carried back against the capital gain realized by the deceased in the year of death. (This planning strategy has been seriously impacted by the introduction of new stop-loss rules in 1995. These rules will be examined in Chapter 6.)

Joint and Several Liability for Income Tax on RRSPs and RRIFs

It is the executor's responsibility to ensure that taxes and other estate liabilities are paid before final distribution of the estate is made to the beneficiaries. Thus, the beneficiaries are not required to pay any of the estate's income tax liabilities, and should receive their inheritance free of tax. The usual procedure, prior to a final distribution of estate assets, is for the executor to obtain a Clearance Certificate from the CRA, which certifies that no further taxes are owing. Failure to obtain this certificate may result in the executor being personally liable for the estate's unpaid taxes.

However, there are special rules in the case of taxes owing in respect of RRSPs and RRIFs. In most cases, of course, there are named beneficiaries under these plans, and the death benefits are paid directly to them by the financial institution, without any tax being withheld. Thus, the estate is liable for the tax without having received the funds. In these circumstances, the Act provides that a named beneficiary under an RRSP or RRIF is jointly and severally liable for taxes owing in respect of these plans. Otherwise, the CRA would have no recourse if the estate failed to make the necessary tax payments.

Payment of Income Tax by Instalments

Another rarely mentioned rule is the one which provides that tax payable in the year of death may be paid by annual instalments over a period of up to 10 years. Interest is, of course, payable on outstanding amounts, and security "acceptable to the Minister" must be provided. This interest is non-deductible and is generally at higher than market rates (8% in the first quarter of 2008).

While this provides a means of financing the payment of large amounts of tax which arise in the year of death, most individuals are reluctant to enter into this type of formal, debtor/creditor relationship with the CRA. The non-deductibility of the interest makes this even less attractive.

This method of paying tax in respect of the "terminal year" will usually pale in comparison to a life insurance solution.

3. Probate Fees

Probate fees have existed for more than a century in many provinces, but continue to be a current topic of conversation for estate planners. In Ontario, for example, probate fees for estates in excess of $50,000 were tripled in 1992 from 0.5% to 1.5% of the value of an estate under probate. This reinforced the view already held by many that probate fees were nothing more than a wealth tax thinly disguised as an anachronistic court fee. In fact, the Supreme Court of Canada subsequently came to the same conclusion. The decision in the *Eurig Estate* case found that probate fees were in essence a tax, and that they were being imposed and collected in an unconstitutional manner. Such fees must now be legislated in the same way as other tax legislation. Among other things, in the future, this will prevent provinces from raising probate fees behind closed doors in a cabinet meeting, as was done in Ontario in 1992. As a result, what were formerly called probate fees are now known in Ontario as "estate administration taxes". Because of its familiarity and its continued use in other provinces, however, the term "probate fees" will be used in this book.

Fee increases also led to a renewed focus by planners on means of reducing these fees. Traditional methods of avoiding probate fees were reemphasized and new planning ideas were developed.

This section will review some of the legal background concerning the concept of probate and will discuss a number of planning alternatives which may be of interest.

Historical Background

The probate rules have been in force in most provinces since the 19th century and had changed little since that time, until the *Eurig Estate* case. Although this case has changed the way provinces must collect probate fees, the general law of probate remains much the same.

Probate provides evidence that the executor of a deceased's will has authority to act, but it is not true to say that the executor requires probate in order to act on behalf of the estate; rather, the executor takes his or her authority from the will itself and may theoretically act as of the moment of death. Probate has evolved primarily as a means of providing legal protection to third parties who must deal with the estate, particularly financial institutions. While probate is not strictly required as a means of proving the executor's authority, practice has evolved over time so that, in many circumstances, it has become a legal requirement. Thus, the necessity of obtaining probate in many circumstances seems to have evolved more through practice and custom than through the law itself.

What Goes In and What Stays Out?

Most readers will be familiar with assets in respect of which probate is typically required. This would include most investments issued by financial institutions, such as GICs, T-Bills, cash on deposit, mutual funds and publicly traded securities. As all readers will know, life insurance proceeds payable to a named beneficiary fall outside of probate. This includes segregated funds, annuities and other investment products, registered or otherwise, issued by insurance companies. Jointly held property is also excluded from probate on the first death, as discussed more fully below.

In 2004, the Ontario Court of Appeal case *Amherst Crane Rentals Limited v. Arlene Clare Perring* significantly changed the landscape involving registered plans, probate fees and creditor protection. In that case, the Court held that RRSP proceeds payable to a named beneficiary did not form part of the deceased's estate, even though the RRSP was not issued by an insurance company. As a result, the proceeds were free from the claims of the deceased's creditors and, by the same reasoning, would not be subject to probate fees. This serves to "level the playing field" amongst registered plans issued by various types of financial institutions. (Changes to the bankruptcy laws are also leading towards providing equality, as regards creditor protection during lifetime, for all types of RRSPs. See Chapter 11.)

Leave to appeal this case to the Supreme Court of Canada was denied in February 2005. Therefore, *Amherst Crane* now represents Ontario law in this area. While not binding in other provinces, this is a strong decision that would likely be influential in other courts.

Probate Planning Ideas

(a) Multiple Wills

Over the years it has become commonplace for estate planners to recommend to clients that, to the extent it is reasonable to do so, assets should be held in joint tenancy and beneficiaries should be named on insurance policies and registered plans in order to keep assets out of an individual's estate for probate purposes. This would avoid probate fees and would also avoid having the assets tied up should there be any problems with the administration of the estate.

While these long-standing planning ideas remain viable, some new planning strategies are emerging which are taking probate planning to a much more sophisticated level. One that has gained significant popularity in the last few years relates to individuals who own shares of private corporations. In most cases, probate should not be required for private corporation shares. Family members will typically authorize the transfer of these shares under the deceased's will without the necessity of probate being obtained.

It has been suggested that, in these circumstances, an individual can execute multiple wills. One will would deal with the person's general estate and would include all those items in respect of which probate was required. A second will could be prepared which would deal exclusively with shares of the individual's private corporation. Fees would be payable only in respect of the former will which, in this case and many others, would represent a relatively small portion of the estate. These two wills are typically executed simultaneously and only the former will would be submitted for probate on the person's death. In Ontario, the *Granovsky* case ruled in favour of the estate when the multiple-will strategy was challenged by the province. The government initially appealed this decision but subsequently abandoned the appeal. Barring a change in legislation, the multiple-will strategy should continue to grow in popularity.

(b) Revocable Trusts

It has also been suggested that property which would otherwise be included in probate may be transferred, during a person's lifetime, to a revocable trust. Under the trust document, the individual transferring the property would name himself or herself as trustee and would retain the ability to collapse the trust and reacquire the trust property at any time. The individual would also have the right to trust income, or to distribute such income to other beneficiaries if he or she wished to do so. On death, because the property would be held by a trust rather than the individual directly, the assets held within the trust would not be part of the deceased's estate for probate purposes.

If planning is to be done with a revocable trust, some caution should be exercised regarding the income tax issues. Individuals should be aware that income generated within the trust will be attributed to the settlor of the trust, but this is no worse from a tax perspective than if the individual had simply retained the assets in his or her own name. A potentially more serious problem arises, however, regarding the possible realization of capital gains upon the transfer of appreciated assets to this trust. It is possible, although the income tax legislation is far from clear, that a capital gain could be triggered on appreciated capital assets that pass to this trust. This issue would not arise if the assets consisted of unappreciated capital property or assets such as T-Bills, GICs and other "near cash" investments. Thus, for the time being, these latter types of assets are best suited to this planning idea.

For taxpayers age 65 or over, the use of an alter ego or joint partner trust may be more attractive than a revocable trust. These trusts are discussed immediately below.

(c) Alter Ego and Joint Partner Trusts

(i) Introduction

In December 1999, the Department of Finance released draft legislation that included unexpected proposals creating two new types of trusts, known as alter ego trusts and joint spousal trusts. The term "joint spousal trust" was subsequently changed to "joint partner trust", and finally, to "joint spousal or common-law partner trust", but for the sake of brevity, this chapter will use the term "joint partner trust". These proposals were passed into law in 2001, effective for trusts created after 1999.

(ii) Structure

An alter ego trust is one created by an individual age 65 or older (the "settlor") for the exclusive benefit of the settlor during his or her lifetime. In other words, as long as the settlor is alive, no other person may receive income or capital from the trust. A joint partner trust is also one created by a settlor age 65 or older, but is for the exclusive benefit of the settlor and his or her spouse during their lifetimes.

Under either type of trust, other beneficiaries would be named to receive trust property after the death of the settlor or, if applicable, that of the survivor of the settlor and the spouse.

By definition, an alter ego or joint partner trust will constitute an *inter vivos* trust (i.e., one created during the settlor's lifetime). It will typically be established under a trust agreement signed by the settlor and the trustees. The settlor will have complete discretion over the selection of trustees — for example, the settlor could act as sole trustee or could be one of many. If the trust is a joint partner trust, the settlor and his or her spouse could act as trustees. In most cases, however, the settlor's main objective will be to retain complete control over trust assets.

The trust agreement would also provide for the appointment of a new trustee or trustees upon the deaths of the original trustees.

(iii) Income Tax Considerations

As an *inter vivos* trust, an alter ego trust or joint partner trust will be taxed at the top marginal tax rate on all of its undistributed income. Income may be allocated to the settlor or, in the case of a joint partner trust, to the settlor's spouse, and will in that case be taxed at the recipient's own marginal rate. In this regard, these trusts are taxed like any other *inter vivos* trust.

However, alter ego and joint partner trusts do have one feature that sets them apart from other trusts. The draft legislation provides that, contrary to the usual rule, there is no deemed disposition of property transferred to these trusts. Rather, the property will be acquired at the settlor's adjusted cost base, resulting in a rollover for income tax purposes. The availability of this rollover provides a degree of tax planning certainty that is missing when, as described above, assets pass to a revocable trust. In the latter case, it is likely that capital gains will arise when appreciated property is transferred to the trust.

In the case of alter ego and joint partner trusts, the deemed disposition is deferred until the death of the settlor, or the death of the survivor of the settlor and the spouse, as the case may be. At that time, a deemed disposition will occur within the trust and, because this will be considered an *inter vivos* trust, tax will be payable at the top marginal rate on realized capital gains.

It would be stretching matters to suggest that alter ego and joint partner trusts present significant tax planning opportunities. Income will not be taxed at any lesser rate than would be the case without the use of the trusts. Similarly, unrealized gains will be taxed on the death of the settlor (or the settlor's spouse, as the case may be) to the same extent as before death.

Rather, the main planning opportunities relating to these new trusts appear to be in the area of estate planning, as described below.

(iv) Planning Opportunities

The following is a summary of the planning considerations for alter ego and joint partner trusts (and of *inter vivos* trusts generally):

- Property held in an alter ego or joint partner trust on the settlor's death is not part of the deceased's estate and is therefore free of probate fees. This is also true of other *inter vivos* trusts. However, there is no rollover for tax purposes when property is transferred to the latter trusts. This will be of particular interest to individuals with large investment portfolios that have significant unrealized capital gains, and to shareholders of private corporations.

- A probated will is a public document, and thus cannot remain confidential or secret. On the other hand, an *inter vivos* trust need never come to the attention of anyone other than the settlor, trustees and beneficiaries. Where secrecy is a concern, *inter vivos* trusts, including alter ego and joint partner trusts, have significant advantages over wills.

- Alter ego and joint partner trusts should, in most cases, be flexible planning instruments. For example, the trust documents should be drafted in a way that, unlike typical irrevocable *inter vivos* trusts, allows some or all of the trust capital to revert to the settlor at any time. In this way, if the settlor decided upon an estate-distribution strategy different from that included in the original trust document, a new arrangement could be implemented by having such capital transferred to a new alter ego or joint partner trust, or by having it dealt with under the individual's will.

- An alter ego or joint partner trust is not a complete substitute for a will. Clients should have a will to deal with any assets not held within the trust. A will can also deal with issues that are not appropriate for alter ego or joint partner trusts, such as guardianship for children.

- All provinces have laws under which interested parties can challenge the validity of a will for reasons such as undue influence or the mental incapacity of the testator. These laws will not apply to property passing to beneficiaries under an *inter vivos* trust, including an alter ego and joint partner trust, making such trusts less susceptible to being weighed down by litigation.

- Where an individual transfers property to an *inter vivos* trust, he or she will generally enjoy a greater level of creditor protection with regards to such property. It is questionable, however, whether alter ego and joint partner trusts will provide a significant level of creditor protection, because by their very nature they exist for the exclusive benefit of the settlor, and perhaps his or her spouse, during his or her lifetime. The best that can be said is that such trusts will provide no lesser level of creditor protection, and possibly more, than would be available if the settlor had simply retained ownership of the property.

- Alter ego and joint partner trusts can, as described above, be at least partial will substitutes. Similarly, they may also act as an alternative to the standard power of attorney for property. Where an individual has transferred assets to a trust, the assets are managed by trustees under the terms of the trust agreement and would not fall under the power of attorney. This will often allow the property to be managed more effectively, as the individual can generally provide more specific directions to trustees under a trust agreement than can be given under a standard power of attorney. For example, a trust agreement can provide detailed provisions regarding the investment and distribution of trust funds held on behalf of minor beneficiaries.

(v) Some Precautionary Notes

While the creation of alter ego trusts and joint partner trusts creates probate planning opportunities, clients and their advisors need to review all available options in order to determine whether these present the best available options. For example, a trust created under an individual's will (a testamentary trust), unlike an *inter vivos* trust, is eligible for graduated income tax rates identical to those applicable to individual taxpayers. This creates income-splitting opportunities, the benefits of which may outweigh the probate fee savings and other advantages available through the creation of alter ego or joint partner trusts.

In addition, as discussed above, all income realized in an alter ego or joint partner trust on the death of the settlor or the settlor's spouse will be taxed at the top marginal rate. In some cases, this may result in a higher amount of tax than would have been paid without the establishment of the trust.

Finally, certain tax planning opportunities that arise at the time of death may not be available where an alter ego or joint partner trust is used. Capital gains realized in one of these trusts at the time of death cannot be offset by capital losses realized in the deceased's terminal return, and *vice versa*.

(vi) Role of Life Insurance

Life insurance is often acquired as a means of funding income tax liabilities that arise on the death of an individual or his or her spouse, and will continue to be a valuable estate planning tool when clients establish an alter ego or joint partner trust.

The deemed disposition will, as noted above, occur within the trust. Technically, therefore, it will be the trust rather than the deceased's estate that is responsible for the payment of income taxes. For this reason, it may be advisable for the trust to be owner and beneficiary of the insurance policy. Insurance premiums could be paid with trust income or capital, or, alternatively, the settlor could pay premiums out of his or her remaining personal resources. Insurance proceeds paid to the trust will not form part of the deceased's estate and will thus be free of probate fees.

(d) Joint Ownership with Right of Survivorship

Where individuals own a property jointly, with right of survivorship, the death of one joint tenant causes the other to become sole owner of the property. This takes place through the right of survivorship and does not cause the property to pass through the deceased's estate nor become subject to probate. Perhaps the most common form of joint ownership is a home or cottage owned by a husband and wife. However, joint ownership of investment assets between spouses, and between parents and children, is becoming more common.

Joint ownership has come under increased scrutiny because of the recent Supreme Court decisions in the *Pecore and Marsden* cases. These cases make it clear that there are different types of joint ownership. For example, a parent may decide that he or she wishes to add an adult child as a joint tenant on an investment account because the parent's wish is that the child ultimately inherit the account. In other cases, the addition of a joint tenant may be for the sake of convenience (e.g., to have another person with signing authority on the account) without any real intention to give the child a beneficial interest in the investment.

In cases such as this, it is critical to determine what the individual's intention was in creating the joint ownership. Proper documentation — not always prominent in the creation of a joint account — is the best way to establish intention.

The death of a joint tenant will typically result in the application of the deemed disposition rules, i.e., this is not a method for avoiding income tax on death. But it can be a convenient way of avoiding probate fees, as well as the time and cost of estate administration.

4. Using Corporate-Owned Life Insurance to Pay Estate Liabilities

Individual business owners frequently purchase life insurance to provide funding for a variety of estate liabilities, such as capital gains tax, probate fees and other estate costs addressed in this chapter. In certain circumstances, however, it is possible to use corporate-owned insurance to solve these same needs.

Consider the example of a husband and wife who each own 50% of the shares of an operating business. The shares have a nominal ACB and a fair market value of $3 million. Each spouse intends to leave his or her shares to the other, meaning that capital gains tax will be deferred until the second death. The spouses have each utilized the capital gains exemption for small business corporations. Assuming that 50% of capital gains continue to be subject to tax, and assuming a personal tax rate of 46%, tax payable on the second death would approximate $690,000. The spouses agree to acquire $900,000 of joint second-to-die insurance, enough to pay estimated income tax liabilities and to allow for future increases in value.

Obviously, it would be open to one of the spouses to purchase the insurance in his or her name, with the estate of the second-to-die named as beneficiary. The spouses could also own the policy jointly. The same objectives could be accomplished, however, by having the corporation as owner and beneficiary of the policy. On the second death, the life insurance proceeds would be received tax-free by the corporation, and the amount of those proceeds, less the ACB of the insurance policy, would be credited to the corporation's CDA. A tax-free capital dividend could then be declared, which would be tax-free to the estate, and the funds used for the above estate purposes.

In this example, the shareholders would be advised to identify the existence of the corporate-owned insurance in their wills. Each spouse could direct his or her executor to take all necessary steps to ensure that the proceeds were collected, distributed and applied in the intended manner. This would be particularly important if, for example, the shares of the corporation were being gifted to the couple's child(ren). The wills would have to provide for the payment of the capital dividend prior to the transfer of shares so that the estate's control of the insurance proceeds was maintained.

In some cases, in the course of an insured share redemption strategy, it is possible to use corporate-owned life insurance not only to pay income tax but to reduce overall tax liability. This is discussed in greater detail in Chapter 5.

5. Personal Insured Annuities

An insured annuity, or "back-to-back" arrangement, consists of the purchase of an immediate annuity in combination with a life insurance policy. In many circumstances, this type of arrangement can result in income tax advantages and favourable investment returns. This section will review the common methods of structuring back-to-back arrangements in the personal and corporate markets, as well as some relevant taxation issues and potential risks.

Structure

The first component of a typical back-to-back arrangement involves the purchase by an individual of an immediate annuity that qualifies as a prescribed annuity for the purposes of the *Income Tax Act.* In order to maximize income, the annuity will generally be paid for the life of the annuitant with no guarantee period.

The second component is the purchase of an insurance policy on the individual's life, using the after-tax portion of the annuity payments to pay premiums. Insurance policies with little or no cash surrender value, such as Term to 100 plans or "minimum-funded" universal life policies, are most commonly used because of the relatively low level of required premiums. The life insurance can be structured to exactly replace the capital that was used to fund the purchase of the annuity.

This kind of arrangement is especially attractive to older individuals who are concerned about depleting capital, to the detriment of their beneficiaries, for the payment of their living expenses. Thus, a properly structured program will provide the desired level of annuity income for life. In addition, it will provide tax-free insurance proceeds that will restore capital for the payment of bequests, liabilities and other estate liquidity needs.

Taxation

By definition, each prescribed annuity payment contains a blend of taxable interest and a tax-free return of principal. These amounts do not fluctuate throughout the term of the contract. This is in contrast to the taxation of a non-prescribed annuity, where each payment contains a much higher level of taxable income in the early years of the contract.

The level taxation of interest under a prescribed annuity, plus the return of the original capital, can provide an after-tax cash flow superior to that available under other savings vehicles, such as GICs. In addition, of course, the capital is replaced on death through the insurance proceeds, providing needed liquidity for estate purposes.

References

Income Tax Act (Canada)

Paragraphs 20(1)(c) to (d) — interest deductibility

Section 54 — definition of "principal residence"

Paragraphs 56(1)(d) and 60(a) — taxation of prescribed annuities

Subsection 70(5) — taxation of capital property held at death

Subsection 70(5.3) — valuation of certain corporate-owned life insurance policies

Subsection 70(6) — transfer of property on death to spouse or spouse trust

Subsection 70(6.2) — election to realize capital gains on property transferred to a spouse or spouse trust

Subsection 73(1.01) — rollover on transfer of property to alter ego or joint spousal or common-law partner trust

Subsection 83(2) — capital dividends

Subsection 89(1) — definition of "capital dividend account"

Section 110.6 — capital gains exemption

Subsection 111(2) — utilization of losses in year of death

Paragraph 148(2)(b) — taxation of life insurance policy held at death

Subsections 159(5) and (7) — payment of tax owing by deceased taxpayer over ten-year period

Section 160.2 — joint and several liability for income tax

Subsection 164(6) — carryback of capital losses realized in first taxation year of estate

Subsection 248(1) — definition of "common-law partner", "alter ego trust" and "joint spousal or common-law partner trust"

Income Tax Regulation

Section 304 — prescribed annuity contracts

Subsection 4301(a) — payment of tax owing by deceased taxpayer over ten-year period

Interpretation Bulletins

IT-66R6 — Capital Dividends

IT-87R2 — Policyholders' Income from Life Insurance Policies

IT-120R6 — Principal Residence

IT-140R3 — Buy-Sell Agreements

IT-305R4 — Testamentary Spouse Trusts

IT-416R3 — Valuation of Shares of a Corporation Receiving Life Insurance Proceeds on Death of a Shareholder

IT-430R3 — Life Insurance Proceeds Received by a Corporation or Partnership

IT-500R — RRSPs: Death of an Annuitant

Information Circular

IC 89-3 — Policy Statement on Business Equity Valuations (see paragraphs 40 and 41 regarding corporate-owned life insurance)

Case Law

Amherst Crane Limited v. Perring, 241 D.L.R. (4th) 176 (Ont. C.A.)

Re Eurig Estate, [1998] 2 S.C.R. 565

Granovsky Estate v. Ontario, (1998) 156 D.L.R. (4th) 557 (Ont. Ct. Gen.Div.))

Marsden Estate v. Saylor, [2007] 1 S.C.R. 838

Pecore v. Pecore, [2007] 1 S.C.R. 795

Singleton v. Canada, 2001 DTC 5533 (S.C.C.)

Chapter 4

Introduction to Corporate-Owned Life Insurance

The most complex, interesting and rewarding estate planning cases typically involve individuals who own and manage their own businesses. In most cases, these businesses are operated through private corporations which have a small number of shareholders, or perhaps just one. Corporations frequently acquire insurance on the lives of their shareholders. This insurance is sometimes used for corporate purposes, but may also be used to satisfy the personal estate needs of the deceased shareholder.

This chapter will discuss some basic issues concerning the ownership of life insurance by a private corporation, including an introduction to the capital dividend account ("CDA"). It will then discuss how an individual who owns a corporation can use corporate-owned life insurance to pay estate liabilities, such as those discussed in Chapter 3. It will conclude with a discussion of some difficult issues concerning the transfer of ownership of life insurance between corporations and their shareholders.

1. The Capital Dividend Account ("CDA")

Life insurance proceeds are tax-free, whether they are received by an individual, corporation, trust or other entity. The CDA is the vehicle through which insurance proceeds received by a private corporation may, in turn, be distributed tax-free to its shareholders. An insurance professional operating in the business insurance market must have familiarity with the CDA in order to properly advise clients and maintain credibility with their other professional advisors.

The Purpose of the CDA

The concept of the CDA originates with the "integration theory", which, as described in Chapter 2, is the fundamental basis on which the Canadian corporate tax system is structured. The integration theory holds that income earned by a corporation and distributed to its shareholders as a dividend should attract no more or less tax than if the income had been earned directly.

The CDA is a notional tax account which includes certain tax-free amounts received by private corporations. The outstanding credit within the CDA may be distributed in the form of tax-free capital dividends to the shareholders. Thus, it represents a further characteristic of the integration theory — that amounts received tax-free by a corporation and distributed to its shareholders should not attract tax in the shareholders' hands, because such amounts would not have been taxable had they been directly received.

Amounts Affecting the Calculation of the CDA

The following amounts (among certain others not mentioned) will be credited to the CDA of a private corporation:

- the tax-free portion of capital gains (currently 50%) realized by the corporation from time to time, net of the non-allowable portion of capital losses (also currently 50%);

- capital dividends received by the corporation on shares it holds in another corporation;

- certain tax-free amounts which the corporation receives from the sale of "eligible capital property", such as the goodwill of a business; and

- the amount of any life insurance proceeds received by the corporation from a policy under which it was beneficiary, less the ACB of the policy to the corporation.

The CDA credit of a corporation will be the aggregate of the above amounts, less capital dividends paid by the corporation from time to time. A negative balance in one of the above categories (for example, where a corporation's capital losses exceed its capital gains) will not reduce the overall positive CDA balance created in the other categories. In that case, the notional negative balance in the capital gains category will be monitored, but it will only affect the overall CDA balance when sufficient capital gains are realized in the future to offset the net capital losses.

It is apparent from the above that some, but not all, amounts received tax-free by a corporation will be credited to the CDA. For example, lottery winnings and disability buyout insurance proceeds are received tax-free by a corporation, but are not eligible for a CDA credit. They cannot, therefore, be distributed to shareholders on a tax-free basis. This simply points out one of the imperfections of the integration theory.

2. Purposes of Corporate-Owned Life Insurance

Corporations acquire insurance for a variety of purposes, many of which will be addressed in detail in this book. The availability of the CDA is sometimes a deciding factor in the purchase of insurance by a corporation, while in other cases it is merely a side benefit. Consider the following examples.

Buy/Sell Funding

Life insurance proceeds received by a corporation can be used to fund a purchase of shares held by a deceased shareholder. Whether the shares are purchased (or redeemed) by the corporation itself, or acquired by surviving shareholders, the ability to finance the purchase through tax-free capital dividends is generally critical in planning the structure of these arrangements. (Buy/sell agreements are discussed in detail in Chapter 6.)

Key Person Insurance

Corporations often have an interest in purchasing insurance on the lives of key shareholders or employees. These proceeds may be used, for example, to hire and train new personnel or to give the corporation a financial cushion to help survive the impact of the key person's death.

However, a side benefit is also available in that the proceeds create a CDA credit. Thus, even though the insurance proceeds may have been used as described above, the opportunity to pay capital dividends to the shareholders out of business profits in future years is still available. Alternatively, the capital dividend could be paid to the shareholders immediately in the form of a promissory note if no further cash was available. This would effectively convert the CDA credit to a shareholder loan, against which the shareholder could make tax-free draws at any time. This has the additional advantage of reducing the value of the corporation's shares for capital gains purposes. (A shareholder loan is not subject to capital gains tax on death. On the other hand, shares of a corporation with a significant pre-existing CDA balance could have an increased value for the purpose of a future deemed disposition on a shareholder's death.)

Collateral Insurance

Lenders often require corporations to secure borrowings with corporate-owned insurance on the lives of shareholders. Under the appropriate circumstances, some or all of the premiums payable under such policies are deductible for income tax purposes.

(a) Historical Background

Prior to the introduction of specific legislation governing this issue in the early 1990s, the determination of whether or not premiums could be deducted was based upon a combination of case law and the administrative practice adopted by the CRA. The Department required, among other things, that only premiums for collaterally-assigned term insurance could be deducted. No deduction was permitted for universal life, whole life or other permanent insurance policies.

This administrative position was challenged in the 1988 case of *The Queen v. Antoine Guertin Ltée*. In that case, the corporation had assigned a whole life policy as collateral for a loan from a financial institution. It then attempted to deduct a portion of the premium as a cost of borrowing. The amount deducted reflected what would have been payable by the corporation for term insurance of an equivalent amount.

The taxpayer was successful in the Federal Court Trial Division, but lost on appeal to the Federal Court of Appeal. The appeal decision not only denied the corporation's deduction, but called into question the deductibility of any insurance premiums, including those for term insurance.

The confusion resulting from the *Guertin* case was resolved by the introduction of specific legislation in the 1991 technical bill. These legislative rules are discussed below.

(b) Legislative Requirements

The legislative changes mentioned above apply to premiums paid after 1989. The major requirements of the legislation are as follows:

- an interest in a life insurance policy must be assigned to a restricted financial institution (such as a bank, trust company or life insurance company) in the course of a borrowing from that institution;

- interest on the loan must be deductible to the borrower as a cost of earning income from a business or property; and

- the assignment of the life insurance policy must be required by the lender as a condition of the loan.

Where the above conditions are met, the borrower may deduct the lesser of premiums payable by the borrower under the policy and the NCPI under the policy. (See Chapter 2 for additional commentary on NCPI.) The amount deducted must reasonably relate to the amount owing to the financial institution from time to time throughout the year. More commentary on the latter point will follow below.

Generally, a policy's NCPI reflects an annual mortality charge provided in a mortality table prescribed in the Regulations. The applicable NCPI for any given policy should be readily available from the insurer. The introduction of the NCPI limitation means that a deduction is available for at least a portion of premiums payable under any type of life insurance policy assigned to a lending institution under the conditions described above. The requirement that the policy be for term insurance is no longer applicable.

(c) CRA Policy

In 1995, the CRA introduced a revised interpretation bulletin that reflected its administrative position concerning the new legislation. The following are some highlights of this bulletin:

- As noted above, the legislation requires that the amount deducted reasonably relate to amounts owing to the lender by the policyholder.

For example, if a $500,000 life insurance policy is assigned as security for a $200,000 loan, the deduction must be prorated accordingly. Where the loan balance fluctuates throughout the year, the deductible amount should be determined on a reasonable basis that reflects amounts owing from time to time.

- No deduction is available where the policy secures an unused line of credit.

- It must be clear that the lender requires the life insurance as a collateral assignment. This is usually evidenced by a letter or other documentation from the financial institution. If the requirement is in reality a mere accommodation to the borrower by the lender, no deduction is permitted.

- In order for the deduction to be available, the borrower must also be the owner of the life insurance policy. This is a change from previous administrative practice. Formerly, one taxpayer (such as a corporation) could obtain a deduction for premiums paid under a collaterally-assigned policy owned by another person (such as a shareholder of the corporation).

(d) Capital Dividend Account Credit

The concept of collateral assignment assumes that ownership of the asset in question remains with the borrower. Where the asset is a life insurance policy, therefore, the policyholder retains the right to designate a beneficiary for the insurance proceeds. On death, the insurer will typically issue a cheque jointly to the beneficiary and the lending institution, at which point the parties are free to determine their respective entitlement to the proceeds.

Where the borrower/policyholder is a private corporation, the corporation will in most cases also be named as beneficiary of the policy. In that case, despite the collateral assignment, the full amount of the proceeds less the ACB of the policy will be credited to the corporation's CDA. This credit is available no matter that all or a portion of the proceeds were used to repay outstanding indebtedness. The legal basis for this is that the proceeds were "constructively received" by the beneficiary, then used to repay the indebtedness.

The CRA agrees with the availability of the CDA credit in the above circumstances, despite having made an announcement to the contrary in early 1997. This intended policy change was quickly reversed after submissions from interested parties.

Creditor Insurance

Banks and other lending institutions typically use creditor insurance as a means of protecting business and other loans. In most cases, the financial institution itself will be named beneficiary of the policy and apply the proceeds against outstanding debt. Until recently it was assumed that, because the lending institution was named beneficiary, no CDA credit would be available to a corporate borrower in these circumstances.

This assumption has changed in light of the 2008 decision in *Canadian Movitel vs. The Queen*. In that case, a corporate taxpayer had a number of business loans outstanding. The shareholders were insured under a Sun Life group policy that named the lender, the Royal Bank, as beneficiary. One of the shareholders died and the proceeds were paid directly to the bank in payment of amounts owing by the corporation. The corporation added the policy proceeds to its CDA and declared a capital dividend to the surviving shareholder. The CRA reassessed the corporation on the basis that it had paid a capital dividend in excess of its CDA balance and levied additional tax under Part III of the Act.

In court, the taxpayer argued that the CDA credit should be available because the corporation had constructively received the proceeds. In other words, as with collateral insurance, the nature of these transactions was the same as if the proceeds had initially been paid to the corporation then directed to the Royal Bank in payment of the outstanding loans. The Crown conceded the argument and agreed to a consent judgment in favour of the taxpayer.

The long term impact of this decision remains to be seen, although in the circumstances it would be difficult for the CRA to go back to the position it originally took in the *Movitel* case. If this case does lead to a change in assessing practice, it eliminates a significant distinction between creditor insurance and collateral insurance, i.e., as of now a corporate bor-rower will be entitled to a CDA credit in either case. However, as discussed below, other differences between these two approaches suggest a significant preference for the collateral insurance rather than the creditor insurance strategy:

- Creditor insurance typically matches outstanding loan balances, whereas collateral insurance has a fixed face amount. This allows collateral insurance to be used for other purposes, such as key person protection, if the proceeds exceed the loan.

- Creditor insurance is not portable or flexible. It will generally expire when loans are repaid whereas a policy being used as collateral can continue and may be used for other purposes. The latter policy could, for example, be converted and used for estate planning purposes if desired, or could be assigned to another lender if the corporation was refinancing.

- Insurance rates charged by lenders for creditor insurance policies are frequently higher than those payable under traditional term insurance policies.

Charitable Giving

Corporate-owned life insurance can be used to provide funds for charitable-giving purposes. In the case of a corporate donation, the funds contributed will, subject to statutory limits, be deductible to the corporation. The CDA credit will remain for the benefit of the continuing shareholders. Any unused deduction can be carried forward and used to offset future income.

Alternatively, proceeds received by the corporation can be paid as a capital dividend to the estate of the deceased shareholder in order to fund charitable donations made by the deceased through his or her will. Subject to statutory limits, this will allow a tax credit to the deceased in the year of death, and potentially the year prior to death.

Charitable giving using life insurance is discussed in detail in Chapter 9.

3. Advantages of Corporate-Owned Life Insurance

The advantages of corporate-owned life insurance are well understood by insurance professionals active in the business and high net worth market. Generally speaking, the preponderance of corporate-owned policies in the business market can be explained by one or more of the following factors:

- Corporations eligible for the small business deduction enjoy income tax rates that are significantly below the top individual rates to which their shareholders are often subject. Where premiums are non-deductible, which is true in the great majority of cases, this means that corporations will usually have more available after-tax dollars. For example, a corporation paying tax at an 16% rate needs to earn $1,191 in order to have $1,000 remaining for the payment of an insurance premium. An individual in a 45% tax bracket must earn $1,819 to have the same $1,000 remaining.

- In many cases, corporate-owned life insurance provides tax planning opportunities that would be unavailable if insurance were held outside the corporation. For example, in the context of a shareholders agreement, proceeds received by a corporation can be used to fund either a redemption of the deceased's shares by the corporation, or a purchase of those shares by surviving shareholders. This allows for flexible buyout strategies to meet the tax planning needs of the various parties. There are also many leveraging strategies and other sophisticated arrangements whose benefits are maximized where insurance is corporate-owned. CDA credits received by corporations facilitate many advantageous *post-mortem* tax planning strategies.

- Corporations often have more cash available for the purchase of life insurance. This is particularly true of retired business owners who may have cash and other investments within personal holding companies, the source of which was proceeds from the sale of an operating company at the time of retirement. Rather than pay the personal tax cost of distributing these assets, shareholders will typically opt for solutions within the corporation itself.

- Income tax and other financial considerations aside, business owners are typically more agreeable to paying for insurance with corporate dollars. Thus, the purchase of insurance by the corporation is the path of least resistance in the sales process.

The focus of this part of the book will be on some critical problems that can arise if the ownership of a life insurance policy in a corporate context is not structured properly. In particular, this chapter will address issues relating to the ownership of permanent life insurance in operating companies. The following specific areas will be considered:

- creditor and income tax concerns with the ownership of permanent insurance (in particular that with CSV) in an operating company;

- income tax issues relating to the transfer of ownership of existing corporate-owned life insurance policies; and

- planning strategies, to be employed at or near the time of sale, which will help avoid future problems.

4. Concerns with CSVs in Operating Companies

Creditors

An operating company ("Opco") has a number of options regarding the utilization of its after-tax profits. Typically, a management bonus will be paid which reduces the corporation's income to the amount that is eligible for the small business deduction. Corporate funds can also be used to pay dividends to shareholders, to pay down debt, or for business expansion.

At a given point, however, the corporation's earnings may grow to a level where they are not required for any of the above purposes. In this case, excess monies may be invested in marketable securities, real estate, permanent life insurance or other passive investments. If such investments are made by the operating company, however, they are exposed to the company's creditors.

In these circumstances, the preferred course of action is to establish a holding company ("Holdco") to own some or all of the Opco shares. Opco profits can be distributed as tax-free intercorporate dividends to Holdco, then invested as desired (this might include the making of a secured loan to Opco). This provides an extra layer of protection from Opco's creditors.

In most circumstances, where there is a need for permanent insurance on the life of a business owner, creditor considerations dictate that the policy not be owned by the operating company. Particularly where the policy has CSV, it should be held by a holding company or by the individual shareholder. As will be seen below, there are also compelling income tax reasons for structuring the ownership of permanent policies in this way.

Income Tax Concerns

(a) Capital Gains Exemption

As already addressed in Chapter 2, each individual taxpayer (not including a trust) is eligible for a lifetime exemption of $750,000 on the disposition of a qualified small business corporation share. The Act contains a predictably complex set of rules for determining a share's eligibility for the exemption. The following is the general framework of these rules:

- the corporation in question must be a Canadian-controlled private corporation;

- at the time the capital gain in question is realized, "all or substantially all" of the fair market value of the corporation's assets must be used principally in an active business carried on primarily in Canada. "All or substantially all" has been interpreted by the CRA to mean 90% or more;

- throughout the 24-month period preceding the disposition, more than 50% of the fair market value of the corporation's assets must have been so used; and

- throughout the same 24-month period, the share could not have been owned by anyone other than the taxpayer or a person or partnership related to the taxpayer.

Corporate-owned life insurance is not considered to be an asset used in an active business. Therefore, the value of such insurance, together with that of other "passive" investments, could disqualify a given corporation's shares from eligibility for the exemption. For these purposes, the Act provides that the value of a corporate-owned policy is, for the most part, its cash surrender value.

For business owners who have yet to fully utilize their capital gains exemption, prudence dictates that permanent policies be held outside of operating companies. A holding company may be used to hold the insurance and other redundant assets, as long as the shareholder personally retains Opco shares with accrued gains sufficient to take advantage of this exemption on a future disposition.

(b) Change of Policy Ownership

In many cases, life insurance that is purchased by a corporation is no longer required for its original purpose. For example, a shareholder may sell his or her shares of the corporation during his or her lifetime, thereby eliminating the need for life insurance to fund a purchase of shares on death. The shareholder may in these circumstances wish to obtain the insurance for personal estate planning purposes. Alternatively, further to the discussion above, a corporate-owned life insurance policy may be creating tax planning or creditor problems.

In the above circumstances, it will usually be necessary to change the ownership of the insurance policies in question, resulting in a disposition of the policies for tax purposes. The unique nature of life insurance has led to a sometimes confusing set of rules concerning the transfer of ownership of insurance policies, some of which are provided for in the Act and some of which must be left to CRA administrative positions and, ultimately, the courts. Depending upon the circumstances, the income tax consequences of a change of ownership, as considered in the commentary below, could be extremely onerous.

5. Planning Options Regarding the Transfer of a Corporate-Owned Life Insurance Policy

The discussion to follow considers the many tax issues involved in the transfer of a life insurance policy from a corporation to an individual shareholder or holding company. While the focus will be on policies with CSV, some issues apply equally to non-cash value plans. The analysis will be based upon the following simple fact situation:

- Herman (age 64) is a Canadian resident who is the sole shareholder of Herman Co., a corporation that carries on an active business primarily in Canada. Herman owns 1,000 common shares and no preferred shares.

- Herman's shares have a fair market value of $2 million and an ACB and paid-up capital ("PUC") of zero.

- Herman Co. owns a permanent insurance policy on Herman's life. It has a face amount of $1.2 million, CSV of $500,000 and an ACB of $300,000. The policy's CSV is included in the $2 million fair market value of Herman's shares.

- Herman has been suffering from ill health and would like to sell his business. He has received an offer from a younger competitor, Henrietta, to purchase his Herman Co. shares. The purchase price would be $1.5 million, i.e., $2 million less the CSV of the insurance policy, which Herman wants to transfer into his own name and use for estate planning purposes.

As the analysis below will show, there is no tax-free method of transferring this policy out of Herman Co., although some methods are more tax-effective than others. Consider the following alternatives:

Transfer from Corporation to Individual Shareholder

The Act provides for a disposition of a life insurance policy at the policy's "value", as defined below, in the following circumstances:

- where a policyholder transfers an interest in a life insurance policy by way of gift, whether during lifetime or under a will, to any person;

- where a policy is transferred by corporate distribution to any person;

- where a policy is transferred by operation of law to any person; and

- where a policy is transferred in any manner whatever to any person with whom the policyholder does not deal at arm's length.

The transfer of the policy to Herman could be considered either a corporate distribution or a non-arm's length transfer. In either case, Herman Co. will be deemed to have received proceeds of disposition equal to the value of the interest at the time of disposition. The recipient is deemed to acquire the interest at the same value. "Value" for these purposes means:

(i) where the interest includes an interest in the CSV of the policy, the amount receivable by the policyholder if that interest were surrendered to the life insurer; and

(ii) in any other case, nil.

Therefore, Herman Co. would be considered to have received $500,000 (the policy's CSV). This amount, less the policy's ACB of $300,000, would result in taxable income of $200,000 to Herman Co. Herman's ACB would equal the deemed proceeds of $500,000.

Unfortunately, income tax consequences to Herman Co. represent only one part of the income tax analysis. The tax impact on Herman must also be addressed. Under the Act, a shareholder is taxed on the value of a benefit conferred by the corporation. (Likewise, the value of benefits received by an employee may be taxed as employment income.) "Value" for these purposes must be calculated without reference to the definition described above, as the definition expressly applies only for the purposes of calculating the proceeds of disposition to the transferor. That definition has no relevance in determining the amount of any taxable benefit to the transferee.

The CRA's views on the valuation of life insurance policies, in circumstances where the Act provides no specific guidance, are considered in Information Circular IC 89-3. It is likely that the CRA would consider the amount of any benefit conferred in the above circumstances as being determined on the basis of the factors listed in the Circular, which are as follows:

- the CSV of the policy;

- the loan value of the policy;

- the face value of the policy;

- the state of health of the life insured and his or her life expectancy;

- the policy's conversion privileges;

- replacement value; and

- the perceived imminence of death.

In Herman's case, the value of his policy could be affected by his poor health and by the fact that his age and insurability would make the existing policy difficult to replace on a cost effective basis. If the CRA disagreed with the amount of the shareholder benefit reported by Herman on his personal tax return, it could assess the benefit it considered appropriate given the criteria listed in the above Circular. That amount could significantly exceed the policy's CSV.

In a worst case scenario, if Herman's ill health led to his demise within a short period of time after the transfer of the policy, the taxable benefit could equal the present value of the policy's face amount at the time of transfer. This would be reduced by the amount, if any, that Herman paid for the policy. This determination would inevitably be made by the CRA with the advantage of hindsight, i.e., on a reassessment after Herman's death. On this basis, therefore, as the taxable benefit would primarily be a factor of the policy's face amount rather than its CSV, it would open Herman to significant income tax liability even if the policy in question were merely term insurance.

To make matters worse, the amount of any shareholder benefit would be non-deductible to Herman Co. as it would not be considered as an expense incurred for the purpose of earning income.

In this example, income tax factors dictate that the transfer of the policy to Herman should not be pursued. Other options, while not without their own costs and risks, will be more attractive. These will be discussed below.

Transfer from Operating Company to Holding Company

The onerous income tax consequences described above may be mitigated through the establishment of a holding company to which Herman Co. would transfer the policy. The holding company could also be used in the process of "purifying" Herman Co. so that its shares became eligible for the $750,000 capital gains exemption on the sale to Henrietta. The following transactions would take place:

- Herman Co. would reorganize its share capital so that Herman's common shares were exchanged for 500 Class A preferred shares and 100 participating (i.e., "new" common) shares. The Class A preferred shares would be redeemable for $1,000 each. The aggregate redemption value of these shares would be $500,000, the CSV of the insurance policy.

- Herman would incorporate a new company ("Holdco") under which he was the sole shareholder. He would then transfer his Class A preferred shares of Herman Co. to Holdco in exchange for Holdco common shares. Herman would retain the 100 new participating shares (fair market value $1.5 million) in his own name.

- Herman Co. would redeem the Class A preferred shares now owned by Holdco, and would satisfy the redemption proceeds "in kind" by transferring the insurance policy, which has CSV of $500,000, to Holdco. Holdco would designate itself as beneficiary of the policy.

- Herman would then sell all of his participating shares to Henrietta for $1.5 million.

The income tax consequences of these transactions would be as follows:

- The reorganization of the Herman Co. shares and the transfer of the Herman Co. Class A preference shares to Holdco would be achieved on a tax-deferred basis.

- Holdco would incur no capital gain or loss on the redemption of its Herman Co. Class A preference shares. It would receive a deemed dividend on the amount by which the redemption proceeds exceeded the PUC of the redeemed shares. As long as Herman Co. had sufficient "safe income" for tax purposes, the dividend would be tax-free to Holdco.

- The transfer of the policy to Holdco would constitute a disposition to Herman Co. As in the example of Herman Co. transferring the policy to Herman personally, this would result in $200,000 of taxable income to Herman Co.

- Herman would realize a $1.5 million capital gain (proceeds less ACB) on the sale of his participating shares to Henrietta. At the time of sale, all of Herman Co.'s assets would be active business assets, as the insurance policy would have been transferred to Holdco. Assuming the Herman Co. shares met the other requirements for the capital gains exemption, Herman would receive a tax-free capital gain of $750,000. An additional $375,000 (one-half of the remaining $750,000 capital gain) would also be tax-free. The taxable portion of the capital gain (also $375,000) would be taxed at Herman's personal tax rate.

Some additional comments are in order regarding this example:

- As the above discussion illustrates, a change of ownership of the insurance policy will be a disposition and any policy gain will be taxed at that time. The use of the holding company strategy, however, reduces concerns regarding the taxation of shareholder benefits. Having said that, there may still be a concern that the CRA would assess a shareholder benefit to Holdco if it was felt that the fair market value of the policy was greater than its CSV, i.e., greater than the amount of dividend declared. In the circumstances, it seems unlikely that the CRA would take this position as even a larger dividend would be tax-free to Holdco (subject to the safe income rules). In any event, Herman should review these complex issues with his tax advisor.

- Following the transactions described above, Holdco will be the owner and beneficiary of the policy on Herman's life. On Herman's death, the proceeds would be paid tax-free to Holdco. The amount of the proceeds, less the ACB of the policy (which would be $500,000 at the time of transfer), would be credited to Holdco's CDA and be eligible for tax-free distribution to Herman's estate.

- Tax is payable on a policy disposition only where, as in Herman's example, the CSV exceeds the ACB. On the other hand, where the ACB is greater than the CSV, there will be no tax payable on a disposition. In that case, the use of the holding company strategy should allow the transfer of the policy to take place on a tax-free basis.

Other Options

There are other options available when it becomes necessary to deal with a corporate-owned life insurance policy in advance of a sale to a third party. A number of these options involve the transfer of corporate business assets so that the life insurance policy(ies), and perhaps other passive investments, are left isolated in the original corporation. In that way, the tax consequences of a policy disposition can be avoided altogether. These options will not be reviewed in detail but will be summarized below:

(a) Asset Sale

Henrietta's purchase of the business can be structured as an asset sale rather than a share sale. In that case, she would pick and choose the Herman Co. assets that she wished to acquire and negotiate a price with Herman Co. After selling the selected assets to Henrietta, Herman Co. would simply continue to be the owner and beneficiary of the policy on Herman's life. Ultimately, the proceeds would be available to Herman's estate through the CDA. The following comments are in order regarding this alternative:

- Purchasers generally prefer to purchase assets rather than shares. For example, purchasers can deduct capital cost allowance (depreciation) against many types of assets such as buildings, machinery and equipment. No such deductions are available on the purchase of shares, although the underlying business can claim these deductions.

- From the vendor's perspective, however, the sale of business assets can result in the recapture of capital cost allowance, and is generally less favourable from a tax perspective than the capital gains treatment available on a share sale, especially where the capital gains exemption would otherwise be available.

- From the perspective of legal documentation and tax planning, an asset sale can be significantly more complex than a share sale. This is dependent on the nature and extent of the assets in question. The resulting additional costs should be weighed against the benefits of avoiding a policy disposition.

(b) Asset Rolldown

In the above example, it would be possible for Herman Co. to transfer its business assets to a newly-incorporated subsidiary, Sub Co., in exchange for shares of Sub Co. Henrietta would then purchase the shares of Sub Co. Herman Co., which would still be wholly-owned by Herman, would continue to own the insurance policy and other non-business assets.

In this case, Herman Co. would realize a capital gain on the sale of the Sub Co. shares, one-half of which would be credited to its CDA and available for tax-free distribution to Herman. No capital gains exemption would be available on the sale as it may only be claimed by individual shareholders.

(c) Butterfly Transaction

A butterfly is a complex transaction, the intimate details of which are beyond the scope of this book, under which corporate assets are "spun off" to another corporation. Unlike the rolldown example described above, there are generally no inter-connected shareholdings between the two corporations after the butterfly is completed. In this case, Herman Co.'s business assets could be transferred to the separate corporation, the shares of which would then be purchased by Henrietta. Herman Co. would continue to own the insurance policy and any other assets not being acquired by Henrietta.

A butterfly transaction is potentially the most complex of all the planning options described in this chapter. If the only purpose of the butterfly is to avoid a policy disposition, great care must be taken to compare the potential costs of implementing the butterfly with the tax otherwise payable on the disposition.

(d) Share Sale without Policy Transfer

In the above example, it would be possible for Herman to sell his Herman Co. shares to Henrietta without changing ownership of the policy. By agreement with Henrietta, Herman would obtain a special class of shares on which a capital dividend could be paid with the insurance proceeds after Herman's death. In these circumstances, Henrietta might be prepared to pay an increased purchase price for the Herman Co. shares because the policy's CSV could be used by Herman Co. as security for additional post-sale bank financing.

This sale would, however, for the reasons previously given, be ineligible for the capital gains exemption. In addition, the policy would now be owned by a corporation in which Herman had only a small minority interest. If Herman Co. suffered financial setbacks after the purchase, the policy could be at risk of seizure by Herman Co.'s creditors. In that case, Herman's estate planning could be severely compromised.

Henrietta would also have to be careful regarding the structuring of this transaction. If the policy's death benefit included the policy's CSV, the funds would be paid to Herman Co. on Herman's death. The corporation could then use the funds to repay loans, or for other purposes. On the other hand, if the death benefit did not include the CSV, the corporation would no longer have the policy as security after Herman's death and would have to refinance.

Rather than having Herman obtain special shares of Herman Co. as described above, it may be preferable for him to incorporate a holding company (or to use an existing holding company) that would be named as irrevocable beneficiary of the policy after the sale to Henrietta. The irrevocable designation would prevent Herman Co. (now controlled by Henrietta) from dealing with the policy without Herman's consent, and would also provide a significant degree of creditor protection. This would help deal with the creditor problem, but would not solve the ineligibility of the Herman Co. shares for the capital gains exemption.

6. Avoiding the Problems: Structuring the Insurance Properly from the Beginning

As the above discussion illustrates, significant problems can be created where policies with CSV are held within operating companies. Many of these difficulties could be remedied with relatively straightforward income tax amendments. This issue will be addressed below. Absent legislative relief, the best way to avoid these concerns is to ensure that ownership of insurance policies is properly structured from the beginning. Consider the following options:

Personal Ownership

Where a business owner has a personal insurance need, personal ownership of the policy should always be considered, especially where there is no holding company. For the reasons given earlier in this chapter, the client may prefer to have the policy owned by his or her corporation. However, where the client has the available cash flow, personal ownership is often the simplest and most attractive option.

Holding Company as Owner and Beneficiary

In many situations, a Holdco will have significant amounts of cash and near cash investments that can be used for the payment of premiums. Alternatively, it may own an Opco from which it can receive tax-free dividends for the same purpose. Insurance proceeds will be received tax-free by Holdco and can then be distributed to the shareholder's estate via the CDA. In this way, a policy owned by Holdco can be easily used to satisfy personal needs and can be funded with corporate dollars that have been subject to a low rate of tax. Therefore, it can provide the best of both worlds in terms of policy ownership options.

Ownership by Holdco will also provide a greater level of creditor protection. It is possible for holding companies to have creditors, and similarly they may provide guarantees for the debts and obligations of others (such as operating companies or personal shareholders). In general, however, holding companies have fewer creditor concerns. Therefore, life insurance and other assets owned by holding companies are less subject to seizure.

Finally, it is much less likely that a holding company will be sold during the shareholder's lifetime. It is much more common, for example, for shares of an operating company to be sold. In other cases, it is the business assets owned by the operating company that are purchased by a third party. In these cases, it will be unnecessary to change ownership of a life insurance policy owned by the holding company, as its shares will continue to be owned by the original shareholder(s).

Shared Ownership

In many situations, Opco will have an insurance need such as buy/sell funding or key person coverage. These needs can typically be satisfied by term insurance, as the insurance is generally required only while the shareholder/employee is active in the business. At the same time, however, the individual shareholder may have permanent insurance needs. In these circumstances, an arrangement known as shared ownership (or split dollar) can satisfy the respective needs of the parties, while limiting the potentially negative aspects of permanent corporate-owned life insurance. The following are the key features of a shared ownership arrangement:

- Ownership of the policy is shared between one party who requires the life insurance coverage (typically Opco) and another who has longer term needs (typically the individual shareholder or Holdco).

- The costs and benefits of the policy, typically a universal life plan, are shared by the parties in accordance with a shared ownership agreement. Generally, the death benefit owner will pay an amount reflecting insurance charges under the policy and will designate a beneficiary for the policy's face amount. Deposits to the policy's investment accounts will be made by the cash value owner, who will designate a beneficiary for that portion of the policy.

- On the death of the life insured, the face amount and cash value portions of the policy will be paid to the respective named beneficiaries. A corporate beneficiary will receive a CDA credit in the amount by which the proceeds exceed the ACB of its interest in the policy. The ACB of the policy to the corporation would equal its share of premiums paid, less the NCPI. The NCPI is a mortality cost prescribed under the Income Tax Regulations and would normally be used to calculate the policy's ACB as a whole. In a shared ownership situation, however, it is arguable that the NCPI may be allocated entirely to the premiums paid by the death-benefit owner (the corporation in this case). This would increase the amount of CDA credit available to the corporation on the shareholder's death. In many cases, however, the parties will wish to terminate the shared ownership arrangement before the death of the life insured. This could arise when the individual retires and sells his or her business (Opco shares or assets) to an outside party. In that case, Opco can simply transfer its interest in the policy face amount to the cash value owner, who will from that time be the sole owner of the policy. This can usually be done on a tax effective basis from Opco's perspective as it does not require a change in ownership of the cash surrender value. (In this regard, however, planners must be cognizant of possible tax issues if the individual is, for example, in ill health at the time of transfer. See commentary earlier in this chapter under the heading "Transfer from Corporation to Individual Shareholder".)

In summary, by allowing the cash surrender value of a policy to remain outside the operating company, a shared ownership arrangement effectively deals with the major issues confronting permanent insurance in a corporate setting. At the same time, shared ownership arrangements are themselves complex, and there can be significant difficulties in monitoring these policies and in tracking the ACB attributable to each owner. In most cases split beneficiary arrangements, as discussed below, are a preferred alternative.

Split Beneficiary

Split beneficiary arrangements are a simpler alternative to shared ownership in many situations. Rather than having more than one party with an ownership interest in the insurance policy, as is the case with a shared ownership arrangement, a split beneficiary arrangement involves only one policy owner, but two or more beneficiaries. For example, Holdco could own a policy on the life of a key shareholder and would name Opco as beneficiary of the face amount. Holdco would designate itself as beneficiary of the cash value portion of the proceeds. Opco could pay tax-free intercorporate dividends to Holdco to provide the funds necessary for the payment of premiums.

This arrangement could be used in the context of a shareholders agreement, where Opco would use the insurance proceeds to fund a buyout of shares owned by the deceased's Holdco. Opco's interest in the death benefit could be protected through an irrevocable beneficiary designation or through a contractual arrangement under which Holdco agrees not to alter the beneficiary designation without the consent of all the Opco shareholders.

In terms of corporate insurance planning, split beneficiary has the same advantages as a shared ownership arrangement. It is also less complex in most cases, as it does not require the same degree of tax, legal advice or administrative support.

Split beneficiary may also allow for the maximization of benefits under the CDA rules. In the above Holdco/Opco example, Opco would have paid no premiums under the policy, and thus would not have an ACB. Arguably, therefore, all insurance proceeds paid to Opco would be credited to its CDA, as any ACB would be attributable only to Holdco, the policy owner. The CRA has expressed some concerns that this might constitute undue tax avoidance. However, a challenge by the CRA on this basis could likely be defended if it could be established that there was a legitimate business purpose, such as creditor protection, for having the arrangement structured in this way.

An additional advantage is that, on the termination of a split beneficiary arrangement, the policy owner need only change the beneficiary designation. This is not a disposition of the policy for income tax purposes. This is in contrast to the termination of a shared ownership plan, where there is a disposition by one party of an interest in the policy.

There may be cases where, because of the respective interests of the parties, a shared ownership arrangement will be necessary. However, where possible, the simpler split beneficiary structure should be used.

7. The Need for Legislative Change

The above discussion illustrates that there is rarely, if ever, justification for holding policies with cash surrender values inside operating companies. Compounding these problems are the potentially punitive income tax consequences of attempting to rectify matters by changing the ownership of a corporate-owned policy. The tax consequences and the cost of obtaining professional advice to remedy problem cases seem out of proportion, especially given the fact that the client is rarely to blame for the faulty planning.

It would be a relatively straightforward matter for the Department of Finance to implement legislative change that allowed life insurance to be transferred on a tax-deferred basis from one corporation to another (or, for that matter, from an individual to a corporation). The Act contains an exclusive list of "eligible property" that may be transferred to a corporation on a rollover basis under section 85 of the Act. The list of eligible properties is a diverse one that includes capital property (such as shares of a corporation), depreciable property, most types of inventory, goodwill and Canadian and foreign resource property.

Life insurance policies are not on the list of eligible properties, although there seems to be no tax policy reason for this exclusion. If a life insurance policy were eligible, it could be transferred to a corporation on a tax-deferred basis as long as the many rules of section 85 were met. Presumably the policy would have to be transferred at an agreed price between its ACB and CSV, and the transferee corporation would have to issue shares in consideration for the transfer. Considerable tax planning might still be required, but could be justified in the spirit of tax deferral.

A simpler legislative alternative would be to allow one corporation to transfer an insurance policy to another corporation at the policy's ACB. To prevent such a rollover from being too widespread, certain limitations could be included. For example, there could be a requirement that the recipient corporation be controlled by the life insured person or his or her spouse.

Alternatively, the rollover could be limited to situations where the recipient corporation held a specified percentage of shares of the transferor corporation. Similar rollovers for certain transfers with families are already provided in the Act. Again, there would seem to be no compelling tax policy reason against allowing intercorporate transfers of this nature to take place on a tax-deferred basis.

In the absence of such legislation, however, insurance professionals and tax advisors should ensure that proper planning is done, at the time a policy is placed, so that the likelihood of a future change of ownership is minimized.

8. An Anomaly: Transfers of Personally-Owned Policies to a Corporation

There is a curiosity in the tax rules relating to the transfer of insurance policies from an individual shareholder to a non-arm's length corporation. (This is essentially a corporation controlled by the individual and/or family members.)

The rules in question provide that, where a policy is transferred in these circumstances, the deemed proceeds will equal the policy's CSV even if the actual proceeds are a different amount. By way of example, assume that Thelma owns a $1 million Term to 100 policy on her own life that she acquired twenty years ago. The policy's CSV and ACB are both zero. Using actuarial principals, and considering Thelma's current insurability and state of health, an actuary has determined that the fair market value (FMV) of the policy is $600,000. On this basis, Thelma sells her policy to her corporation, Thelma Inc., for $600,000. The tax consequences of this transfer are as follows:

Actual proceeds:	$600,000
Deemed proceeds for tax purposes (CSV):	0
ACB of policy to Thelma Inc.:	0
Taxable income to Thelma:	0

As a result of this transaction, Thelma receives $600,000 from Thelma Inc., tax-free, in exchange for the policy. Payment would be in the form of cash and/or a promissory note that could be paid down, without tax, at any time. This result assumes that the fair market transfer value of the policy can be substantiated if challenged by the CRA.

Although Thelma Inc. paid fair market value for the policy, it is deemed to have acquired the policy for proceeds equal to the CSV of zero. This means that on Thelma's death the full death benefit of $1 million will be credited to Thelma Inc.'s CDA and can be distributed as a tax-free dividend to her estate or the surviving shareholders.

The CRA and the Department of Finance are aware of this anomaly in the Act and legislative change is always a possibility. In the meantime, this planning idea seems to be gaining in popularity.

References

Income Tax Act (Canada)

Subsection 15(1) — benefit conferred on shareholder

Paragraph 20(1)(e.2) — deduction for premiums on life insurance used as collateral

Subsection 70(5.3) — valuation of certain corporate-owned life insurance policies

Subsection 83(2) — capital dividends

Subsection 85(1.1) — definition of "eligible property" for purposes of a s. 85 rollover

Subsection 89(1) — definition of "capital dividend account"

Section 110.6 — capital gains exemption

Subsection 110.6(15) — impact of corporate-owned life insurance on eligibility for capital gains exemption

Subsection 112(1) — intercorporate dividends

Section 121 — dividend tax credit

Subsection 148(7) — transfer of life insurance policies by corporation and between non-arm's length parties

Subsection 148(9) — definition of "value"

Interpretation Bulletins

IT-66R6 — Capital Dividends

IT-87R2 — Policyholders' Income from Life Insurance Policies

IT-309R2 — Premiums on Life Insurance Used as Collateral

IT-355R2 — Interest on Loans to Buy Life Insurance Policies and Annuities (Archived by the CRA)

IT-416R3 — Valuation of Shares of a Corporation Receiving Life Insurance Proceeds on Death of a Shareholder

IT-430R3 — Life Insurance Proceeds Received by a Corporation or Partnership

Information Circular

IC 89-3 — Policy Statement on Business Equity Valuations (see paragraphs 40 and 41 regarding corporate-owned life insurance)

Case Law

Canadian Movitel v. The Queen (Docket #2006-30761 (IT)G), dated March 18, 2008

The Queen v. Antoine Guertin Ltée, 1988 DTC 6126 (F.C.A.)

Chapter 5

Family Business Succession

The term "estate planning" as it applies to owner/managers inevitably involves the central question of business succession. As soon as the business owner is able to decide upon and articulate his or her business-succession goals, one or more of the almost limitless number of available planning strategies can be recommended. Life insurance is one of several key tools that can be used to help the client and the client's family members and business associates deal with succession problems.

As discussed in Chapter 1, an insurance professional is in a unique position to help the client identify and come to grips with his or her estate problems, and to act as a catalyst in finding the appropriate solutions. Succession issues are frequently aired at an early stage of the estate planning process when the client's other advisors are not yet involved. In the case of the owner/manager, a smooth business transition is often the most important of these objectives. The main focus should be to provide for business succession while at the same time ensuring that family members not involved in the business are adequately provided for.

Estate problems faced by any clients are unique, particularly so as they pertain to business owners. Thus, there is no "right" estate planning solution that suits every case. For the purpose of analysis, however, it may be helpful to separate business clients into different groups and to suggest the ways life insurance may be used to solve business succession problems faced by those in each group. At the risk of generalizing, it can be suggested that business clients fall into one of three categories:

- the client involved in a business which, it is hoped or expected, will remain in the family and ultimately be taken over by the next generation;

- the client who has partners or fellow shareholders who are not members of the family and who would continue to operate the business after the client's death; and

- the client who effectively "is" the business and has no successor either inside or outside of the family.

This chapter will focus on planning strategies for the business owner who wishes to pass the business to the next generation. Chapter 6 will deal with business succession outside the family using shareholders and partnership agreements. As usual, the discussion will assume that the business in question is operated through a Canadian-controlled private corporation.

In many respects, family-owned businesses (large and small) represent the backbone of the Canadian economy. As successful as family enterprise may be, however, Canadians have not generally been successful in providing for the smooth transition of businesses from one generation to the next. The difficulty in providing for this transition is not for lack of legal avenues or planning techniques. Rather, it seems to have much more to do with human nature, with family dynamics and, in many cases, with a failure to plan properly or take advantage of available planning strategies.

This part of the chapter will review some basic estate planning issues faced by family business and describe some long-standing strategies, such as estate freezes, which can allow for tax-effective business succession from parents to children.

1. Capital Gains

Capital Gains Tax in Canada

In simple terms, a capital gain arises when property is sold for proceeds that exceed its original purchase price. From the time of their inception in 1972, capital gains taxes steadily increased, until they declined dramatically in 2000. Here is a summary of inclusion rates since the introduction of capital gains tax:

- Prior to 1972 — no tax on capital gains
- 1972–1987 — 50% of capital gains subject to tax
- 1988–1989 — 66⅔% of capital gains subject to tax
- 1990–February 27, 2000 — 75% of capital gains subject to tax
- February 28, 2000–October 17, 2000 — 66⅔% of capital gains subject to tax
- October 18, 2000 to present — 50% of capital gains subject to tax

Capital Gains Issues Regarding Shares of Family Business Corporations

Despite reduced rates and the increase of the capital gains exemption to $750,000, capital gains tax remains a major concern of any business owner. In the case of a family business, this is an estate planning issue because it is likely that the shares will never be sold, and thus never taxed, during the business owner's lifetime. Instead, after the deaths of the business owner and his or her spouse, the shares are typically redeemed or gifted to the next generation and become subject to taxation at that time. Having said that, changes in dividend tax rates have made it more attractive for some business owners to redeem their shares and pay tax during lifetime. This will be discussed later in this chapter under the heading "The Wasting Freeze". (For further information on capital gains, see the discussion in Chapter 2 on the capital gains exemption and in Chapter 3 regarding the taxation of property held at death).

2. Estate Freezes

One of the cornerstones of the life insurance business in Canada is providing liquidity to estates facing such tax liabilities, and there is no doubt that this will continue to be the case for the foreseeable future. However, many taxpayers are not prepared to have their capital gains exposure subject to unpredictable and continual increases. Tax and inclusion rates may go back up, as will (it is hoped) the value of businesses — factors which ultimately result in greater tax liability to an estate unless tax planning is done. And while life insurance is often the most effective means of dealing with tax liabilities in an estate, it may not be the only piece of the estate planning puzzle for a business owner. This is why the "estate freeze" has become one of the fundamental estate planning tools for business owners and other high net worth clients.

Although there are several ways of accomplishing an estate freeze, the two most common methods are the "Section 85 Freeze" and the "Section 86 Freeze", both of which will be discussed below. The examples to follow will assume that the assets being "frozen" are shares of a small business corporation, although it is possible to freeze most kinds of properties in ways similar to those described below. Section references are to the *Income Tax Act.*

Section 85 Freeze

A section 85 freeze involves the transfer of a parent's common shares of an operating company to a holding company. In exchange, the parent receives preferred shares of the holding company, while its common shares are acquired by the child or children who are to benefit from the freeze.

> Mike and Phil, who are unrelated, each own 100 common shares of Southpaw Supplies Inc., a manufacturer specializing in tools and sporting equipment for left-handed people. The fair market value of the Southpaw shares is $2 million. The ACB of the shares is nominal in each case.
>
> Phil would like to retire in five years or so. His daughter, Freda, is active in the business and is anxious to become a shareholder. Mike has no children who are active in the business. He is happy to continue working indefinitely and to have Freda as a partner.
>
> One way for Freda to become a partner, and for Phil to do some income tax planning, is for Phil to undertake a section 85 estate freeze. Phil would incorporate a holding company ("Phil Co.") and would transfer his 100 common shares of Southpaw to the new corporation. In exchange, Phil would receive 10,000 preferred shares of Phil Co. These shares would have the following attributes:
>
> - The shares would carry a fixed redemption price equal to the fair market value of the common shares of Southpaw, i.e., they would not fluctuate in value like common shares.

- The shares would carry enough votes to allow Phil to control Phil Co. (alternatively, the preferred shares could be non-voting and Phil could subscribe for a separate class of nominal value voting shares in order to achieve voting control).

- The shares would be redeemable and retractable. In other words, either Phil or Phil Co. could at any time require the redemption of some or all of the preferred shares for their redemption amount.

- Phil's preferred shares would likely have dividend privileges in preference to the common shares, and would also have preferential treatment on any future wind-up of Phil Co.

A section 85 freeze is a tax-deferred transaction. In order to ensure the desired income tax results, Phil's accountant will file an election with the Canada Revenue Agency in the form prescribed under the Act. Under this form, Phil and Phil Co. may choose any purchase price between the ACB of Phil's Southpaw shares (nil) and their fair market value at the time of the transaction ($1 million). No capital gain will be realized if the elected amount equals the ACB of Phil's Southpaw common shares.

At the time of the freeze, Freda would acquire new common shares of Phil Co., either by way of subscription or as a gift from Phil. These would have nominal value at the time of the freeze, but would reflect all the future growth of Phil Co., i.e., half the future growth of Southpaw. For example, if the value of Southpaw rose to $2.6 million in five years' time, the shares owned by Phil Co. and Mike would each be worth $1.3 million at that time. Assuming Phil Co. had no other assets, its shares would have a value of $1.3 million, of which $1 million would be reflected in Phil's preferred shares, the same value as at the time of the freeze. The remaining $300,000 would be reflected in Freda's common shares. In this way, $300,000 of capital gains otherwise taxable to Phil would shift to Freda.

Section 86 Freeze

In a section 86 freeze, the parent would exchange his or her operating company shares for preferred shares having attributes identical to the preferred shares of Phil Co. described in the previous example. The children would at the same time acquire common shares of the operating company at a nominal price.

The section 86 freeze is somewhat more popular than the section 85 variety because it does not require another corporation nor an income tax election. As long as the reorganization meets the relatively straightforward rules contained in section 86, the tax rollover is automatic. Clients should consult their professional advisors to determine which method is better for them.

> Bertha is the sole shareholder of a successful bakery known as Bertha's Bundt Cakes Inc. ("Bertha Inc."). The ACB of her shares is nil and the fair market value is $1.2 million. Bertha wants to do an estate freeze, and to bring in her son, Bert, as a shareholder.

> Under a section 86 freeze, Bertha would exchange her Bertha Inc. common shares for preferred shares with a combined redemption amount of $1.2 million. Bert would acquire new common shares that would have nominal current value, but would reflect all future increases in the fair market value of Bertha Inc.

> As mentioned above, the income tax rollover in these circumstances is automatic. Bertha will realize no capital gain as she will be considered to have sold her common shares for their nominal ACB, and to have acquired the preferred shares for the same amount.

Capital Gains Crystallization

The capital gains exemption, recently increased to $750,000, has been a feature of the Canadian income tax system since 1985. In many cases it is prudent to consider crystallizing capital gains in order to take advantage of this exemption. It is often convenient to do so in the course of implementing an estate freeze.

(a) Example

A capital gains crystallization can be illustrated using the example of Bertha Inc. illustrated in the above section on section 86 estate freezes. Consider the same fact situation, but with the added planning wrinkle of a capital gains crystallization being implemented by Bertha. The example assumes that the Bertha Inc. shares qualify for the capital gains exemption and that Bertha has not used any of the exemption to date.

As in a typical section 86 freeze, Bertha would exchange her Bertha Inc. common shares for preferred shares having a combined redemption amount of $1.2 million. As the previous example illustrated, if no other steps are taken the rollover is automatic and no capital gain is realized. However, even in a situation that has all the appearances of a section 86 rollover, the Act provides Bertha with the option of filing a section 85 election form, as described above, in order to cause the disposition of her common shares for an amount greater than their ACB.

In the election form, Bertha and Bertha Inc. would elect that her common shares be disposed of for $750,000. This would create a $750,000 capital gain that Bertha would report on her income tax return for the year. The gain would be offset by the capital gains exemption.

Bertha's preference shares would have an ACB of $750,000. On a future sale of the shares, or on her death, her capital gain would be $450,000 ($1.2 million less $750,000). On the other hand, if Bertha had not undertaken a crystallization and if the capital gains exemption had been abolished (or if her shares ceased to qualify for the exemption), her capital gain would be $1.2 million.

(b) Other Tax Issues Regarding Crystallization

The capital gains exemption rules are extremely complex. Prior to undertaking any crystallization transactions, clients should consult their advisors to ensure that there are no unexpected problems. The following are two potential complications:

- Access to the exemption can be limited if the taxpayer has a cumulative net investment loss. This would arise if he or she had investment expenses in excess of investment income, as calculated on a cumulative basis since 1987.

- The impact of alternative minimum tax ("AMT") should also be considered. The exemption is an allowable deduction for the purposes of AMT, however this does not fully offset the fact that the entire amount of the capital gain must be included in income, rather than just the 50% taxable portion. This could result in AMT liability which, although potentially refundable in future years, may nonetheless represent an unwanted side effect of a crystallization.

Use of Trusts in an Estate Freeze

Occasionally, young children are the beneficiaries of an estate freeze. Children under the age of majority cannot subscribe for shares nor should they own any kind of investment property in their own names. On these occasions, a trust is often established to hold shares on the children's behalf. The parents could act as trustees for the children and give themselves the power, through a written trust document, to manage the trust assets on the children's behalf. The trust document could also give the trustees the discretion to ultimately distribute shares to any one or more of the children in such proportions as the trustees determine. Thus, children who became active in the business might eventually acquire shares in their own name to the exclusion of non-active children.

In some cases, both the children and the parents themselves are beneficiaries of the trust. If the parents subsequently decide that they do not wish to distribute shares to any of their children, they can unwind the freeze by transferring the shares to themselves as beneficiaries of the trust. At that point, the parents would once again be the sole shareholders of the corporation. In most cases, the distribution of shares to trust beneficiaries is tax-deferred.

Generally speaking, the need for a trust is not as great where the children benefiting from the freeze are adults. However, where the parents wish to undertake a freeze but also wish to retain flexibility, a trust can hold the shares pending an outright distribution of the shares at a future date.

In structuring estate freezes for minor children, attention must be paid to the attribution rules. Where children are under the age of 18, dividends paid on shares held by a trust could be attributed, for tax purposes, to the parent(s).

Trusts and the attribution rules are examined in greater detail in Chapter 10.

Planners should also bear in mind the potential impact of the 21-year "deemed disposition" rule. The Act provides that, for most trusts, there will be a deemed disposition of their capital property every 21 years. This can create a significant liquidity problem in a trust that has few liquid assets, such as one designed to hold common shares of a family corporation. The easiest way to avoid this deemed disposition is to transfer trust property to the beneficiaries before the 21-year mark arrives. This can be done on a tax-deferred basis. Trust agreements should be drafted in a way that permits such a distribution to be made.

Frequently, the effect of this rule is to force a distribution of trust property before the deemed disposition arises. In the context of an estate freeze, the rule creates a deadline before which the parent must decide which of the children are to own shares, and in what proportions.

On the other hand, shares held within a trust may be sold long before the 21-year rule becomes a problem. This might occur, for example, where the business owner felt that none of the children were suitable for business management, resulting in a decision to sell the shares to a third party. In that case, there could be the realization of capital gains on shares held within the trust. These gains could be allocated amongst all the trust beneficiaries and, assuming the shares were eligible, the $750,000 capital gains exemption could be available to each of the beneficiaries. This can greatly reduce, and sometimes eliminate, the overall tax liability on the sale of a family business.

Partial Freezes

If a parent is unwilling to undertake a complete freeze of his or her shares, or to establish a trust as described above, it is possible to do a halfway measure known as a partial freeze. Rather than having children obtain all of the common shares under a freeze, the parent could subscribe for a given percentage of those shares, and in that way have an interest in the future appreciation of the underlying business. It would, of course, always be possible for the parent to complete the freeze at a later date.

The Wasting Freeze

The preferred shares a parent receives under an estate freeze often pay dividends that can be used to provide retirement income. It is also possible for the parent to redeem shares from time to time as a means of cashing out their interest in the business and providing additional retirement capital. This is sometimes called a "wasting freeze".

Typically, a redemption of shares will create a dividend in the shareholder's hands to the extent the redemption proceeds exceed the shares' paid up capital ("PUC"). Prior to the recent changes in the taxation of dividends, this approach could be unattractive as dividend tax rates, depending on the province of course, were often 8% or so higher than capital gains tax rates. However, where a corporation is in a position to pay eligible dividends, the tax rate in some provinces may be lower than the capital gains rate. This can be even more attractive where the payment of the dividend would generate a dividend refund to the corporation under the RDTOH rules. See Chapter 2 for a discussion of the new dividend tax rules and RDTOH.

Wasting freezes may become more common in light of the changes to the taxation of dividends. In certain cases, this may have an impact on the parents' insurance needs, i.e., where shares are redeemed during lifetime there may be a lesser need for the funding of tax liability on death. Careful planning is required as client needs will vary greatly in these circumstances.

Relating Planning Ideas

(a) Shareholders Agreements for Family Corporations

Life insurance can also be used to fund, in appropriate cases, a shareholders agreement between the parent's estate and his or her children. For example, where one or more children will be active in the business after the parent's death, and others will not, an agreement could provide for the active children to use insurance proceeds paid on the parent's death to purchase shares from the estate. The estate could then use these funds to pay bequests to the non-active children. In this way, insurance can be used to help equalize estate distribution.

Whether or not there is a need for a funded buy-out on a shareholder's death, a shareholders agreement may be a critical planning strategy when an estate freeze is undertaken and children are involved in ownership of shares for the first time. Such an agreement might give the father, mother or siblings the right (or obligation) to purchase shares if one of the children died, became disabled, or simply ceased working in the business.

(b) Family Law Act (Ontario)

In Ontario, the *Family Law Act* should be reviewed when an estate freeze is being considered, especially where a married child is the beneficiary of the freeze. If the child subscribes for the common shares directly, the shares become part of net family property and are potentially subject to division on marriage breakdown. On the other hand, if the parent subscribes for the shares then immediately gifts them to the child, the shares are excluded from net family property.

The *Family Law Act* is discussed in greater detail in Chapter 13.

Conclusion: Don't Let the Tax Tail Wag the Dog

The avoidance or reduction of future capital gains tax liability is attractive and sometimes leads to freezes being undertaken prematurely. Clients must understand that by undertaking a freeze they are relinquishing future values upon which they could base retirement income or which could be used to finance other business ventures. A freeze is a real economic transaction, not something done merely for tax purposes and that has no real effect. Clients should also understand that, once a freeze is put into place, it can be extremely difficult to reverse course (although this can be made easier by using a trust, as described above). Thus, they should resist "letting the tax tail wag the dog".

In most cases, the ideal client for a freeze is someone within a few years of retirement with a child or children active in the business who are a position to assume increasing management responsibility. In these cases, it makes both business and tax sense to pass future corporate values to the children. In cases where children are very young, or are uninvolved in the business, the tax advantages of bringing them in as shareholders may be more than overcome by other factors.

3. Estate Equalization

In family business succession cases, the business typically represents the bulk of the client's estate. It is also common to find situations where, for example, one or two adult children are active in the business and are in a position to succeed their parent(s), while other children may be totally uninvolved in the family's business affairs. In these situations, a key estate planning objective may be the "equalization" of the client's estate between those children who are active in the business and those who are not.

Determining an appropriate estate division amongst the various children is often the most emotionally draining aspect of estate planning for business owners. Many clients choose to deal with these difficult issues by ignoring them. As discussed in Chapter 1, lawyers and accountants are often less inclined to motivate the client. This frequently leaves the insurance professional as the advisor best able to demonstrate to the client that inaction is the worst plan of all.

When confronting questions of estate division, owner/managers usually understand the wisdom of having the family corporation owned only by those family members who are active in business management. On the other hand, they are concerned about the impact this will have on their other children. There is rarely a simple solution to this dilemma. One strategy that may be helpful, however, is to help the business owner understand that an "equal" division of his or her estate does not necessarily equate to a "fair" division. This may be illustrated by the following case study:

Fact Situation:

To use a simple example, consider the case of a husband and wife, Ferdie and Nadine, who own shares of a family business corporation with an estimated fair market value of $2 million. Their other property, including the family home, has a combined value of $600,000. For the sake of discussion, assume that both values are net of income tax and other estimated estate expenses.

Ferdie and Nadine have two adult children, one of whom (Gertie) is active in the business and is ready, willing and seemingly able to succeed her parents. The other child, Manfred, has no business aspirations. They have stated clearly that they wish to treat their children as equally as possible in the distribution of their combined estates.

Option 1: Equal but Unfair?

One option would be to divide the combined $2.6 million equally between the two children. Manfred could, for example, inherit $700,000 worth of shares and the $600,000 of other property, while Gertie could be given the remaining $1.3 million in shares. While this would represent an equal division of their estates, Ferdie and Nadine should consider whether it would be fair. For example:

- If Gertie is successful in running the business, her shares will appreciate in value accordingly. However, so will those of her brother, who will benefit from an increase in net worth solely as a result of his sister's efforts. In addition, Manfred's share ownership will entitle him to all the legal protection afforded to shareholders under corporate law, including the ultimate right to make a court application if he feels he is being treated "oppressively" by his sister. In the worst case, such an application could result in a court-ordered winding-up of the corporation.

- If Gertie is unsuccessful in running the business, the value of Manfred's net worth will depreciate accordingly, through no fault of his own.

Therefore, while option 1 may represent an equal distribution of Ferdie's and Nadine's estates between their children, it has the potential for creating animosity between the siblings, and for unfairness to one or the other.

Option 2: Unequal but Fair?

Another option for Ferdie and Nadine would be to give all of their shares to Gertie. This recognizes that she is the only logical successor, and that as a result, she should benefit from any business growth, or suffer the consequences of any setbacks. As a non-participant in the business, Manfred should not be a shareholder, but should be treated generously in his parent's estates.

If Ferdie and Nadine agree that this is the better approach, it means that Gertie will inherit property with a value of $2 million, and Manfred's inheritance will be $600,000. The alert insurance professional will see the opportunity for using life insurance as a means of providing additional capital to Manfred. For example, insurance on the joint lives of Ferdie and Nadine, payable on the second death, could be used both to pay their capital gains tax liability and to provide money to Manfred to "top up" his $600,000 inheritance.

If life insurance is to be used for these purposes, Ferdie and Nadine should carefully consider how much is required. Insurance of $1.4 million, when combined with the $600,000 of other assets, would give each sibling a $2 million inheritance, but is likely not a realistic solution. Arguably, a discount ought to be applied to Manfred's share of his parent's estates in recognition of the risk inherent in his sister's inheritance. In other words, the value attributable to Gertie's shares is dependent upon her efforts in managing the family business, whereas Manfred's inheritance is purely passive and can be invested with minimal risk. There is no correct answer; the amount of insurance paid to Manfred should simply be an amount that recognizes these factors and with which Ferdie and Nadine are comfortable.

Another approach is to acquire enough insurance to fully fund a redemption of the shares owned by Ferdie and Nadine on the second death. This would create enough liquidity to satisfy their estate equalization needs. For an example of this strategy see below under the heading "Using the 50% Solution to Fully Redeem Shares".

As part of the tax planning process, it would also be appropriate to discuss an estate freeze with Ferdie and Nadine. As discussed earlier in this chapter, this would limit the future growth in the value of their shares, thereby reducing their ultimate capital gains tax liability. A freeze would also simplify the estate equalization issue because it would establish a permanent value for the shares owned by Ferdie and Nadine. Without a freeze, the fair market value of their shares is a moving target, which makes equalization a more difficult, ongoing challenge.

4. Role of Life Insurance in Estate Freezes and Family Business Succession

In summary, the following are the key uses of life insurance in cases where clients are considering an estate freeze.

Payment of Capital Gains Tax

One advantage of a freeze is that it fixes the parent's capital gains exposure and makes this liability, and thus the insurance need, easier to calculate. Of course, the capital gains inclusion rate, marginal tax rates and the future availability of the capital gains exemption continue to be variables in this analysis. Life insurance can play an important role in funding this liability. In many cases, the redemption of shares using corporate-owned life insurance and the "50% solution", as detailed later in this chapter, is the ideal mechanism.

Estate Equalization

As discussed below, where children active in a family business might otherwise inherit a disproportionate share of the estate, life insurance can be a simple tool for benefiting the other children.

Key Person Insurance

The need for key person insurance is not limited to situations involving an estate freeze, but is nonetheless a common topic of discussion for clients involved in this process. In many cases, the premature death of one or both parents would place the business, and by inference the children, in a degree of financial difficulty. With this in mind, it may be appropriate for the corporation to acquire insurance on the lives of one or both of the parents. The proceeds could then be used to alleviate bank debt, pay trade creditors or simply provide a financial security blanket that helps overcome the death of a key shareholder.

Using the 50% Solution to Pass Shares of a Family Business Corporation to a Child

As discussed below, the redemption of shares using corporate-owned life insurance will not only provide a source of funds for the payment of taxes owing by the estate of a deceased shareholder, but will in many cases cause a reduction in taxes otherwise payable.

(a) Fact Situation

The 50% solution, as it applies to family businesses, will be illustrated using the following simple example:

- Bill Bugelman, age 60, operates a lucrative chain of pie shops through a corporation called Bugelman's Bakery Inc. (fair market value $3 million). The only child of Bill and his wife Hazel is Betty, age 28. She also works in the business and is expected to take over its management when her parents retire.

- Bill did an estate freeze in 2008. As a result, he holds preference shares of Bugelman's Bakery Inc. with an ACB and PUC of nil, and a fair market/redemption value of $3 million. Hazel and Bill have both utilized the $750,000 capital gains exemption on the sale of a previous business.

- Under the freeze, Betty acquired all the common shares of Bugelman's Bakery Inc. These shares have little value at present, but will reflect any future growth in the value of the corporation.

- Hazel and Bill have mirror wills under which each leaves all of his or her property to the other. The property will pass to Betty on the second death. For the sake of discussion, it will be assumed that Hazel predeceases Bill.

(b) Capital Gains Tax on the Deaths of Bill and Hazel

Applying current tax rates, absent any special tax planning, a capital gains tax liability of approximately $690,000 would arise on the death of the survivor of Bill and Hazel. This tax would arise if, for example, the shares of Bugelman's Bakery were simply gifted to Betty on the second death.

Conventional insurance planning strategy would suggest that a policy in that amount be acquired, on a joint second-to-die basis, to fund this liability.

(c) Using the 50% Solution to Reduce Taxes Payable

The 50% solution is an alternative to the conventional strategy described above. It applies where the shares are not eligible for grandfathering under the stop-loss rules, and involves the use of corporate-owned life insurance to redeem shares held by a deceased shareholder. (See a detailed discussion of the stop-loss rules in Chapter 6.)

The stop-loss rules contain a relieving provision that forms the essence of the 50% solution. The rule currently states that the capital loss realized in the estate is reduced only by the extent to which capital dividends exceed 50% of the lesser of:

(i)   the capital gain resulting from the deemed disposition on death; and

(ii) the capital loss in the estate as otherwise determined (i.e., as determined without reference to the stop-loss rules).

In many cases, this means that 50% of the redemption proceeds could be paid in the form of a tax-free capital dividend (hence, the "50% solution"). While this does not eliminate tax payable by the estate, it does result in significant savings.

In the case of Bill and Hazel, the 50% solution can be used to reduce their tax liability from $690,000 to $600,000, a savings of 13%. The $600,000 figure can be determined using the following formula, which allows for differences in tax rates amongst the various provinces:

Amount of insurance (i.e., the reduced tax liability) = tax otherwise payable/1 + (marginal tax rate - dividend tax rate)

Using current Ontario rates, the tax otherwise payable is $690,000, the marginal tax rate is 46% and the dividend tax rate (for ineligible dividends) is 31%. Therefore, the amount of insurance needed equals the following:

$$690,000/1 + (.46 - .31) = 600,000$$

After the deaths of Bill and Hazel, their tax advisors would calculate the number of shares that could be redeemed using double the amount of insurance ($1.2 million). The redemption would be accomplished using a combination of $600,000 of insurance proceeds and a $600,000 promissory note. One-half of the deemed dividend paid on the redemption would be elected as a capital dividend arising from the payment of the insurance proceeds. The other half would be a taxable dividend. The stop-loss rules would not apply because of the 50% rule described above. Any shares not redeemed would be gifted to Betty and would be subject to normal capital gains rates.

The tax liability would be calculated as follows:

Tax on $600,000 capital dividend	0
Tax on $600,000 taxable dividend (assumed ineligible)	186,000
Tax on remaining $1,800,000 of shares (capital gain)	414,000
Total tax	**$600,000**

(d) Using the 50% Solution to Fully Redeem Shares

Rather than acquiring enough insurance to simply pay tax liability on death, as illustrated in the example of the Bugelmans above, business owners can acquire insurance to redeem the full value of their shares. Once again, if the stop-loss rules would otherwise apply, this redemption can take place using the 50% solution. This strategy may not be required in the case of the Bugelmans, as Betty is their only child and she is taking over the business. However, if Betty had siblings, as was the case in an example earlier in this chapter under the heading "Estate Equalization", extra funds might be necessary to provide adequately for all beneficiaries.

So let's assume that Betty Bugelman has siblings and that Bill and Hazel have decided to fully insure the $3 million value of their shares to free up cash for all of their children. Again, it is assumed that their shares have an ACB and PUC of zero. They have insured the shares with a corporate-owned policy that has a face amount of $3 million and an ACB of zero at the time the proceeds are paid.

Using the 50% solution, the redemption would create a capital dividend of $1.5 million and a taxable dividend of $1.5 million. The stop-loss rules would not apply because of the 50% rule. Tax on the taxable dividend (assumed ineligible) would be $465,000, significantly less than the capital gains tax of $690,000 otherwise payable. In addition, because a capital dividend of only $1.5 million was declared on the redemption, an additional credit of $1.5 million remains in the corporation for Betty's benefit.

This is an ideal method for generating tax savings and providing estate liquidity for the benefit of active and inactive children alike. Share redemption strategies for arm's length situations are discussed in detail in Chapter 6.

References

Income Tax Act (Canada)

Section 38 — taxable capital gains and allowable capital losses

Section 54 — paragraph (j) of definition of "proceeds of disposition" exclusion for amount of deemed dividend on redemption of shares

Subsection 70(5) — taxation of capital property held at death

Subsection 70(5.3) — valuation of certain corporate-owned life insurance policies

Subsection 70(6) — transfer of property on death to spouse or spouse trust

Sections 74.1–75.1 — attribution rules

Subsection 83(2) — capital dividends

Subsection 84(3) — deemed dividend on redemption of shares

Section 85 — rollover on transfer of certain property to corporation

Section 86 — tax-free reorganization of share capital

Subsection 89(1) — definition of "capital dividend account"

Subsection 104(4) — deemed disposition rules for trusts

Subsection 107(2) — rollover on transfer of trust property to beneficiary

Subsection 110.6(1) — definition of "qualified small business corporation share"

Subsection 110.6(15) — impact of corporate-owned life insurance on eligibility for capital gains exemption

Subsections 112(3)–(3.32) — stop-loss rules

Section 121 — dividend tax credit

Subsection 164(6) — carryback of capital losses realized in first taxation year of estate

Interpretation Bulletins

IT-66R6 — Capital Dividends

IT-140R3 — Buy/Sell Agreements

IT-291R3 — Transfer of Property to a Corporation under Section 85

Chapter 6

Buy/Sell Agreements

T he use of life insurance as funding for buy/sell agreements has long been one of the most prominent features of the business market. Even lawyers and accountants, who might normally be unaware of the many benefits of insurance, will usually understand the need for funding in the event of a shareholder's death. Other funding options, such as borrowing from the bank, liquidating assets or financing the purchase out of business profits, are too expensive and financially risky in most cases. And it is usually foolhardy to assume that business owners will self-insure by saving money in a sinking fund for that far-off day when his or her partner encounters actuarial maturity. Business owners with excess cash will always find more current uses for the money. Life insurance is tax-free and is usually cheaper than other options. Most important, it is there when you need it.

While life insurance is a well-accepted part of buy/sell agreements, issues and complexities arise in how to structure the ownership of the insurance in a corporate setting. There are strategies which are beneficial in one case, but detrimental in others. Tax planning opportunities and pitfalls abound.

Of course, it is not the job of the insurance professional to do tax planning for the client. In the final analysis, this is the territory of the client's accountant or lawyer. On the other hand, the insurance professional's credibility with clients and their other advisors is greatly enhanced if he or she is able to provide some input into the many tax planning strategies available. This enhanced credibility will lead directly to referrals, which are critical in the upscale insurance business.

This section will explore some common methods of using life insurance to fund the purchase of shares held by the deceased shareholder of a private corporation.

1. Popular Methods of Structuring Buy/Sell Agreements (Individual Shareholders)

Hypothetical Fact Situation

For simplicity's sake, most of the examples which follow assume that two shareholders, Harry and Hortence, are Canadian residents who are equal shareholders in a private corporation (Opco) which carries on business in Canada. They are not related to each other and have spouses who are uninvolved in the business. Opco has a fair market value of $2 million and the ACB of the shares to each shareholder is nil.

The Need for an Insured Buyout

The insurance professional's first job is, of course, to convince Harry and Hortence that they require insurance to fund the purchase of shares in the event one of them dies. Undoubtedly, they will both see the wisdom of a life-insured buyout. As mentioned previously, this is usually the most cost effective and efficient financing method. Adequate insurance funding will also ensure that the survivor can carry on the business as its sole owner, while leaving the deceased's spouse with needed cash from the sale of the shares. This is usually much preferred to having the surviving spouse inherit the deceased's shares — smooth business operations are difficult where one of the original shareholders is attempting to run the business with the spouse of his or her ex-partner.

The above is true notwithstanding the many changes which have taken place in the taxation of life insurance over the years. In other words, the need for life insurance as funding for shareholders agreements will exist no matter what twists and turns may be taken by income tax law.

Once Harry and Hortence understand the way insurance can facilitate business continuation, the various buy/sell structures need to be reviewed. The structure that is best for them can be incorporated into their shareholders agreement. Some common options are discussed below.

Method 1: Cross Purchase — Personally-Owned Insurance

The shareholders agreement might provide that shares held by a deceased shareholder would be sold to the surviving shareholder for a purchase price determined under the agreement. Normally, this price would be the shares' fair market value. The agreement would be funded with personally-owned insurance — Harry would be the owner and beneficiary of the policy on Hortence's life, and vice versa. On Hortence's death, for example, Harry would use the insurance proceeds to pay for her shares. If the purchase price for the shares was greater than the available life insurance, the balance might be paid in instalments over an agreed upon period of time, usually five years or less.

The tax consequences of method 1 are as follows:

- Immediately before Hortence's death, she would be deemed to have sold her Opco shares for their fair market value of $1 million. This amount less the ACB of her shares would represent a capital gain realized by Hortence in the year of her death. In this example, because her ACB is nil, the capital gain would be the full $1 million.

- Under the Act, one-half of this gain ($500,000) would be added to Hortence's income in the year of her death. At a 46% marginal rate, tax of $230,000 would be payable. This would be reduced if the Opco shares were eligible for the $750,000 capital gains exemption, and if Hortence had not fully used this exemption at the time of her death. (The capital gains exemption is discussed more fully in Chapter 2.)

- Hortence's estate would be deemed to acquire her shares at their fair market value of $1 million. This would represent the ACB of the shares to her estate. The estate would realize no capital gain or loss when the shares were sold for $1 million to Harry under the shareholders agreement.

- Harry would receive the life insurance proceeds tax-free. After purchasing the shares from Hortence's estate, he would have an ACB equal to the $1 million purchase price. The fair market value of his shares would be $2 million, representing his original holdings plus the shares purchased from Hortence.

When to use Method 1:

This method is rarely used, mainly because shareholders usually prefer to have their corporation own and pay for life insurance coverage. It is best-suited to cases involving smaller corporations where the shareholders' income is not at the top marginal rate, and where the shareholders have not fully utilized the $750,000 capital gains exemption.

Method 2: Cross Purchase — Corporate-Owned Insurance

This method is similar to the first, in that the purchase takes place between the estate of the deceased shareholder and the survivor. The purchase is funded, however, with insurance under which the corporation is both owner and beneficiary. The following transactions would occur on Hortence's death:

- Opco would receive the life insurance proceeds.

- Harry would purchase Hortence's shares for their fair market value, in exchange for which he would issue to her a promissory note equal to the purchase price.

- After the purchase, Harry would arrange for Opco to distribute the insurance proceeds to him as a capital dividend. The proceeds would be used to pay down Harry's obligations under the note. As with method 1, any remaining purchase price would be paid by instalments over a period of time stipulated in the shareholders agreement.

The interim step of having Harry purchase Hortence's shares with a promissory note is necessitated by corporate law. If the capital dividend were declared before her shares were transferred to Harry, Hortence's estate would be entitled to its 50% *pro rata* share of the dividend. This would give Harry only 50% of the funds needed to complete the purchase, thus partially defeating the purpose of the insurance arrangement.

The following are the income tax consequences of method 2:

- The capital gains consequences to Hortence and her estate are the same as in method 1.

- Opco would receive the life insurance proceeds tax-free. The amount of the proceeds less the ACB of the insurance policy would be credited to Opco's capital dividend account ("CDA").

- Any capital dividends paid to Harry would be tax-free. As with method 1, his new ACB would equal the purchase price of $1 million.

When to use Method 2:

This method be used where it is anticipated that any purchase and sale of shares would entitle the deceased to the capital gains exemption, i.e., where the capital gain realized would not exceed $750,000. It is more common than Method 1 because it allows for the use of corporate-owned, rather than personally-owned, insurance.

Method 3: Share Redemption Before the Stop-Loss Rules

Method 3 also involves the use of corporate-owned life insurance, but in this instance, the corporation itself is the purchaser of the shares. Insurance proceeds received by Opco would be used to redeem shares held by Hortence's estate. This is sometimes also known as a purchase for cancellation of the shares. As with the other methods, the shareholders would likely provide for the unfunded portion of the purchase price to be paid to Hortence's estate over time.

This popular buy/sell technique was significantly affected by the introduction of the "stop-loss rules" on April 26, 1995. Method 3 involves the rules which were in effect prior to the introduction of the stop-loss rules. This method is still available for the many situations which are eligible for the transitional, or "grandfathering", rules which were introduced with these new amendments. The grandfathering rules are considered in detail below.

The following is an overview of the tax consequences on Hortence's death where the stop-loss rules do not apply. For simplicity's sake, it is assumed that the redemption can be fully financed with life insurance proceeds:

- As in methods 1 and 2, Hortence would be deemed to realize a capital gain of $1 million immediately before her death, and her estate would acquire the shares for an ACB equal to that amount.

- As in method 2, Opco would receive the life insurance proceeds tax-free. The amount by which the proceeds exceeded the ACB of the life insurance policy would be credited to Opco's CDA. For the sake of discussion, it is assumed that a CDA credit would be available for the full amount of the proceeds.

- On the redemption of the shares, Hortence's estate would receive a deemed dividend equal to the amount received, less the paid-up capital of the shares. The paid-up capital in this example is assumed to be nil, resulting in a dividend for the full $1 million.

- Opco would elect to treat the deemed dividend paid to Hortence's estate as a capital dividend. This would allow the estate to receive the dividend tax-free.

- The redemption of Hortence's shares is also considered to be a disposition by her estate for the purposes of the capital gains rules.

  However, the proceeds of disposition ($1 million) may be reduced by the amount of any deemed dividend received on the redemption (also $1 million). For capital gains purposes, therefore, Hortence's estate has proceeds of disposition of nil with an ACB of $1 million, resulting in a capital loss of $1 million. If realized in the first taxation year of her estate, and where the stop-loss rules do not apply, this capital loss can be carried back and fully applied against the capital gain realized in the year of death.

- The net result is that Hortence and her estate have received $1 million for her shares without income tax consequences. Harry now owns all of Opco's shares, with a total fair market value of $2 million. His ACB remains at nil, however, as he has paid nothing for the additional $1 million in value that he has acquired. In effect, the capital gains deferred on Hortence's death have been passed on to Harry, the surviving shareholder. Despite his additional income tax liability, Harry has benefited from these transactions, as he has essentially acquired $1 million of shares at no personal cost.

When to use Method 3:

Method 3 was the most common form of buy-sell agreement prior to the introduction of the stop-loss rules in 1995. Where grandfathering is available, this is still the most appropriate structure. Where the deceased may still have entitlement to the capital gains exemption on death, use this in conjunction with a sale of a limited number of shares to the surviving shareholder(s), as described in method 6.

Method 4: Share Redemption After the Stop-Loss Rules

(a) The 50% Solution

Under the 50% solution, corporate-owned life insurance is used to fund the redemption of shares held by a deceased shareholder in circumstances where grandfathering under the stop-loss rules is not available. The latter rules contain a relieving provision that state that the capital loss realized in the estate is reduced only in the amount by which capital dividends exceed 50% of the lesser of:

(i)   the capital gain resulting from the deemed disposition on death; and

(ii) the capital loss in the estate as otherwise determined (i.e., as determined without reference to the stop-loss rules).

In accordance with the above example, assume that Harry died and that, under the shareholders agreement, his shares were redeemed using the $1 million of insurance proceeds. In accordance with the 50% solution, 50% of the resulting deemed dividend would be treated as a capital dividend, with the balance being taxable. As shown in Schedule 1, the total tax payable by Harry and his estate would be $155,000. This is significantly less than the $230,000 that would have been payable (subject to the capital gains exemption) had Harry simply sold his shares to Hortence and realized a capital gain.

From Hortence's perspective, the 50% solution also has benefits. She does not obtain an increase in the ACB of her shares because she is not the purchaser. However, as only 50% of the $1 million CDA credit was utilized in the redemption of Harry's shares, a total credit of $500,000 remains. This is entirely to Hortence's benefit, as she is the sole remaining shareholder. This allows her to pay tax-free dividends out of future business earnings. Alternatively, she could declare the capital dividend right away and, in the absence of any available cash, pay the dividend in the form of a promissory note. This note could be paid down over time on a tax-free basis.

(b) The 100% Solution

In many cases, it will now be worth paying the maximum available capital dividend on the redemption of shares (the "100% solution"), even where this causes the stop-loss rules to come into play. Once again, the following example assumes that Harry dies and that his shares are redeemed. However, in this case the full $1 million deemed dividend is elected as a capital dividend.

The tax consequences of the 100% solution, which are shown in Schedule 1, may be summarized as follows:

- The capital dividend received by Harry's estate ($1 million) exceeds 50% of the lesser of the capital gain realized on his death and his capital loss determined without reference to the stop-loss rules (50% of the latter two amounts is, in each case, $500,000).

- The difference between the above amounts ($1,000,000 - $500,000 = $500,000) represents the amount of capital loss generated in Harry's estate that, because of the stop-loss rules, may not be carried back against the capital gain realized on his death. Nonetheless, the remaining $500,000 capital loss may be carried back, reducing Harry's capital gain to $500,000, on which tax of approximately $115,000 would otherwise be payable. This compares with the $155,000 payable by Harry and his estate under the 50% solution. Thus, the 100% solution provides the lowest amount of tax to Harry.

- From Hortence's perspective, as with the 50% solution, she obtains no increase in the ACB of her Opco shares. In addition, there is no remaining CDA credit for her to access following the redemption of Harry's shares. This is a significant disadvantage of the 100% solution to the surviving shareholder.

When to use Method 4:

Method 4 should be used in situations where the stop-loss rules are applicable, i.e., where grandfathering is not available. As with method 3, it can be used as part of the hybrid approach described in method 6 (sale of shares to survivor(s) to fully utilize capital gains exemption, followed by a redemption of balance of shares). In some cases, method 5 (spousal roll and redeem) will be preferable to method 4 where the deceased leaves a surviving spouse because method 5 involves complete tax deferral. Method 4 can be a "fall back" position where there is no surviving spouse.

The decision as to whether the 50% solution or 100% should be used may not be an easy one. To use the above example as a reference point, under the 100% solution, Harry and his estate pay $40,000 less tax than would be payable under the 50% solution. This is an immediate tax savings of almost 26%. From Hortence's perspective, the 100% solution means that she would lose access to a potential CDA credit of $500,000 that would be available if the 50% solution were used. Absent this credit, a future dividend of that amount would generate approximately $155,000 of income tax.

It is difficult to make general recommendations that will apply in all cases. The 100% solution is the most tax-effective from the deceased's point of view, but involves an element of "CDA wastage", i.e., the maximum capital dividend is paid to the estate but the deceased still has tax liability — and there is no CDA remaining for the survivor. The 50% solution is a more balanced approach, allowing the deceased to pay less than capital gains rates, but more than is payable under the 100% solution. And the remaining CDA credit leaves something for the survivor. This is all a matter for negotiation between the parties.

Before adopting either the 50% or 100% solution as the preferred strategy, however, other tax planning options should be considered. One attractive method can, in the right circumstances, provide complete tax deferral on a shareholder's death, even where the stop-loss rules apply. This involves a transfer of shares to the surviving spouse of the deceased shareholder, as will be addressed in method 5.

SCHEDULE 1 — Tax Consequences

TO HARRY:	50%	100%
Deemed disposition of shares	$1,000,000	1,000,000
ACB of shares	0	0
Capital gain	1,000,000	1,000,000
Less capital loss carryback	1,000,000	500,000
Capital gain/loss	0	500,000
Tax on capital gain	0	115,000

TO HARRY'S ESTATE:		
(a) Deemed Dividend		
Redemption proceeds	$1,000,000	1,000,000
PUC of shares	0	0
Deemed dividend	1,000,000	1,000,000
Capital portion of dividend	500,000	1,000,000
Taxable portion of dividend	500,000	0
Tax on taxable dividend (31%)	155,000	0
(b) Capital Loss		
Proceeds of disposition	$1,000,000	1,000,000
Less deemed dividend	1,000,000	1,000,000
Net proceeds of disposition	0	0
Less ACB of shares to estate	1,000,000	1,000,000
Stop-loss limitation	0	(500,000)
Capital loss (carried back against Harry's capital gain)	1,000,000	500,000
Total tax payable by Harry and his estate	155,000	115,000

TO HORTENCE:		
Increase in ACB of shares	0	0
Available CDA credit	500,000	0

Method 5: Spousal Put/Call Options

Under this arrangement, the spouses of Harry and Hortence would be parties to the shareholders agreement. Assume that Hortence dies leaving her husband, Buster, surviving. Under Hortence's will, Buster would inherit her shares, but under the shareholders agreement, he would have the right to require Opco to redeem the shares within the time frame stipulated in the agreement. The agreement would also give Opco and/or the surviving shareholders a corresponding right to redeem or purchase the shares. These "put/call" options would be funded with corporate-owned life insurance on the lives of Harry and Hortence.

Assuming Opco redeems Hortence's shares under one of these options, the following income tax consequences would arise:

- Hortence's shares would pass tax-free to Buster under the spousal rollover rules. Buster would acquire the shares at Hortence's nil ACB.

- The insurance proceeds would be received tax-free by Opco and credited to its CDA as described in previous examples.

- On the redemption, Buster would receive a deemed dividend of $1 million, all of which would be declared as a tax-free capital dividend.

- Buster would also be deemed to have disposed of his shares for capital gains purposes, but his proceeds of disposition would be reduced by the amount of the dividend received, leaving him with net proceeds of nil. He would therefore have no capital gain or loss, as his ACB is also nil.

The income tax result under method 5 is essentially identical to that of method 3 (the traditional corporate redemption technique that is so attractive where the stop-loss rules do not apply). Neither Buster, Hortence, nor her estate is taxable on the disposition of the shares, while Harry's interest in Opco doubles to $2 million and his inherent capital gains exposure increases accordingly.

This method is available even with the advent of the stop-loss rules because, under the arrangement described above, the deceased does not have a capital gain. No offsetting capital loss is available or even needed, which makes the stop-loss rules irrelevant.

When to use Method 5:

Method 5 should be used in situations where the stop-loss rules are applicable, i.e., where grandfathering is not available. It can provide complete tax deferral where the deceased leaves a surviving spouse. Agreements should always provide a "fall back", such as method 4 or method 6, in the event that the deceased does not leave a surviving spouse.

Method 6: The Hybrid Method (Individual Shareholders)

The continually changing income tax laws have made it more important than ever for shareholders agreements to be flexible in their approach.

Under the hybrid method, the deceased's shares can either be redeemed by the corporation or sold to the survivor. Or, a combination approach may be taken where some shares are redeemed by the corporation and the balance sold to the survivor. Typically, the deceased's executor is given the choice as to how and to whom the shares are sold, and will make the decision based upon the various income tax issues affecting the deceased shareholder.

The hybrid method first became popular following the introduction of the $750,000 capital gains exemption in the 1980s. At that time, it became advantageous for the deceased to sell to the surviving shareholder whatever number of shares was necessary to allow the exemption to be utilized in full. This would be done under a process similar to that described in method 2. The balance of the shares would be redeemed as in method 3. The income tax consequences would be as described in the above discussion of these methods. This combination may still be effective in situations where grandfathering under the stop-loss rules is available.

Method 6 is also advantageous where the stop-loss rules apply. The capital gains exemption continues to be of benefit to many shareholders and may dictate a sale of some or all of the deceased's shares to the surviving shareholder. The balance of the shares could be redeemed using the 50% or 100% solution, for example.

When to use Method 6:

This method is attractive where the deceased has remaining entitlement to the $750,000 capital gains exemption, but where a sale of all of his or her shares to the survivor(s) would create a capital gain greater than the available exemption. Relatively simple tax calculations can determine how many shares the survivor(s) purchase, leaving the remaining shares to be redeemed in accordance with the agreement and/or the executor's wishes. Method 6 can be used whether or not the deceased's shares are eligible for grandfathering.

2. Popular Methods of Structuring Buy/Sell Agreements (Corporate Shareholders)

Different considerations apply when an individual owns shares of a holding company that in turn owns shares of an operating company. In these cases, the same compelling reasons exist for a purchase and sale of shares on the individual's death. However, in most cases the sale will involve shares owned by the deceased's holding company, rather than those owned personally by the deceased. The involvement of a holding company as a vendor naturally introduces additional income tax rules, as will be described below.

For purposes of illustration, assume that two unrelated individuals, Mack and Mitzi, each own all of the shares of a holding company ("Mack Co." and "Mitzi Co.", respectively). Mack Co. and Mitzi Co. are equal shareholders of Opco, whose shares have an aggregate fair market value of $4 million and an ACB and PUC of nil. The examples below, which all assume that Mack predeceases Mitzi, illustrate some common methods of structuring a purchase and sale of shares owned by Mack Co.

Method 1: Cross Purchase

Under this method, after Mack's death, Mack Co. would sell its Opco shares to Mitzi Co. for their fair market value of $2 million. Life insurance could be used to fund this purchase in one of several ways:

- Mack Co. and Mitzi Co. could have a criss-cross arrangement under which Mitzi Co. was the owner and beneficiary of a policy on Mack's life and vice versa. On Mack's death, the insurance proceeds would be paid to Mitzi Co. and applied towards the purchase price of the Opco shares owned by Mack Co.

- Alternatively, Opco could be the owner and the beneficiary of the policies. In that case, following Mack's death, Mitzi Co. would purchase the Opco shares owned by Mack Co. for a $2 million promissory note. Opco would then pay a $2 million capital dividend to Mitzi Co., which would use the funds to pay off the note.

- As a refinement on the structure described immediately above, Mark Co. and Mitzi Co. could each own a policy on the life of its shareholder, with Opco as beneficiary in each case. This would be a split beneficiary arrangement (see Chapter 4 for additional information on the benefits of these arrangements). The proceeds would be used in the same way as described in the immediately preceding bullet point.

The income tax consequences of this cross-purchase arrangement can be summarized as follows:

- Mack Co. would realize a $2 million capital gain (sale proceeds less the ACB of the shares). Like the case of an individual taxpayer, one-half of the gain is taxable and one-half is tax-free. As Mack Co. is a private corporation, the tax-free portion is credited to its CDA. As a corporation, Mack Co. is not entitled to the $750,000 capital gains exemption.

- The taxable portion of the capital gain is taxed to Mack Co. at the rate applicable to corporate investment income. Depending on the province, this rate is usually just under 50%. As with other investment income, the corporation receives a credit to its refundable dividend tax on hand ("RDTOH") account equal to 26.67% of the taxable capital gain. This entitles Mack Co. to a tax refund of $1 for every $3 paid as a taxable dividend to the shareholder(s). See a discussion of RDTOH in Chapter 2.

- Life insurance proceeds received by Mitzi Co. or Opco, as the case may be, would be tax-free. The amount of the proceeds less the ACB of the insurance policy would be credited to the beneficiary corporation's CDA.

- Where the strategy involves Opco paying a capital dividend to Mitzi Co., it will reduce Opco's CDA by the amount of the dividend, and will increase Mitzi's CDA by the same amount. Mitzi Co. will retain the CDA credit after the purchase of Mack Co.'s Opco shares, thus allowing Mitzi to receive tax-free dividends in the future.

Method 2: Redemption with Full Capital Dividend

Under this method, Opco would redeem (or purchase for cancellation) all of the shares owned by Mack Co. Assuming that there was a sufficient CDA credit, Opco could declare all of the resulting deemed dividend as a capital dividend. This would be tax-free to Mack Co. and would also leave Mack Co. with a corresponding increase in its CDA.

Mitzi Co. would receive no increase in the ACB of its Opco shares but would, as a result of the redemption, become the sole shareholder of Opco. The value of Mitzi Co.'s shares would have increased to $4 million, which means that Mitzi Co. will have effectively inherited the income tax liability deferred by Mack Co.

Method 3: Redemption with 50% Capital Dividend

Where a corporation redeems shares owned by another corporation, the shareholder corporation will receive a deemed dividend in the amount by which the redemption proceeds exceed the PUC of the shares. Even if the dividend is not a capital dividend, it will be tax-free if:

- The shareholder corporation owns shares having more than 10% of the votes and more than 10% of the value of the corporation whose shares are being redeemed; and

- The amount of the dividend does not exceed the holding company's share of the subsidiary corporation's "safe income". Safe income, which must be calculated by the corporation's accountant, generally represents the holding company's share of the subsidiary's retained earnings. If the dividend exceeds this level, onerous income tax consequences can arise. In particular, these rules can essentially convert what was thought to be a tax-free intercorporate dividend into a capital gain that is subject to tax.

Therefore, a deemed dividend that arises on a redemption of shares owned by a holding company can be tax-free, even if the dividend is not a capital dividend. In the above example, this might lead to an arrangement under which a portion (say, 50%) of the dividend received by Mack Co. on the redemption of its Opco shares was treated as a capital dividend and the balance as an ordinary dividend. Assuming the above requirements are met, even the latter dividend will be tax-free to Mack Co. This will also leave Mitzi Co., as the sole shareholder, with access to the credit that remains in Opco's CDA.

Method 4: Hybrid Method

As with situations involving individual shareholders, it is open to holding companies to have a hybrid arrangement under which shares can either be sold to the survivor's holding company or redeemed by the operating company. In this situation, the decision as to which method was used, or as to whether a combination of the two would be used, could be left to the deceased's holding company. The buyout could then be structured in accordance with the tax rules and the holding company's circumstances at that time.

Considerations Regarding the Holding Company Shares Owned by the Deceased

As the above discussion indicates, the Opco shares owned by Mack Co. can be sold tax effectively after Mack's death. Tax issues remain, however, regarding the taxation of Mack and his estate. If Mack's shares are transferred after his death to his spouse, or to a qualifying spouse trust, taxation on any inherent gains in the Mack Co. shares will be deferred until the spouse dies or otherwise disposes of the shares. Otherwise, the shares will be subject to a deemed disposition immediately before Mack's death.

In many cases, the most advantageous strategy from an income tax point of view is to wind up the holding company after the shareholder's death, and to distribute the assets to the estate. This can be particularly attractive where there is a significant CDA credit in the holding company.

3. Commentary on Eligible Dividends, Changing Tax Rules and Related Drafting Issues

As discussed in Chapter 2, certain dividends are now eligible for a lower rate of tax. As some of the above examples illustrate, it is possible for taxable dividends to arise on the redemption of shares. In that case, if there is a balance in the corporation's general rate income pool (GRIP), it is to the estate's advantage that such dividends are paid out of the GRIP account. On the other hand, the survivors would prefer to preserve the GRIP for themselves. For this reason, the shareholders agreement should stipulate how the GRIP should be shared amongst the deceased and the other shareholders.

Existing shareholder agreements should be reviewed in light of these proposals. Depending on the circumstances, it may be appropriate to amend agreements in order to deal with issues such as the allocation of the GRIP. Similarly, these rules should be addressed in the structuring of new shareholders agreements. More than ever, it is critical that the clients' tax advisors be consulted in the drafting stage.

Agreements should provide a mechanism for determining whether or not a taxable dividend arising on a share redemption should be paid out of the GRIP (if available). The agreement should also provide a mechanism for allocating the GRIP amongst the shareholders. Should the deceased be entitled to dividends out of the GRIP to the maximum available? Alternatively, should the GRIP be shared ratably amongst the shareholders, so that the deceased may only claim a *pro rata* portion upon the redemption of his or her shares? In many cases, these questions will become a matter of negotiation as the agreement is prepared.

With continuous changes in the taxation rules that apply to shareholders agreements, it is difficult to identify one or two buy-sell methods that will be ideal in every case. This issue is complicated by the fact that the parties under a shareholders agreement have competing interests regarding which buy-sell method is most advantageous. In light of these issues, it would be beneficial if shareholders agreements include a statement that sets out a philosophical basis for determining the buy-sell method that will be used to buy out a deceased shareholder. Agreements could provide for the mandatory purchase and sale of shares owned by a deceased shareholder but provide one party, such as the deceased's representative, with the ability to determine the methodology.

4. Marketing Opportunities Relating to the Stop-Loss Grandfathering Rules

The original version of the stop-loss rules provided no transitional relief for arrangements that were already then in place. However, a concerted and well-reasoned lobbying effort by interested groups led to a series of transitional measures, commonly known as grandfathering rules, which provide a level of protection to those pre-existing arrangements. This section will provide an overview of these grandfathering rules and will also discuss some opportunities for corporate-owned life insurance relating to these changes. It will also consider potential pitfalls and the need for due diligence on the part of legal, accounting and insurance professionals who advise small business clients.

(a) Overview of the Grandfathering Rules

As shown above, the stop-loss rules have their widest impact on the popular strategy of using the proceeds of corporate-owned life insurance to redeem shares held by a deceased shareholder. As the above commentary indicates, before the stop-loss rules this strategy created a capital loss in the estate, which could be carried back against capital gains realized by the deceased in the year of death. Where the stop-loss rules apply, however, the amount of available loss is reduced in most cases to 50% of that formerly available.

The grandfathering rules are designed to protect arrangements which were in place on April 26, 1995, the day the stop-loss rules were introduced. This date will be referred to hereafter as the "Effective Date". Where grandfathering is available, taxpayers will be able to avoid the impact of the stop-loss rules and rely upon the more favourable "old rules". This section will focus on what are likely the two most important grandfathering rules:

- Grandfathering will be available where a corporation was the beneficiary of a life insurance policy on the life of a taxpayer on the Effective Date, where the main purpose of the insurance on that date was to redeem shares held by the taxpayer, or by the taxpayer's spouse.

- Grandfathering will also be available where shares are redeemed pursuant to an agreement in place on the Effective Date.

These rules are discussed in greater detail below.

(b) Grandfathered Life Insurance

(i) Overview

This is the most generous of all of the grandfathering rules. In order to meet this test, it is not necessary to establish that the sole purpose, or the primary purpose, of the insurance was to redeem shares, only that this was *a main purpose*. In this regard, a few comments are in order:

- Under this rule, the reason for the purchase of the insurance may be irrelevant. It requires that a "snapshot" be taken to determine the purpose of the insurance on the Effective Date. For example, if a policy originally acquired for share-redemption purposes was assigned as collateral to the bank on the Effective Date, grandfathering may not be available.

- If the only purpose of the insurance on the Effective Date was to fund a purchase of shares by surviving shareholders, grandfathering is not available. "Redemption" is a purchase by the corporation, not by shareholders. On the other hand, some buy/sell agreements provide for one or more alternative buy-out mechanisms following a share-holder's death. If one of these possible mechanisms is share redemption, it should be enough to meet the purpose test. An example of this is Method 6 for individual shareholders (the hybrid method).

- If grandfathering is available under this rule, it applies to any policies acquired on the shareholder's life after the Effective Date, under which the corporation is beneficiary, even where this involves an increase in coverage from the amount in force on that date. It also applies where the grandfathered policy is converted or replaced, or if it lapses and is subsequently reinstated.

(ii) The Problem of Proof

While the rules concerning grandfathered life insurance are quite generous, it seems inevitable that, in the future, taxpayers and the CRA will disagree as to whether or not they apply in given circumstances. In this regard, it is critical to note that if the CRA assesses a tax return, the onus is on the taxpayer to establish that the assessment is wrong. Absent proper documentation, it may be difficult for a taxpayer to overcome an assertion by the CRA that "a main purpose" of a particular insurance policy was not share redemption. This will be particularly difficult where the issue is being addressed many years, or even decades, after the insurance was acquired.

In many cases there will be ample documentation, created at the time the insurance was acquired, which supports the purpose of these policies. This might include notations on the insurance application, correspondence from the insurance broker or other advisors, and corporate resolutions. In many other cases, however, there may be a lack of documentation, which could ultimately doom any effort to avoid the stop-loss rules.

At the present time, there are undoubtedly thousands of insurance policies that may be eligible for grandfathering. Legal, accounting and insurance professionals would be well-advised to review existing client situations to determine whether such policies exist within their client portfolios and whether there is documentation to support the purpose of such policies on the Effective Date. If there is a reasonable argument that grandfathering is available, but nothing exists in writing to support that position, it may be advisable to have documentation prepared. This might include correspondence from the insurance broker, a corporate resolution, or even sworn affidavits from parties who can attest as to the purpose of the policy in question. While such documentation would be self-serving, in that it would be prepared years after the Effective Date, it would clearly be better than having no written evidence with which to dispute a future reassessment.

Those involved in advising business owners in this area should always do so with an eye to the grandfathering rules. Part of the necessary due diligence should be inquiring as to the purpose of any corporate policies that may have been in force on the Effective Date. Even if the corporation does not currently have any insurance, it may in the past have owned policies which would provide relief from the stop-loss rules. And even if the corporation currently has insurance not held for share redemption, inquiries should be made as to whether that policy was in force on the Effective Date and what its purpose was at that time.

(c) Grandfathered Agreements

Generally speaking, the rules regarding grandfathered agreements are less generous than those dealing with grandfathered insurance. Where an arrangement receives relief under the latter rules, grandfathering is theoretically available as long as the shareholder or his or her spouse continues to own shares of the corporation. On the other hand, where a taxpayer is relying on a grandfathered agreement, for the reasons discussed below, there is less certainty that grandfathering will always be available.

The CRA has stated that an agreement will retain its grandfathered status only if it "is not altered or modified in any way". This has been taken to mean that any amendment after the Effective Date, no matter how minor or unrelated to buy/sell provisions, will cause a grandfathered agreement to lose its protected status. Time will tell whether this unduly rigid administrative position will survive the scrutiny of the courts.

The CRA has also stated that the parties to a grandfathered agreement may alter their legal relationship by executing a separate agreement. Grandfathering would be lost if the latter agreement was considered to "cancel, modify or replace" the original agreement. This presumably means that a separate agreement, which merely adds new terms to the grandfathered agreement, without amending or replacing it in any way, would not cause the loss of grandfathering.

An agreement that is grandfathered under the stop-loss rules may need to be changed for a variety of reasons: shareholders come and go; new corporations may be added to the business structure; or there may be any number of legal or business reasons to revise existing terms and conditions provided under the agreement. Usually it will be best to make these changes, and to have an up-to-date agreement that meets all of the present needs of the shareholders and the business, even if it means grandfathering under the stop-loss rules is lost. There are still many attractive ways of structuring insurance plans to meet buy/sell needs, even where the stop-loss rules apply.

The grandfathering rules present an opportunity for insurance advisors to review client situations and to ensure that the necessary tax and insurance planning is done. Insurance professionals should also take it upon themselves to assist the lawyers and accountants with whom they work, many of whom are not familiar with these issues, as to the importance of grandfathering. Other advisors should be grateful for this assistance, as these difficult provisions contain traps for inattentive advisors who fail to thoroughly investigate whether transitional relief is available. Due diligence is necessary to ensure that potential opportunities and pitfalls are not overlooked.

5. Partnership Buy/Sell Agreements

(a) Introductory Comments

For a variety of reasons, some of which will be addressed below, corporations are the most common form of business structure in Canada. There are occasions, however, where a partnership structure is either advantageous or is required for regulatory reasons (the latter typically being the case for professionals such as doctors, lawyers and accountants).

A partnership is not a separate taxpayer under Canadian law. Instead, income earned or losses realized at the partnership level are allocated to the partners as they may agree. The partner then reports the income or loss individually for tax purposes.

Partnerships do not provide the same level of creditor protection as corporations, as a partner may be personally liable for partnership obligations. These concerns are mitigated somewhat in limited liability partnerships (LLP's), the form in which virtually all law and accounting firms, for example, carry on their practices.

This section of the book will briefly discuss buy/sell strategies as they apply to partnerships with individual partners, and to partnerships with corporate partners.

(b) Buy/Sell Agreements for Partnerships with Individual Partners

A partnership with individual partners is sometimes found in the case of very small businesses that do not have the size or revenue stream to justify incorporation. In the upscale business market, a partnership with individual partners will typically be a firm of professionals such as accountants or lawyers.

Life insurance held at the partnership level may be used in these circumstances to fund a buyout of a deceased partner's interest on death. In that case, the buyout may consist simply of a repayment by the partnership of the partner's capital account, which is essentially the deceased's equity in the firm. Amounts paid in excess of the ACB of the deceased's partnership interest would be treated as a capital gain to the deceased's estate.

It is also possible for a deceased's partnership interest to be purchased by the surviving partners. This may be funded using insurance payable to the partnership or to the partners themselves. Again, any amount received by the deceased in excess of the ACB of his or her partnership interest would be taxed as a capital gain. The survivors would receive an increase in ACB equal to their relative share of the purchase price. This type of buyout is more complicated in firms with large numbers of partners, as there are that many more potential purchasers. It is generally simpler to have the partnership itself pay funds directly to the estate as a means of buying out the deceased's partnership interest.

Insurance proceeds are received tax-free by a partnership. The amount of the proceeds attributable to each partner, net of the policy's ACB, will increase the ACB of each partner's partnership interest. This is a calculation similar to that of the CDA for private corporations.

The CRA has taken the position that the insurance proceeds cannot increase the ACB of the deceased's partnership interest, as he or she ceases to be a partner on death. Therefore, the increase in ACB would be shared by the surviving partners, and would allow them to receive capital from the partnership in future without tax consequences. In calculating the deceased's capital gain, therefore, no adjustment to his or her ACB would be made as a result of the insurance payment.

(c) Buy/Sell Agreement for Partnerships with Corporate Partners

(i) Introduction

As mentioned, the most common form of business structure in Canada is the corporation. The main reasons for this are creditor protection (shareholders are generally not liable for the obligations of the corporation) and income tax (small business corporations enjoy a low tax rate on the first $400,000 of business income earned each year and their shares often qualify for the $750,000 capital gains exemption — see Chapter 2). Estate planning strategies such as estate freezes are also more easily utilized in a corporate setting (see Chapter 5).

It is becoming more common, however, to see structures that have an operating partnership as a key component. By using unique structures that include corporations as partners of these partnerships, the same creditor protection and estate planning advantages are available, but ongoing tax savings from business earnings may be multiplied. As will be demonstrated below, these savings are achieved by utilizing a second tier of corporations to hold the shares of the corporate partners.

Partnerships referred to in this section may carry on an active business, as would a typical private corporation, or may carry on a professional practice such as law, accounting, medicine or dentistry. However, in the case of the professions, many provinces have placed restrictions on the ability of a professional corporation to have a holding company as shareholder. This would prevent utilization of the strategy described below.

This section will briefly describe how corporate partnership arrangements are structured and will identify the income tax advantages that make them increasingly popular. It will then suggest a method of using life insurance as a vehicle to fund the purchase and sale of partnership interests on the death of one of the principals.

(ii) Example

By way of example, assume that Moe, Larry and Eleanor are arm's length individuals who manage a partnership known as Maple Leaf Engraving ("MLE"), which specializes in engraving trophies for professional hockey leagues. A recent decision to move the focus of the business away from Ontario and into the broader North American market has significantly increased business prospects. The business currently has a fair market value of $3 million ($1 million to each partner).

MLE is owned equally by three corporations, Moe Partner Inc., Larry Partner Inc. and Eleanor Partner Inc. The three corporate partners are wholly-owned, respectively, by Moe Holdings Inc. (controlled by Moe), Larry Holdings Inc. (controlled by Larry) and Eleanor Holdings Inc. (controlled by Eleanor).

(iii) Multiplying the Small Business Deduction

Assume that MLE earns $1.2 million of income in its 2008 fiscal year and allocates it equally to its partners pursuant to the partnership agreement. Absent any other planning, the *Income Tax* Act would treat this as "specified partnership income" and would allocate the $400,000 small business limit to the three partners. It would presumably be equally shared amongst them. Therefore, depending on the province, the corporate partners would collectively pay tax of approximately $68,000 on income eligible for the small business deduction ($400,000 x 17%) and $264,000 on the balance ($800,000 x 33%). Total tax payable would be $332,000.

However, rather than having partnership income taxed at the corporate partner level, each partner could pay its $400,000 share of MLE income to its holding company as a management fee. The payment would be deductible to each corporate partner (after which it would have no taxable income) and would be treated as business income to the holding company. After receiving the management fees, each of Moe Holdings Inc., Larry Holdings Inc. and Eleanor Holdings Inc. would have $400,000 of income, but this would not be partnership income from MLE as the holding companies are not partners of MLE. Therefore, each holding company would be entitled to the full $400,000 small business limit, which in this example exactly matches each company's income. Collective tax would be $204,000 rather than $332,000, a savings of $128,000.

(iv) Structuring the Buy/Sell Agreement

The partners' accountant, lawyer and insurance advisor have met and recommended a method for structuring a buy/sell in the event of the death of Moe, Larry or Eleanor. Under their proposal, Moe Partner Inc. will acquire an insurance policy on the life of Moe. Larry Partner Inc. and Eleanor Partner Inc. will also purchase insurance on the lives of Larry and Eleanor, respectively. MLE will be the beneficiary of each policy, perhaps on an irrevocable basis, so that the designation cannot be unilaterally changed. The face amount of the policies will be $1 million each, reflecting the current fair market value of each partnership interest.

Using Moe's death as an example, the insurance proceeds would be paid to MLE then used pursuant to the partnership agreement to purchase the partnership interest owned by Moe Partner Inc. (similar to a share redemption where a corporation is being used rather than a partnership). The tax consequences of this strategy would be as set out below. For purposes of illustration, the analysis assumes that there are no significant assets other than the various interests in MLE:

- On Moe's death, he would be deemed to have disposed of his shares of Moe Holdings Inc. for their fair market value of $1 million. Assuming an ACB of zero, he would have a capital gain of $1 million unless the shares passed to Moe's spouse or a spouse trust. Tax on the capital gain would be approximately $230,000.

- The life insurance proceeds would be received tax-free by MLE. Each partner's share of the proceeds less the policy's ACB (assume a policy ACB of zero) would be added to the ACB of its partnership interest. As Moe Partner Inc. would be entitled to all of the proceeds under the partnership agreement, the ACB of its interest in MLE would increase by the full $1 million. (This is in contrast to what would occur if Moe owned his partnership interest directly. In that case, as discussed above, he would not be entitled to an ACB increase because he would cease to be a partner on death.)

- On the "redemption" of its partnership interest, Moe Partner Inc. would receive $1 million, the amount by which its ACB increased when the proceeds were paid to MLE. Thus, the payment would be tax-free to Moe Partner Inc. as a return of capital.

- Under its administrative guidelines, the CRA would also permit Moe Partner Inc. to receive a credit to its CDA upon receipt of payment from MLE. It would therefore have cash and a CDA of $1 million, and would have disposed of its partnership interest without tax consequences.

Following the above transactions, it would be open to Moe Partner Inc. to pay a $1 million capital dividend in cash to its parent company, Moe Holdings Inc. The latter company could in turn pay a capital dividend to its shareholders or use the funds to redeem shares owned by the estate.

The two remaining corporate partners would now have an equal share in a partnership that is worth $3 million without any corresponding increase in the ACB of their partnership interests. As such, this buy-sell structure merely shifts the capital gain (and resulting tax liability) into the hands of the two other corporate partners (and indirectly to their controlling shareholders).

The result of the above transactions is similar to what would occur if MLE were a corporation. See earlier in this chapter under the heading "Popular Methods of Structuring Buy/Sell Agreements (Corporate Shareholders)" (method 2). If Moe did not leave the shares of Moe Holdings Inc. to a surviving spouse, he would pay tax at the personal level on the deemed disposition of his shares. If the shares did pass to a surviving spouse, there would be complete tax deferral until the spouse's death, similar to the spousal put/call strategy also described earlier in the chapter.

The above example includes what might be considered aggressive tax planning to multiply access to the small business tax rate. Therefore, a future CRA challenge is possible. From a buy-sell structuring point of view, however, the method described will work in any situation where partners hold their partnership interests through corporations. This will be the case whether or not there are multiple tiers of corporations as described above, and whether or not the arrangement involves an attempt to maximize the benefits of the small business tax rate.

References

Income Tax Act (Canada)

Section 38 — taxable capital gains and allowable capital losses

Subparagraph 53(1)(e)(iii) — addition to ACB of partnership interest when partnership receives life insurance proceeds

Section 54 — paragraph (j) of the definition of "proceeds of disposition" exclusion for amount of deemed dividend on redemption of shares

Subsection 55(2) — potential conversion of tax-free intercorporate dividend to a capital gain

Subsection 70(5) — taxation of capital property held at death

Subsection 70(6) — transfer of property on death to spouse or spouse trust

Sections 74.1–75.1 — attribution rules

Subsection 83(2) — capital dividends

Subsection 84(3) — deemed dividend on redemption of shares

Section 85 — rollover on transfer of certain property to corporation

Section 86 — tax-free reorganization of share capital

Subsection 89(1) — definition of "capital dividend account"

Subsection 104(4) — deemed disposition rules for trusts

Subsection 107(2) — rollover on transfer of trust property to beneficiary

Subsection 110.6(1) — definition of "qualified small business corporation share"

Subsections 112(3)–(3.32) — stop-loss rules

Section 121 — dividend tax credit

Section 125 — small business deduction

Subsection 125(7) — definition of "specified partnership income"

Subsection 164(6) — carryback of capital losses realized in first taxation year of estate

Interpretation Bulletins

IT-66R6 — Capital Dividends

IT-140R3 — Buy/Sell Agreements

IT-291R3 — Transfer of Property to a Corporation under Subsection 85(1)

IT-430R3 — Life Insurance Proceeds Received by a Private Corporation or a Partnership as a Consequence of Death

Chapter 7

Using Legal Documents as Sales Tools

I t is questionable how much tax and legal knowledge is required for an insurance professional to be successful in the estate planning market. There appears to be only a limited correlation between technical knowledge and the ability to generate a high volume of sales in this lucrative marketplace. However, while a high level of tax and legal expertise will not guarantee success in the business market, it is almost certain that complete ignorance is a forerunner of failure. It is unnecessary for agents to become tax or legal experts *per se*, but a reasonable level of expertise is essential to achieving a high degree of success in this field. This is largely because agents who deal in this market will regularly encounter lawyers, accountants and other professionals who act for the agent's clients. In order to be included as part of the client's professional team, and not just be seen as a salesperson, the insurance professional should attempt to achieve a measure of sophistication in dealing with tax and legal matters which impact the products and services he or she provides.

Developing the ability to read and understand legal documents is an important step in making the transition from salesperson to advisor. The insurance professional who is able to analyze documents such as shareholders agreements and wills enjoys enhanced credibility with the client and the client's other advisors. Beyond that, a client's existing shareholders agreement and will can become powerful sales tools. This does not mean that agents have to review and understand these agreements as a whole, but they should at least be able to discuss those few sections of an agreement which deal specifically with insurance and related issues.

1. Reviewing Shareholders Agreements

The review of documents is part of the fact-finding procedure, the first stage in the estate planning process described in Chapter 1. Legal documents, such as shareholders agreements, wills and trust agreements, can be excellent sales tools for insurance professionals who work, or hope to work, in the owner/manager market. Rather than shying away from the task of reading these (admittedly less than riveting) documents, you should instead try to get as many of them as possible from your clients. This section will focus on shareholders agreements, although many of the benefits discussed below will arise from a review of wills and other documents. (Some tips on reviewing wills are included later in this chapter.)

The Benefits of Reviewing Shareholders Agreements

There are many reasons why reviewing shareholders agreements could be of benefit:

- The agreement will usually outline the shareholders' business continuation plans. It should tell you what will happen if a shareholder dies or becomes disabled. Understanding the clients' present plans, as outlined in their agreement, will open the door to discussions about whether their objectives have changed since the agreement was prepared.

- Reviewing and understanding these documents, or at least those sections dealing with insurance issues, will make you better at what you do. The more you understand about shareholders agreements, the better will be your positioning with your clients' lawyers and accountants. Once they appreciate your expertise in this area, they will look upon you less as a salesperson and more as a business advisor.

- Speaking of lawyers and accountants, it is apparent that there is little insurance-related expertise in these professions. This is evidenced by the many "bloopers" which can be found in these agreements. These gaffes can provide a modest bit of entertainment, as illustrated in some of the examples considered below, but also present opportunities for you to begin the process of putting your clients' affairs back on sound footing. In fairness to these other professionals, they rarely get any training in the insurance field, and often must rely on insurance advisors for their education in this area. This can be an important role for the insurance professional and a good way of cementing relationships with centres of influence. Good lawyers and accountants will understand their limitations in this area and will look upon a knowledgeable insurance advisor as an ally in helping to put together agreements that work the way they are supposed to.

- There have been situations where an agent has asked for a copy of a client's shareholders agreement only to be given an unsigned draft or, in one case, the client's Articles of Incorporation. Therefore, your involvement can help your clients understand that their plans may not be as well documented as they thought.

- A shareholders agreement, like any legal document, is confidential. If a copy is provided to you, it is a sign that the client trusts you and sees you as someone who can offer a valuable service, not just sell a product.

Assuming the client does have a signed shareholders agreement, agents should focus on four main areas of the agreement in order to try to understand what is being proposed and what is flawed. In the great majority of cases, there are areas in these agreements that are seriously flawed, or at least deficient in some manner, because of bad drafting or legislative changes that have rendered the agreement obsolete. These four areas are as follows:

- What happens to the shares of the corporation owned by a deceased shareholder?

- How are the shares valued?

- What, if anything, does the agreement say about life or disability insurance acquired as funding for the buy/sell portion of the agreement?

- What, if anything, does the agreement say about a shareholder's disability?

Case Studies

To illustrate some of the above points, we will look at five mini-case studies. Each one includes paraphrased excerpts of problems uncovered in the review of actual shareholders agreements.

Case Study Number 1

This case was a bit unusual as it involved a shareholders agreement, first uncovered and reviewed by an insurance agent, between mother ("Mary") and son ("Marvin"). It made sense to have an agreement between them as Mary was in her early sixties and still active in the business. On Marvin's death, it would certainly have made some sense to have his shares purchased so that his wife and children, none of whom worked in the business, would have cash from the sale of his shares. At the same time, Mary would be able to continue to run the business as the sole shareholder, without having a grieving daughter-in-law as a partner. These good intentions got lost in some incompetent drafting, however, as follows:

> On Marvin's death, Marvin's estate shall sell and Mary shall purchase his shares, the purchase price for which shall equal the amount of any proceeds received by Mary under any insurance policies she may own on Marvin's life.

This agreement was drafted at a time when Marvin first became a shareholder and when his shares were of minimal value. Mary acquired a $750,000 term insurance policy on his life which, had he died in the next year or two, would have produced a most generous purchase price for his shares.

However, when this agreement was first reviewed, Marvin's shares had grown to a value of more than $3 million but the insurance remained at $750,000. Had Marvin died, and had Mary insisted upon following the terms of the agreement, as was her right, the result would have been a disastrous commercial deal for Marvin's estate. (Don't be too hard on Mary here, though, since the agreement did not require her to have any insurance at all.)

In addition to the lack of sufficient insurance, some nasty income tax issues also reared their ugly heads, which only multiplied the potential problems for Marvin's estate:

The CRA does not necessarily accept the purchase price agreed to in a shareholders agreement between family members. The Department's position is supported to a large extent by the *Income Tax Act*, which states that property passing between non-arm's length parties, such as parent and child, is deemed to have been sold at fair market value. In other words, even if Marvin's shares had been sold to Mary for $750,000, his estate could have been considered for tax purposes to have sold them for $3 million. This would have left the estate liable for Canadian taxes of $1 million (at then current rates), representing a 133.3% income tax rate on a $750,000 sale!

To make matters worse, Marvin was a U.S. citizen, even though he was a permanent resident of Canada. U.S. tax experts estimated that, on his death, estate tax of another C$1 million would have been payable.

From Mary's perspective, the ACB of the shares she purchased from Marvin would be the actual purchase price of $750,000, not the deemed sale proceeds of $3 million. Therefore, when Mary died or sold her shares to a third party, an additional unnecessary layer of tax would have been paid.

Luckily for Marvin, he was, and remains, very much alive. Most readers will by now have come up with the obvious solutions to his problem:

- Marvin was grossly underinsured, a matter which the insurance agent was more than happy to rectify without delay. A combination of term and permanent insurance was acquired, some personal and some relating to the shareholders agreement, all of which put Marvin's beneficiaries in a much more secure position.

- The shareholders agreement was subsequently amended to provide that, on Marvin's death, his shares would be sold to Mary for fair market value. This was much more businesslike than having an artificial price which related only to the amount of insurance Mary owned on his life. The purchase price under the agreement should determine how much insurance is needed, not the other way around.

This case is an ideal example of how an agent's willingness to obtain and review an agreement led directly to a large insurance sale. The key is that the agent did not know all the answers, but was wise enough to see that there were issues that needed to be reviewed and to find others who could help solve the problems.

Case Study Number 2

Share valuation always presents unique problems in the drafting of shareholders agreements. In theory, as discussed in case study number 1, shares should be bought and sold for their fair market value on a shareholder's death. In the case of a private corporation, however, it can be difficult to arrive at a determination of fair market value that is acceptable to all parties. A shareholders agreement will sometimes require the shareholders to stipulate a value each year; others will have a formula, such as a multiple of earnings, which can be used at any point in time to determine fair market value.

In the following situation, the lawyer tried (and failed miserably) to provide a method for the corporation's accountant to determine an appropriate purchase price after a shareholder's death. If this bit of drafting doesn't debunk the presumed omnipotence of the legal wordsmith, nothing will:

> *The purchase price for the shares shall be their book value as determined by the accountant, who shall use good accounting principles and take into account the true value of the Corporation's assets on the date of calculation. Goodwill may be included at the option of the parties.*

Most of you will readily see the following problems with this clause (among many others no doubt):

- Using "book value" in reference to the purchase price of shares is usually inappropriate. Book value generally has nothing to do with fair market value. Of course, given the wording in the balance of the clause, it is hard to say what the role of book value is in the determination of the price.

- It is unlikely that any accountant or valuations expert can say what is meant by "good" (as opposed to "generally accepted") accounting principles or by "true value" (other than as the name for a chain of American hardware stores).

- To suggest that goodwill can be included at the option of the parties is to suggest that the purchaser can voluntarily pay more for the shares than he or she would otherwise have to pay. Not likely.

- The valuation by this undoubtedly confused accountant is to be as of "the date of calculation". Theoretically, this could take place at a time when the shareholder's death has caused a significant decline in business values, much to the detriment of his or her estate. Ideally, the valuation should be as of the date of death. Sufficient insurance can guarantee a proper purchase price to the estate. In addition, key person insurance can be used by the business to help hire and train new management and/or to overcome financial problems caused by the shareholder's death.

From a comic-relief standpoint, the above clause is a favourite. It would be a lot less funny, however, if a shareholder actually died and the agreement had to be relied upon.

Case Study Number 3

In this case there were two individuals, John and Jenny, who each owned 20% of the shares of a corporation, the balance of which was controlled by a large public corporation. The shareholders agreement contained the following two clauses, many pages apart, in two totally different sections of the agreement:

> *On the death of John or Jenny, the estate of the deceased shall sell and the corporation shall purchase all of the shares owned by the deceased at the time of his or her death.*

> *On the death of John or Jenny, the estate of the deceased shall sell and the survivor of John and Jenny shall purchase all of the shares owned by the deceased at the time of his or her death.*

The first clause says the deceased's shares will be sold to the corporation, the second that they will be sold to the surviving shareholder. In other words, the clauses are completely contradictory.

The only explanation for this may be that the lawyers who drafted the agreement were in effect retained by the majority shareholder and that little attention was paid to how the agreement affected the minority shareholders. No matter who retained the lawyers, however, it is hard to understand this degree of carelessness. Despite the significant legal fees charged, it seems the drafting lawyer never read the agreement.

It is not unusual to find situations where a lawyer is retained by a corporation to prepare a shareholders agreement. However, each shareholder is entitled to independent legal advice. Even if John and Jenny had retained one lawyer to act for both of them, this mistake could have been avoided.

Case Study Number 4

Another agreement provided that life insurance would be paid to a particular individual who had an option to purchase the shares of the deceased shareholder. If the beneficiary of the life insurance chose not to exercise this option, she was simply to give the insurance proceeds to the deceased's estate. Therefore, she could either give the insurance proceeds to the estate in exchange for something (the shares), or give these funds to the estate in exchange for nothing. The agreement did not indicate what would happen if she chose instead to take the insurance proceeds, jump on a plane and leave the country.

One possible remedy for this faulty language would be to use a trustee to hold the insurance policy. On the individual's death, the trustee would hold the funds pending the prospective purchaser's decision. This would be a means of ensuring that the purchase transpired the way the deceased intended or, alternatively, that the proceeds were paid to the estate if there was no purchase.

Case Study Number 5

Agreements occasionally provide that the purchase price of a deceased individual's shares is to be determined after the shareholder's death by the company's accountant, whose decision would be binding on all parties. This approach does not consider the position of the accountant who would be dealing, on the one hand, with an estate whose interest would be to obtain as high a price as possible and, on the other hand, with a surviving shareholder who would be after as low a price as possible. What is the accountant to do, particularly if he wants to retain the surviving shareholder as a client?

Case Study Number 6

One agreement read, "Any life insurance proceeds received by the corporation, net of any proceeds paid to the corporation's bank, will be applied towards the purchase price of the deceased's shares". This language suggests that at least some of the corporation's insurance is being used as collateral for bank loans, meaning that only those proceeds remaining after repayment of the bank debt would be available for buy/sell purposes. This in turn suggests that the client is attempting to use one policy (or set of policies) for two distinct purposes, buy/sell funding and collateral. These are separate needs requiring, wherever possible, separate policies.

Case Study Number 7

Another agreement read, "For the purposes of this agreement, corporation shall maintain life insurance policies payable to the shareholders". The use of the word "maintain" suggests that the corporation is to own the policies and pay the premiums. The clear wording of the clause indicates that the shareholders are to be beneficiaries of the policies. Knowledgeable insurance advisors will realize that, where a corporation owns a policy under which a shareholder is beneficiary, it gives rise to a taxable shareholder benefit equal to the premium. In a worst case scenario, the proceeds themselves might be taxable.

As indicated in many of the buy/sell scenarios described in Chapter 6, even where a corporation is a beneficiary of the policy, it is a straightforward matter to have the insurance proceeds distributed to shareholders on a tax-free basis. It is unnecessary to take the income tax risk of having individual shareholders named as beneficiaries of a corporate-owned policy.

The Key Areas of Interest to the Insurance Professional

A shareholders agreement can cover a wide range of issues governing the legal relationship among the shareholders and the corporation. In most cases, it is not necessary for the insurance professional to undertake a thorough review of the entire agreement. Instead, a focus on the following key areas is usually sufficient:

- the disposition of shares held by a deceased shareholder;

- ownership of insurance policies;

- share valuation; and

- the disposition of shares held by a disabled shareholder.

Each of the above will be dealt with below.

(a) Transactions on the Death of a Shareholder

Virtually all shareholders agreements will have provisions that deal with the disposition of shares held by a deceased shareholder (or by his or her holding company). Usually, the deceased's shares will either be purchased by the surviving shareholders or redeemed by the corporation. Occasionally, put and call options will be provided where the deceased's personal representative or holding company has an option to sell, and the survivors and/or the corporation have the option to purchase. It is also this area of the agreement that should describe exactly how the life insurance proceeds (if any) on the life of the deceased will be used. In other words, it should explain how the shares get to the purchasing party and how the life insurance proceeds get to the selling party. The following are some crucial points to look for:

- Determine whether or not the buyout of a deceased's shares is mandatory or optional. Most of the time, it is preferable that certainty prevail and that a sale of a deceased's shares is mandatory. Put and call options generally have the same effect, as each party has the right to trigger the agreement.

- Pay attention to the method of purchase. Are the shares to be acquired by surviving shareholders or by the corporation itself?

Discuss with your client's advisors whether the method provided in the agreement is appropriate from an income tax perspective. An agreement that is several years old may have been rendered obsolete by changes to tax legislation.

- Where corporate-owned insurance is involved, the parties will normally assume that the proceeds will be flowed out either to the estate or to the surviving shareholders in the form of a tax-free capital dividend. Too many agreements neglect to take note of this, however. In most cases, the corporation should be required to declare a capital dividend at the time the insurance proceeds are flowed out to the relevant party(ies). This is particularly important in the case of a share redemption where a dividend is paid only to the estate of the deceased. If the corporation is not required to declare this as a capital dividend, the directors of the corporation might simply choose to declare an ordinary taxable dividend, in which case the deceased's estate would lose all of the tax benefits normally associated with life insurance funding. Not only that, the survivors would benefit from the payment of capital dividends in the future, contrary to the original intention of the parties.

(b) Ownership of Life Insurance Policies

Shareholders agreements often fail to provide all of the necessary terms and conditions relating to the ownership and use of life insurance policies that are to be used for funding the agreement. This section will review some of the key insurance-related points which shareholders agreements should cover.

(i) Ownership and Beneficiary Designation

The agreement should clearly identify both the owner and beneficiary of each policy to be used as buy/sell funding. The lawyer and the insurance professional should also ensure that the policies themselves reflect what is contemplated under the agreement. There have been many situations where, for example, the shareholders agreement provided for the corporation to be the owner and beneficiary of the policies, but where the actual owners, as reflected on the policies themselves and on the records of the insurance company, were the shareholders.

It is also helpful to attach a schedule to the agreement which specifically identifies each of the policies being used as buy/sell funding. This schedule would indicate the owner, beneficiary and life-insured, as well as identifying the insurance company and policy numbers. This schedule can be amended as required to reflect changes, such as the addition of new policies or the deletion of old ones. By clearly identifying policies being used for buy/sell funding, there will be no confusion with policies acquired for other purposes (such as key person coverage or collateral security). The use of a schedule, rather than providing policy details in the body of the agreement, means that changes to insurance coverage can be reflected without the necessity of amending the agreement.

The agreement should also give the corporation and/or the shareholders the right to purchase additional insurance in the future, as required.

(ii) Payment of Premiums

The agreement should also make it clear who is responsible for the payment of premiums. In most cases, of course, this will be the policy owner. Affected parties who are not policy owners should, however, have the right at any time to confirm that the policies are in good standing and that premium payments are up-to-date. For example, if the corporation is responsible for premium payments, any shareholder should have the right to inspect relevant books and records to ensure that all premiums have been paid. If not, the shareholder should have the right to pay outstanding premiums and to be reimbursed by the corporation.

(iii) Consent to Medical Examinations

Any shareholders whose lives are to be insured should be obliged, under the shareholders agreement, to the applications for insurance to be made on their lives, and to undergo any necessary medical examinations. This should include insurance being obtained at the time the shareholders agreement is being prepared, as well as any insurance that may be obtained at a future date.

(iv) Future Changes in Ownership of Life Insurance Policies

The shareholders agreement should contemplate the possibility of a change in ownership of the life insurance policies acquired for buy/sell purposes. This might be required where, for example, a shareholder sells his or her shares prior to death and is no longer a party to the agreement. It might also be required where individual shareholders own insurance on each other's lives, and one of them dies owning an insurance policy on the life of the other. In these circumstances, the surviving shareholder may wish to acquire the policy for his or her own estate planning reasons.

Under the above circumstances, the shareholders agreement might provide the shareholder in question with the right to purchase the policy on his or her life. In most cases, the purchase price could be stipulated in the agreement as being the greater of one dollar and the policy's CSV.

On the other hand, there may be situations where it is not appropriate to give an individual the right to purchase such a policy. For example, if an individual's shares are being bought out over time, the corporation and/or the other shareholders may wish to retain ownership of the policy. Then, if the individual dies before the shares have been fully paid for, funds will be available to pay the balance of the purchase price.

The parties to an agreement should consider these various options at the time the shareholders agreement is negotiated and make an informed decision as to which is preferable.

Where insurance is held at the shareholder level to fund a "criss-cross" buy/sell, there should be terms dealing with insurance policies held by the estate of a deceased shareholder. For example, after shareholder A's death, A's estate would continue to hold insurance on shareholder B's life. The agreement should give shareholder B the ability to purchase the insurance on his or her life from shareholder A's estate, normally upon the same terms described above.

(v) Stop-Loss Rules

Stop-loss rules, introduced by the Department of Finance in April 1995, have significantly affected tax planning strategies regarding corporate-owned life insurance. These rules include grandfathering provisions that allow certain arrangements in existence on April 26, 1995 (the "Effective Date") to avoid the stop-loss rules.

As discussed in greater detail in Chapter 6, one of these grandfathering rules applies where a corporation was beneficiary of a life insurance policy on the Effective Date, and a main purpose of the policy was to redeem shares owned by the shareholder on that date. In many cases, grandfathering will continue to be available even where one or more shareholders agreements or amended agreements are executed after the Effective Date. Where grandfathering is available because of life insurance in place on the Effective Date, such agreements should specifically identify the policies as being eligible for grandfathering. While not binding on the CRA, this will at least be a form of notice to the shareholders and their advisors that tax planning opportunities may exist regarding the purchase and sale of shares on the shareholder's death.

(vi) Restrictions on Ownership Rights

In most cases, where an individual or corporation has acquired a life insurance policy for buy/sell funding, the policy should not be used for other purposes. For example, it is common for a corporation to assign a policy on the life of a shareholder as collateral security for bank financing, and to take advantage of rules that allow a full or partial deduction for insurance premiums in those circumstances. These income tax advantages have tempted some corporations to use as collateral security policies that were originally acquired for buy/sell purposes. This creates a risk that, when the shareholder dies, the proceeds will not be available for the purchase and sale of shares, but will instead be subject to the rights of the lending institution. Where possible, the corporation should acquire a separate life insurance policy for collateral purposes.

The shareholders agreement should usually contain terms restricting the ownership rights of parties who hold the insurance policies being used for buy/sell purposes. These policy owners should be prohibited from assigning policies as collateral security, and from absolutely assigning the policies to third parties, without the consent of all parties.

(vii) Flow of Funds/Declaration of Capital Dividend

The agreement should describe the flow of funds that follows the payment of the life insurance proceeds. Where the beneficiary of the insurance proceeds is a surviving shareholder, the agreement will simply require the shareholder to pay this amount to the estate of the deceased shareholder.

Where the beneficiary is the corporation itself, the proceeds may be paid to the estate in the course of a redemption of shares held by the deceased. Alternatively, the surviving shareholder may purchase the deceased's shares using a promissory note. After the purchase, the corporation would distribute the proceeds to the survivor in the form of a dividend which, in turn, would be paid to the estate as a payment against the note. In either case, assuming it is the intention of the parties, the agreement should stipulate that any such dividends be designated as capital dividends to the extent that a capital dividend account credit is created by the receipt of the life insurance proceeds by the corporation.

(viii) Valuation of Life Insurance Policies

Shareholders agreements will typically provide a method for determining the purchase price for shares bought and sold thereunder. The CSV of corporate-owned life insurance may be included as a corporate asset for these purposes. The proceeds themselves, however, if used for buy/sell purposes, should not be included in the value of the corporation. This is generally consistent with the treatment of the proceeds under the Act. An express statement to this effect should be included in the agreement.

(ix) Excess or Deficiency of Life Insurance Proceeds

The agreement should contemplate the possibility that, on a share-holder's death, there will be either an excess or a deficiency of insurance proceeds. In the former case, the agreement should stipulate which party (most often the policy owner) is entitled to the excess proceeds. In the latter case, the agreement should provide that the insurance proceeds will represent the down payment for the shares, payable within a stipulated period after death. The balance of the purchase price would be represented by a promissory note payable on whatever terms may be negotiated in the shareholders agreement.

(c) Share Valuation

Without question, the most difficult area to deal with in most shareholder agreements or corporate reorganizations is that of share valuation. As readers will know, there is usually no market *per se* for private corporations, and the determination of value is an inexact science at best, notwithstanding the proliferation of valuation experts whose services are available. Although some knowledge in the area of valuation is helpful to the agent, normally the client's accountant or an experienced valuator should be called upon when-ever appraisals are required.

Nonetheless, although neither a lawyer nor an insurance agent should be providing appraisals, each should still pay attention to those sections of a shareholders agreement that deal with share valuations. Some of the fol-lowing points may be helpful in this review:

- In most cases, when dealing with the death or disability of a share-holder, the purchase price for that person's shares should be their fair market value. This is the price to which a willing buyer and a willing seller, dealing in an unrestricted market, would agree. It is also the amount typically of greatest importance for income tax purposes. As evidenced by the above case studies, some agreements contemplate a purchase of shares for their book value, which usually bears no resemblance to fair market value (book value would normally use the historical cost of assets rather than their present fair market value, and would also ignore goodwill in most cases).

- A method of valuation should be stipulated. Some agreements con-tain a valuation formula, while others call for an annual valuation by the shareholders and/or the accountants of the corporation. This latter method is acceptable as long as the parties fulfil their obliga-tions to do the valuation annually, which they rarely do. Any agree-ment providing for an annual valuation should provide a means of updating the value if, for example, the existing valuation is more than two years old. The insurance agent can play an important role in these circumstances by reminding the parties of the need to re-value the company on a regular basis. This will also help to keep everyone abreast of the adequacy of the life insurance funding.

- Too often, the convenience of using life insurance as the buy/sell funding vehicle encourages drafters of the agreement to stipulate the purchase price for a deceased's shares as the value of any life insurance held on his life pursuant to the agreement. The basic rule should be that the purchase price determines the amount of the insurance, not the other way around. Otherwise, potential disasters may result. What happens, for example, if the insurance lapses or if the fair market value of the shares becomes much higher than the insurance coverage? In this regard, see case study number 1 above.

(d) Disability and Critical Illness

While most shareholders agreements will contemplate a shareholder's death, and deal, adequately or otherwise, with the disposition of the deceased's shares, the treatment of a disabled shareholder is much more of a hit-and-miss proposition. In many cases, a shareholders agreement will be silent on the issue of disability. This is unfortunate, given the actuarial evidence that an individual is much more likely to become disabled than die prior to age 65.

Please see Chapter 12 for a discussion of disability buyouts and the potential role of critical illness in shareholders agreements.

The above is just a sample of what might be uncovered upon an examination of a client's shareholder agreement. The ability to review an agreement, and discover obvious or subtle flaws, will invariably present sales opportunities. Perhaps most important, knowledgeable agents will earn the respect of other professionals and make themselves referable, a critical advantage in the business insurance and estate planning market.

Other Provisions of Interest

A shareholders agreement can be designed to deal with a wide range of other issues that can arise in a business setting. Each agreement is different and should be geared to the individual needs of the client. The following issues may be dealt with:

- distribution of profits;
- responsibilities of directors and officers;

- day-to-day corporate management;

- shareholders' obligations regarding the capitalization of the corporation; and

- non-competition (to limit a shareholder's ability to leave the corporation and establish a competing business).

Following are situations involving the purchase and sale of shares which could be covered in a shareholders agreement.

(a) First Right of Refusal/Third-Party Offers

If one of the shareholders wished to sell his or her shares to an outside party, the others should have a right of first refusal. In other words, they should be given the opportunity to purchase the shares on the same terms and conditions as those being offered by the third party. The agreement can also provide that, if the other shareholders do not wish to purchase the shares owned by the selling shareholder, they can require the third party to purchase their shares.

It is likely that the Articles of Incorporation of the various corporations have provisions limiting one shareholder's ability to transfer shares to another party by their requiring the approval of either the corporation's board of directors or its shareholders. However, the Articles will not likely contain any provisions that would allow the other shareholders to require the third party to purchase their shares; this kind of protection can typically be obtained only through a shareholders agreement.

(b) Shotgun Buy/Sell

A "shotgun" provision is a commonly found mechanism designed to be the ultimate means of resolving shareholder disputes. In a corporation with two equal shareholders, Phil and Sally, a shotgun purchase and sale would work in the following manner:

- Phil would issue a notice to Sally (or vice versa) under which the shotgun clause would be invoked.

- The notice would stipulate a purchase price for the shares. Sally would have the choice of purchasing Phil's shares, or selling her shares, for that price.

- Sally would be given a period of time, as stipulated in the agreement, to make a decision as to whether she was going to buy or sell. In the end, either Phil or Sally would be left as the sole shareholder.

A shotgun is a weapon to be used only when the shareholders have exhausted all other efforts to resolve their differences. The philosophy behind it is that it will force a termination of the relationship at a fair price. The offering shareholder (Phil in the above example) is motivated to offer a price that is neither too low nor too high. If the price is too low, Sally would presumably decide to purchase Phil's shares at that low price; if it is too high, she would require him to buy. Thus, Phil is forced to find a middle ground and price the offer reasonably.

The shotgun mechanism is an efficient method of terminating a relationship between shareholders. It tends to be unfair in certain circumstances, however, particularly where one shareholder is financially stronger than the other. Also, some individuals are concerned about constantly having the threat of the "trigger being pulled". It is not a strategy that should be entered into without proper consideration.

(c) Termination of Employment or Retirement

A shareholders agreement might also contemplate the departure of a shareholder because of termination of employment due to retirement or resignation. In those circumstances, the agreement would give the other shareholders the option to purchase the shares of the departing shareholder.

Without an agreement, a shareholder who was no longer employed in the corporation could refuse to sell his or her shares, and would thus retain all the rights of a shareholder. Assuming the value of the corporation continued to grow, these shares would also increase in value, even though the departed shareholder would no longer be contributing to the business.

(d) Bankruptcy

In the event one of the shareholders was insolvent or became bankrupt, the others could be given the right to purchase his or her shares. Otherwise, there would be a risk that the shares might be taken over by a trustee in bankruptcy. In some agreements, the buyout price on bankruptcy or insolvency is a percentage of the price that would apply on death or disability, for example.

(e) Matrimonial Dispute

In many circumstances, shares that an individual owns may become the subject of matrimonial litigation. In a worst case scenario, the shares could be transferred to the shareholder's spouse in satisfaction of property rights under provincial family law. Some agreements attempt to deal with this by providing the other shareholders with the option of purchasing shares that become subject to this type of dispute. This is surely preferable to having the shares acquired by a fellow shareholder's aggrieved spouse.

2. Reviewing Wills

The will is, in many cases, the focal point of the client's estate planning. As is the case with shareholders agreements, insurance professionals wishing to provide full service to their clients would be well-advised to obtain and review their clients' existing wills. Some of the benefits of doing so are suggested below, a couple of which are similar to those that apply to shareholders agreements:

- An important part of the agent's job is to help the client articulate his or her estate objectives. By reviewing the client's will, the agent can determine whether these objectives are being adequately met.

- Clients will often tell their financial advisors what they think is in their will. A subsequent review of the document will often disclose, however, that it does not say what the client thought it said. This usually motivates the client to take steps to update the will. In that case, the advisor has performed a valuable service to a client who might otherwise have died in blissful ignorance of the unintended consequences of his or her death.

- An insurance professional who is able to analyze a will and other legal documents is more credible, and therefore more referable, than one who focuses solely on selling insurance.

- Sales opportunities will inevitably result from a review of a will. These usually relate, of course, to the need for estate liquidity (see discussion in Chapter 3).

Following is a checklist of things to look for when reviewing a client's will.

Executor

In many cases, the choice of executor (sometimes known as "estate trustee") is as important a decision as any in the will planning process. Most wills begin by stating that any previous will of the individual is revoked, then go on to name the executor or executors. This is typically the first point of substance that you will encounter.

In many cases, an individual will name the surviving spouse as executor. This is particularly appropriate where the spouse is also the sole or major beneficiary of the estate. In larger or more complicated estates, one or two other persons might be named as co-executor(s).

It is critical that an alternate executor be appointed in the event that the first-named executor is unable or unwilling to act, or predeceases the person making the will. Adult children, other relatives or a trusted family friend are usual candidates. If the client's will does not contain an alternate executor, this omission should be pointed out.

Occasionally, the person making the will, known as the "testator", will name a trust company as primary or alternate executor. No doubt there are many fine trust companies, but this is sometimes considered a last resort, to be exercised when the testator knows of no individual who could act in this capacity. Trust companies are expensive, and trust officers often lack the intimate knowledge of, and sensitivity towards, the testator's family attributes which are often critical in the administration of an estate. Nonetheless, trust companies have the advantage of permanence (subject to corporate take-overs) and have all the required expertise. They can play a uniquely beneficial role in the right circumstances.

Trusted advisors, such as a lawyer or accountant, are sometimes named as executor. This may be advantageous in particularly complex estates, especially involving business owners. A professional advisor may also be a more desirable (though no less expensive) option than a trust company if there are no family members or friends whom the testator wishes to name.

The ideal choice in most cases, however, is a family member or friend who has common sense and can be counted on to "do the right thing". Remember that an accountant, lawyer or trust company can always be retained by the executor if and when their services are required. It is not necessary to name them as executor in order to have access to their particular areas of expertise. A sensible executor will know when to retain the services of an expert.

Occasionally, clients will ask their insurance agent or financial advisor to act as executor. This should be approached with caution. As an executor, an individual has a fiduciary obligation to act in the best interests of the beneficiaries of the estate; an insurance agent has a personal interest in the possible sale of financial products to the estate. Even if the individual carried out both duties with the utmost integrity, the appearance of a conflict of interest would always be there. The best solution may be for the client to appoint someone else as executor, and then request in the will that the executor consult a specific advisor regarding the estate's financial affairs.

Distribution of the Estate

This, of course, is the most important part of the will. After directing the executor to deal with the estate's taxes, debts and other liabilities, this part of the will tells you who gets what property, and how and when they get it. It will also be the area of the will in which the greatest number of sales opportunities will lurk. Here are a few things to look for:

(a) Gifts to Spouses and Spouse Trusts

A married client, or one with a common-law or same sex partner, will most often leave his or her estate to the surviving spouse or partner, which is appropriate in most cases. There may be situations, however, where it is preferable to leave the property to a trust for the spouse. A typical trust would allow the spouse to receive a lifetime income and the potential to encroach on capital at the discretion of the trustees. The main advantage of a trust is that the testator can control what happens to the trust property on the spouse's death. For example, with no trust in place, the spouse could remarry and eventually gift the property to the new spouse. Using a trust, the testator could ensure that his or her children inherited the property on the spouse's death. Whether the client's will provides for an outright gift to the spouse, or to a spouse trust, there will be the opportunity to explore the advantages of joint second-to-die insurance to pay income tax on the second death.

(b) Gifts to Persons Other than the Spouse

Where property is gifted to someone other than the spouse, any capital gains tax owing on that property cannot, in most cases, be deferred. (One common exception to this is the gift of a farm property to a child.) This may prompt a discussion of insurance on the testator's life alone as a means of paying tax liability. Clients are often unaware of these income tax issues and will be open to helpful suggestions from their advisors. For example, the gift of an investment portfolio to children may trigger tax liability. A better strategy might be to gift the portfolio to the spouse or a spouse trust, taking advantage of the available tax deferral, and to make a simple cash gift to the children.

(c) Gifts to Charity

Individuals will often make a gift to charity in their wills. These clients may be interested in the many ways that life insurance can be used as a charitable gift (see Chapter 9).

(d) Estate Equalization Opportunities

The will of a business owner will often disclose whether or not an adequate amount of estate planning has been done. If the shares of the business are to pass to family members who are not active in the business, it is likely that the client is in need of estate planning advice. Perhaps the shares should be left to a spouse trust if the spouse is not able to manage the business. The trustees could be active family members, or others who are familiar with the business. You might also recommend that, upon the spouse's death, only children who are active in the business should inherit shares. This opens up the possibility of using insurance for estate equalization purposes. Family business succession planning is discussed in greater detail in Chapter 5.

(e) Family Law Issues

There are situations, particularly in the case of second marriages, where the bulk of the testator's estate is left to someone other than the spouse (children from the first marriage, for example). This may open up the possibility of the will being challenged by the surviving spouse under provincial matrimonial law. Where your review of a client's will reveals this potential problem, the use of life insurance payable to the spouse may be a convenient method of forestalling future estate problems. See Chapter 13 for a discussion of the Ontario *Family Law Act.*

(f) Dependants' Relief

Provincial law also requires that an individual make adequate provision for dependants in his or her estate. This could include children, parents and former or separated spouses to whom the testator owes a financial obligation. Failure to make adequate provision for a dependant could trigger a future court challenge. Insurance payable to the dependant could be a means of providing the necessary level of support.

(g) Gifts to Minor or Disabled Children

Minor children, usually children or grandchildren of the testator, will often be potential beneficiaries under a will. As an example, a will might state that if the testator's child predeceases the testator, the children of the deceased child will inherit the property. Sometimes the testator's grandchildren will inherit some property, even if their parent is still alive. Yet another example is where young children inherit under the wills of their deceased parents.

Read your client's will carefully to determine how and when minor children might inherit property. Some wills contain a standard "boilerplate" clause which states that, if any such children are under the age of majority (usually 18) when the testator dies, the property is to be held in trust until they reach that age. At that time, the property will simply be given to them.

Most clients, if they are asked to consider this issue carefully, will conclude that 18 is too young an age at which to inherit significant amounts of property. The trouble sometimes is that the drafting lawyer does not review this question thoroughly enough with the client.

A better approach is usually to provide formal trust provisions that require the trustees to hold the property for a longer period of time. If the amounts in question are significant, age 25 may be an acceptable age at which to inherit the property. Alternatively, distributions can be made at different ages (for example, one-third at each of age 25, 30 and 35). Trusts can be drafted in a way that allows the trustees to make discretionary distributions to a beneficiary at any time, so that the child can enjoy the benefits of the property while still too young to acquire full ownership.

Testamentary trusts (i.e., those established under a will) also have tax planning potential. A testamentary trust has graduated marginal tax rates like individuals, although it is not eligible for the personal tax credit. Income earned in a testamentary trust can often be partially taxed within the trust itself and partially taxed to the beneficiaries. This allows for significant income-splitting potential.

Trusts allow a maximum of flexibility and should always be considered when there are potential minor beneficiaries. Creative planning can take into account the specific circumstances of the client and the client's beneficiaries. If the will you are reviewing takes the simplistic approach of allowing children to inherit their gifts at the age of majority, speak to the client about other planning alternatives.

Many of the same considerations apply if the client has a child who is disabled to the extent that, even as an adult, he or she could not properly handle money. In that case, the parents' wills should provide for a trust to be created, usually on the second death, which will exist for the balance of the child's lifetime. Such trusts are usually completely discretionary in nature, which means that the trustees are not required to make any distributions to the child if, for example, it would interfere with the child's access to government benefits or programs.

The terms of a testamentary insurance trust may also be contained in the client's will. This and other strategies involving trusts are discussed in Chapter 10.

References

Income Tax Act (Canada)

Subsection 69(1) — transfer of property for inadequate consideration

Subsection 70(5.3) — valuation of certain corporate-owned life insurance policies

Subsection 70(6) — transfer of property on death to spouse or spouse trust

Subsection 83(2) — capital dividends

Subsection 89(1) — definition of "capital dividend account"

Subsection 110.6(15) — impact of corporate-owned life insurance on eligibility for capital gains exemption

Subsections 112(3)–(3.32) — stop-loss rules

Section 117 — tax rates for individuals and testamentary trusts

Interpretation Bulletins

IT-66R6 — Capital Dividends

IT-140R3 — Buy/Sell Agreements

IT-305R4 — Testamentary Spouse Trusts

IT-405 — Inadequate Considerations: Acquisitions and Dispositions (Archived by the CRA)

Chapter 8

Accumulation and Leveraging Strategies

1. Wealth Accumulation

T he primary purpose of life insurance is to provide liquidity on death. However, the tax rules also permit the CSV of exempt life insurance policies to grow on a tax-deferred basis. While the tax-sheltered nature of insurance products can be attractive, changes in the tax and interest rate environment over the past fifteen years, as well as other factors, have made insurance policies relatively less effective as accumulation vehicles in relation to "traditional" investments. Consider the following changes that have taken place over this period:

- Interest rates are significantly lower. In the early 1990s it was not uncommon to see rates in the 10% range, whereas rates of 3% to 4% are more appropriate today. The tax savings on these types of investments within an exempt policy have consequently been reduced.

- Dividend scales in participating whole life policies have decreased. While returns typically remain higher than guaranteed interest rate assumptions in universal life policies, dividend scales will likely continue to decline over time, reflecting the current low interest rate environment.

- On an after-tax basis, the relative performance of a tax shelter will always be better in a high tax rate environment. As readers will know, personal tax rates have fallen. Top marginal rates in Canada generally exceeded 50% in the early 1990s, but are now generally in the 45% to 48% range, with Alberta the lowest at 39%.

- Capital gains inclusion rates, once as high as 75%, have returned to their original level of 50%.

- Dividends paid out of corporate business earnings that do not qualify for the small business deduction are now subject to much lower tax rates.

Investors also have more choice. There are many opportunities to acquire capital gains-based vehicles which are designed for equity growth and have limited ongoing realization of gains. These types of products provide a significant element of tax sheltering, and also tend to have lower management expense ratios ("MER's") than life insurance policies.

Other factors should also be considered:

- Sex, age, insurability and smoking status are all factors that influence rates of return. A policy on the life of a person who is a smoker, or is in an older age group, or who is not insurable at standard rates, will not enjoy the same investment results as a policy on the life of a young non-smoker to which equivalent deposits are made. This is because a greater proportion of the premium must be used for mortality expenses.

- Savings within exempt insurance policies are generally not readily accessible. Policy loans and partial surrenders will often attract income tax consequences. Traditional back-end leveraging arrangements, as described below, are attractive methods of accessing values, but are available only after a number of years of accumulated savings, and are not without their own risks.

- Exempt policies are not effective short-term savings vehicles. Insurers tend to take a significant share of initial premiums for the payment of expenses, such as administrative costs and commissions. In addition, most insurance contracts have charges that make it unattractive to surrender policies for cash within the first ten years or so. Therefore, clients wishing to take advantage of the tax-deferral opportunities within exempt policies should only do so with funds that will not be needed in the short term. Clients should also maximize available contributions to their registered retirement savings plans, and be relatively debt free, before considering the use of life insurance as a savings vehicle.

2. Back-End Leveraging Strategies

The term "back-end leveraging" suggests the use of a policy's CSV as collateral for a loan from a financial institution after a period of years during which funds have accumulated inside the policy.

There are several key reasons for the use of this strategy:

- As mentioned above, funds can accumulate in exempt life insurance policies on a tax-sheltered basis, which allow for correspondingly greater leveraging room in the future. In addition, external loans are tax-free, which can make leveraging more attractive than potentially taxable policy loans and withdrawals. Although the use of life insurance as a tax shelter is less effective in the current tax and interest rate environment, there are still many policies that have been in force for many years and have significant cash values. These are all potential sources for leveraging of this nature.

- The advent of universal life, and the increased (but still limited) flexibility of whole life, have provided the consumer with more choices than ever before, including flexible premium payment options, and a myriad of different investment and death benefit options. This results in a form of self-administered life insurance that can perform more than one role in the client's financial planning.

This chapter will discuss different methods of leveraging, highlighting the advantages as well as some of the risks and drawbacks associated with the various strategies.

Overview of Back-End Leveraging Strategies

Leveraging is an alternative to the more traditional methods of accessing policy values by way of policy withdrawals or loans. The latter methods involve either a direct withdrawal of funds from the policy, or a loan from the insurer on the security of policy values. In either case, if the CSV of the policy exceeds its adjusted cost basis ("ACB") for income tax purposes, a taxable disposition will result (see Chapter 2). On the other hand, a properly structured leveraging arrangement does not involve the payment of income tax.

Leveraging in its simplest form involves the following steps:

- An individual purchases a permanent insurance policy on his or her own life. It can be a universal life policy, which pays a death benefit equal to the policy face amount plus its fund value, or a participating whole life plan with term enhancements.

- The premiums paid are the highest allowable to permit the policy to maintain its tax-exempt status under the Act, or are at least high enough to allow significant accumulation of cash values.

- At some future point, typically many years after the policy is issued, the individual collaterally assigns the policy as security for a loan, or series of loans, from the bank. Banks will generally lend up to 90% of the CSV of a policy whose funds are invested in guaranteed accounts, or up to 50% if the funds are invested in equities. These limits will vary from lender to lender, borrower to borrower, and policy to policy.

- Interest on the loan is not paid out of the policyholder's pocket. Instead, additional loans are advanced to pay the interest and are added to the principal of the loan.

- When the individual dies, a portion of the death benefit is used to repay the loan, including loans to pay interest, and the balance is paid to the beneficiaries named under the policy.

Income Tax Consequences

The following are the income tax consequences of the above arrangement under current income tax rules:

- The policy in question is an exempt policy, in which case there is no income tax on accumulating policy reserves.

- The assignment of the policy as collateral for the bank loan is not a disposition for income tax purposes.

- Loan payments received by the policyholder are tax-free.

- Interest on loans taken to pay interest is deductible if it can be said that the loans are being obtained for the purpose of earning income from a business or property. Many times, leveraging is shown as a means of supplementing the individual's retirement income, in which case there would be no interest deductibility. Unlike front-end leveraging, discussed later in this chapter, interest deductibility is not a necessary feature of back-end leveraging.

- No tax is payable on the receipt of the life insurance proceeds and repayment of the loan.

Given the above rules, the popularity of leveraging is not surprising. As with any financial transaction, however, there are risks that prospective purchasers must consider, as outlined below.

Income Tax and Commercial Risks of Back-End Leveraging

(a) Income Tax Risks

The attractiveness of leveraging from an income tax perspective relies upon the following favourable rules:

- the tax-free accumulation of cash values in exempt policies;

- the tax-free nature of life insurance proceeds; and

- the fact that there is no disposition, and thus no income tax consequences, when a life insurance policy is assigned as collateral for a bank loan.

As regards the first two points, the Department of Finance is, of course, free to change the tax rules at any time, to the detriment of leveraging strategies, though heaven help them if the mandarins decide that insurance proceeds should be taxable. It is likely, however, that any changes of this nature introduced in the future would be accompanied by transitional rules protecting existing arrangements. The Department has considered changes to the exempt test rules from time to time although, at the present time, it is not being accorded high priority.

As regards the final point, legislation could be introduced to treat the collateral assignment of an insurance policy as a disposition for tax purposes, a change which would essentially defeat the purpose of leveraging arrangements. This would, however, be highly discriminatory unless it applied equally to all types of property so as to cause inherent gains to be realized when real estate, shares and other types of assets were assigned as collateral. This kind of fundamental change would cause chaos in the commercial markets where assets of all kinds, valued in the billions, are subject to bank security. It seems unlikely that the Department of Finance would take such a drastic step.

It has also been argued that a leveraging arrangement could fall under the general anti-avoidance rule ("GAAR"). GAAR is essentially a statutory "smell test" that allows the CRA to attack transactions which it considers abusive. The CRA could conceivably use GAAR to characterize payments made by the bank as policy loans (i.e., as partial dispositions of the policy). However, taxpayers should be allowed to rely upon a law which clearly provides that a collateral assignment is not a disposition for income tax purposes. GAAR ought not to apply simply because a taxpayer chooses a non-taxable alternative, rather than a taxable one, when the Act specifically endorses the former.

(b) Commercial Risks

The commercial risks of back-end leveraging are perhaps of greater concern than the income tax risks. Some key commercial risks are as follows:

- Policy illustrations used to promote the back-end leveraging concepts are not guaranteed. If interest rates do not perform as illustrated, the policy's cash surrender value will not attain the levels shown and the expected amount of bank loans may not be available. For safety's sake, conservative interest rate assumptions should be made in these circumstances.

- Illustrations should assume that there will be a spread between the interest rate charged by the bank and the earnings rate within the policy. If the spread is greater than assumed, the debt will grow at a faster than anticipated rate in relation to the policy's CSV. The potential gap between the illustrated savings rate and the loan rate constitutes a significant unknown and could result in the financial institution requiring additional security or calling the loan.

- Most major Canadian banks are becoming familiar with the leveraging concept and will provide "comfort letters" indicating their interest in participating in these arrangements. However, banks will not commit themselves until such time as the loan is actually negotiated, years down the road. In other words, there is no guarantee that the loan will be available as illustrated.

- Even if interest rates perform as anticipated (which is highly unlikely over an extended period of time) if the borrower lives significantly beyond life expectancy, accumulated loans and interest may be greater than anticipated. This might cause the bank to ask for additional security, or perhaps for a repayment of capital and/or interest. As a last resort, the bank will be entitled to require a surrender of the policy in order to enforce its rights. This would be a disastrous result for the policyholder for two reasons: the surrender of the policy would be a disposition for income tax purposes, and he or she would be deprived of the life insurance protection afforded by the policy.

These commercial risks should not be underestimated. In a "worst case" scenario, the policy's investment returns will fall short of expectations, and loans will either be subject to higher than anticipated interest rates or not be available at all.

Corporate Back-End Leveraging

A business owner, like anyone else, can take advantage of the leveraging concept using a personally-owned exempt life insurance policy. However, leveraging can also be used where the owner and beneficiary of the policy is the corporation of which the individual is owner/manager. For example, assuming there is sufficient CSV in a corporate-owned policy, bank loans could be made directly to the shareholder. The corporation would guarantee these loans, using the insurance policy as collateral. This process would continue until the death of the life-insured, at which point the life insurance proceeds would be paid to the corporation (or perhaps jointly to the corporation and the lender). The full amount of the proceeds would be credited to the CDA (net of the ACB of the policy). A capital dividend would then be paid to the estate (with the appropriate release from the bank) and the funds used to repay the bank loan. Excess proceeds would be available for estate purposes.

The involvement of a corporation in this process introduces additional risks and concerns that do not apply in the more basic leveraging arrangements. In the above scenario, it would be open for the CRA to argue that, by guaranteeing a personal bank loan, the corporation was conferring a taxable benefit on the shareholder. It may be prudent, therefore, to have the shareholder pay a commercially reasonable guarantee fee to the corporation in order to avoid this issue.

Many leveraging illustrations will include the payment of an annual guarantee fee in their assumptions. Suggested fees are usually in the range of 0.5% to 1.5% of the outstanding loan, but clients should determine what the prevailing acceptable rates are at the time the loan is negotiated. In some cases, it may be appropriate for the corporation to pay salary or bonus to the shareholder that is equal to the guarantee fee. This would restore the parties to their original position. The involvement of the client's tax advisor is crucial in order to ensure the appropriate result in the circumstances.

Use of the Borrowed Funds

Leveraging is often illustrated as a method that allows an individual to supplement retirement income received from more conventional sources, such as RRSPs and pension plans. In that case, interest on the money borrowed under the arrangement is not tax deductible, as the borrowing is not undertaken for a business or investment purpose. Typically, however, the lack of deductibility is not fatal to a back-end leveraging plan of this nature.

On the other hand, the client may use the borrowed funds for one of the following purposes:

- to acquire stocks, bonds, segregated funds, mutual funds or other marketable securities;

- to finance the purchase of shares held by a retiring shareholder of a private corporation; or

- to fund the payment of capital or income to individuals retiring from professional partnerships.

In the above three cases, interest on the loan would generally be tax deductible.

The Ideal Client

Back-end leveraging has become commonplace in the insurance market. However, these concepts do not work for everyone, and thorough fact-finding is critical in order to identify the best prospects for this type of planning. Here are some guidelines:

- The most important reason for buying a life insurance policy should be the availability of a death benefit to solve the client's estate liquidity needs. The ability to leverage should be seen as an enhance-ment to the life insurance, perhaps giving the client a reason to buy permanent rather than term, or to "maximum fund" rather than "minimum fund" a universal life plan.

- Savings strategies with life insurance work best over the medium and long term. Clients should therefore fund a back-end leveraging plan with money that is not needed in the short term. In this regard, it should go without saying that the younger and healthier the client, and the longer the accumulation period, the better these strategies will work.

- The ideal client for living benefits will also be maximizing his or her RRSP contributions and will not be devoting significant cash flow to servicing debt (particularly where the interest is of the non-deductible variety).

3. Front-End Leveraging Strategies

Fixed-Rate Policy Loans

Many insurance companies are now offering unique policy loan programs in conjunction with their universal life products. Under these programs, where a policy loan is taken by the policyholder, an identical amount is allocated to a special tax-sheltered account within the policy. The plans offer a guaranteed spread between the rate credited on funds in the special investment account, and that charged under the policy loan. The spread is typically 2%, with current loan rates generally at 10%, and credited rates to the investment account at 8%. In the right circumstances, this can provide significant economic benefits to the client.

The key attribute of the fixed-rate policy loan program, and of the collateral loan program described later in this chapter, is the guaranteed 2% hedge between the loan rate and the rate credited to the special investment account within the insurance policy. This alleviates much of the uncertainty that applies to back-end leveraging strategies which, as described above, are subject to non-guaranteed rates that can impair their effectiveness.

This section will review how a fixed-rate policy loan program is typically structured and will also consider the related income tax considerations and risks.

(a) Client Profile

The target client for this program is a business owner or high net worth individual, with a permanent insurance need. The client will also have business or investment income against which interest charges from the program may be deducted. The insurance can be acquired by the individual, by a holding company that the individual controls or by a trust.

(b) Structure of the Fixed-Rate Policy Loan Program

The discussion below describes how a fixed-rate policy loan program is typically structured:

- A universal life policy is issued to the client where the cash accumulation will be added to the face amount on death. As mentioned above, the policyholder could be an individual or holding company.

- In addition to paying the premiums necessary to maintain the life insurance coverage within the policy, the policyholder makes significant additional deposits into the plan. The amount and duration of the deposits will vary, but in general will be designed to provide a funding level at or near the maximum that is allowable in order to maintain the policy's tax exempt status for income tax purposes. The deposits will initially be made into one or more of the investment accounts provided under the universal life plan.

- In accordance with the contractual terms contained in the policy, the policyholder receives a policy loan from the insurance company. He or she may also decide to receive additional loans in the future. Depending on the terms of the policy in question, loans will be made for up to 100% of the policy's CSV. Under the fixed-rate policy loan strategy, the interest rate on the policy loan is a fixed, guaranteed amount. As noted above, most current programs set this loan rate at 10%.

- The proceeds of the policy loan are invested by the policyholder in investments such as stocks, bonds, mutual funds or segregated funds. The policyholder might also invest in a business.

- An amount equal to the principal of the outstanding policy loans will be transferred into a special account of the universal life policy under which a fixed rate of return is guaranteed (typically 2% less than the rate charged on the policy loan). This account is available only where, and to the extent that, a loan under fixed-rate policy loan strategy is being made to the policyholder.

- If the policy loan is still outstanding at the time the policyholder dies, the loan is repaid out of the insurance proceeds.

The interest rates offered by insurance companies may vary. For example, it is possible that the program may guarantee a 2% spread, but not the actual rates currently offered. If rates decline from the fixed-rate policy loan levels, even while maintaining a 2% spread, the program will not work as effectively (for reasons that will be explained below). On the other hand, loans outstanding under this program may be repaid by the policyholder at any time without penalty if, for example, it becomes more advantageous to eliminate the debt or to replace it with conventional institutional loans.

(c) Advantages of the Fixed-Rate Policy Loan Program

A major premise of the fixed-rate policy loan strategy is that a client can be in an improved financial position when the interest payments under the policy loan are tax deductible. For an individual in the 46% tax bracket, a 10% interest expense that is fully deductible results in an after-tax cost of 5.4%. When compared with non-taxable interest earned within an exempt universal life policy at a rate of 8%, the client enjoys a positive spread of 2.6%. The result can be of significant economic benefit to the policyholder.

The net spread in the client's favour will fluctuate in accordance with marginal tax rates and interest rates. The higher the rates, the more effective the program will be.

(d) Taxation of Policy Loans

"Policy loan" is defined in the Act to mean "an amount advanced by an insurer to a policyholder in accordance with the terms and conditions of the life insurance policy". A policy loan is considered to be a disposition of an interest in a life insurance policy and the funds received by the policyholder on account of the loan are considered proceeds of disposition. If the amount of the loan exceeds the policy's ACB, the excess will be included in the policyholder's income. This is a limitation on the fixed-rate policy loan program that does not apply to the collateral loan strategy, discussed below.

The policyholder may deduct the amount of any loan repayments initially included in income. Loan repayments in excess of those deductible under these provisions are added to the policy's ACB.

See Chapter 2 for additional discussion on the taxation of policy loans and the calculation of a policy's ACB.

(e) Interest Deductibility

The success of the fixed-rate policy loan strategy depends upon the ability of the borrower to deduct interest paid annually on the policy loan. It is critical not only that the borrowed funds be used for an eligible purpose, as discussed below, but that the borrower has sufficient income each year against which the interest may be deducted.

The tax effectiveness of the fixed-rate policy loan strategy increases with the borrower's marginal income tax rate. For example a $1,000 interest deduction for an individual in a 46% tax bracket results in an after-tax interest cost of $540 ($1,000 × .46). The same deduction for an individual in a 39% tax bracket results in an after-tax cost of $610 ($1,000 × .39). The benefits of the program cannot be properly addressed without a careful review of the client's income tax situation.

Interest deductibility has been the subject of dispute between taxpayers and the CRA for many years. The 2001 Supreme Court of Canada decisions in *Singleton* and *Ludco*, both of which were decided in the taxpayer's favour, represent a significant step in support of interest deductibility in many circumstances. Interest deductibility in the context of GAAR was an issue in the *Lipson* case, which was heard by the Supreme Court in April 2008. This decision had not been rendered at the time of the publication of this edition.

Interest deductibility was also potentially affected in proposed amendments introduced by the Department of Finance in October 2003. These amendments provide that losses from property or business will not be allowed unless the taxpayer had a "reasonable expectation of profit", as defined in the proposed legislation. These have come to be known as the proposed "REOP" rules and would, if passed, have a significant impact on policy loan strategies and a myriad of other commercial transactions. A long period of public consultation followed the introduction of these proposals, with representations from many groups that were highly critical of the changes. The government subsequently acknowledged that the REOP test might have unintended consequences and indicated that new proposals would be forthcoming. These have yet to appear.

During this period of uncertainty, the CRA has stated that taxpayers may continue to rely on Interpretation Bulletin IT-533, which contains helpful commentary on the department's current views on interest deductibility.

With specific reference to policy loans, the Act requires that the policyholder indicate on Form T2210 the amount of any policy loan interest to be deducted under the Act. On the same form, the insurance company must verify that such amount has not been added to the policy's ACB. (As noted above, interest on policy loans is added to the ACB only when it is non-deductible.) The form must be filed in each taxation year in which the policyholder pays policy loan interest that he or she intends to deduct.

It is critical that clients consult their income tax advisors to ensure that interest expenses are deductible, and that proper reporting is made to the CRA.

(f) Deductibility of NCPI

As discussed in Chapter 4, the Act allows a taxpayer to deduct the lesser of the insurance premium and the policy's NCPI where:

- an interest in the policy is assigned to a restricted financial institution in the course of borrowing from that institution;

- interest payable in respect of the loan is deductible; and

- the assignment of the policy is required as collateral for the borrowing.

While an insurance company is considered to be a restricted financial institution, policy loans are a contractual right under the policy rather than being a separately negotiated commercial loan. As such, they are not subject to repayment terms or to repayment on demand as is the case with other loans. The insurer's rights are also contractual, i.e., they may offset outstanding loans against benefits payable under the policy. These rights are similar, but not identical, to the rights of a financial institution under a collateral assignment.

For these reasons, the NCPI deduction is not available under a fixed-rate policy loan program.

(g) Taxation of Life Insurance Proceeds and Loan Repayment

Life insurance proceeds are, of course, tax-free to the beneficiary. Where there is a policy loan outstanding at the time of death, the insurance company will use whatever portion of the insurance proceeds required to pay off the loan. The balance of the proceeds will be paid to the named beneficiary.

The CRA has stated that, where the beneficiary is a private corporation, its CDA credit will be reduced by the amount of proceeds that are used to repay a policy loan. This reflects what would have occurred had, for example, the loan been repaid immediately prior to death. In the latter case, the policy's ACB would have increased by the amount of the repayment, which would in turn have resulted in a lower CDA credit.

Collateral Loan Programs

(a) Overview of Program and Benefits

A collateral loan program provides high net worth individuals, private corporations and trusts with a means to borrow funds from an insurance company using the cash values of an insurance policy as collateral security. It is similar to the fixed-rate policy loan strategy described above, but does not involve an actual policy loan. The program can be structured in a number of ways but typically has the following common elements:

- The policyholder or borrower (these need not be the same party) is an individual in the top marginal tax bracket or is a holding company or trust with significant investment assets. A need for permanent life insurance exists for personal or business reasons.

- The policyholder acquires a special universal life policy from an insurance company that offers the program. The death benefit under this policy will equal the required insurance protection plus the cash value of the policy at the time of death.

- The policyholder liquidates investment assets or uses available cash to maximize deposits into the universal life policy.

- The policyholder or a related party uses the collateral loan program to borrow funds from the insurer using the universal life policy as security and invests the borrowed funds in a business or a portfolio of securities.

The collateral loan program differs from more traditional insurance leveraging programs in these important respects:

- The funds are borrowed directly from the insurance company issuing the insurance policy rather than through a policy loan feature under the policy, or from a third party financial institution.

- The interest rate on the loan (currently 10% in most cases) is generally guaranteed for 10 years and the loan is repayable without notice or penalty.

- Interest on the loan cannot be capitalized, but is paid in cash or through additional loan advances from the insurance company secured by the policy's cash values.

As with the fixed-rate policy loan, the insurance cash values being used to secure the loan are placed in a special investment account with a guaranteed return equal to the loan interest rate less 2%. This ensures that the interest credited on the funds in the special investment account will track the interest rates charged on the loan, providing a hedge against interest rate fluctuations and other economic advantages.

A collateral loan program provides greater potential advantages than the fixed-rate policy loan program. Loans under the collateral loan program are not considered to be policy loans, and therefore are not subject to tax even where they exceed the policy's ACB. The program therefore allows for a greater level of borrowing, and improved results.

(b) Taxation of the Collateral Loan Program

(i) *While the Policyholder is Alive*

Assuming the policy is exempt for tax purposes, the cash values of the insurance policy will accumulate on a tax-deferred basis as long as they remain in the policy.

If the borrowed funds are invested for the purpose of earning income from a business or property, subject to legislative change or new court decisions, the interest expense should be deductible. Correspondingly, the income earned on the investments acquired through the borrowed funds would be subject to taxation under normal rules.

Further, the policyholder (if also the borrower) may be entitled to a deduction for the lesser of the premium and the NCPI because the policy is being collaterally assigned to the insurance company (see Chapter 4). This is another feature that separates the collateral loan program from fixed-rate policy loans.

If properly structured, as referenced above, the advance of funds by the insurance company should not be treated as a policy loan, and will therefore not constitute a disposition for tax purposes. The collateral loan differs from a policy loan as the advanced funds must be repaid at the end of the term unless the facility is renewed. Further, unlike a policy loan, interest must be paid on advances under these arrangements. If there is a default, the insurance company will use its secured interest in the policy's cash values to enforce repayment.

(ii) *Upon the Death of the Policyholder*

Upon the death of the life insured, proceeds representing the cash surrender value of the policy are withheld by the insurance company pursuant to the collateral assignment to retire the loan. The remaining death benefit (typically equal to the original face amount) is paid to the named beneficiary(ies) under the policy. All proceeds are tax-free.

If a private corporation is the beneficiary, the entire death benefit (including the proceeds used to repay the outstanding debt) less the ACB of the policy is credited to the corporation's CDA. This allows the corporation to pay out tax-free capital dividends to the surviving shareholders.

(c) Risks Associated with the Collateral Loan Program

There are a number of tax and financial risks associated with the collateral loan program as outlined below:

- The success of a collateral loan program is dependent on the ability of the borrower to deduct the interest paid on the secured loan. It is therefore crucial that the borrowed funds be used for an eligible purpose. It is equally important that the borrower have sufficient taxable income to utilize the interest and NCPI deductions. Over time as the loan grows in value, the policyholder may need substantial income to fully deduct the interest expense. The tax effectiveness of the collateral loan program is also dependent on the marginal tax rate (or corporate tax rate) of the borrower. The lower the tax rate, the fewer tax benefits are generated from the interest and NCPI deductions. Court decisions and legislative changes must, of course, be monitored.

- The CRA could challenge the collateral loan program on the basis that the loans being advanced by the insurance company are actually policy loans. As discussed above, this would result in less attractive tax results to the policyholder. However, proper structuring of the program can significantly minimize this risk.

- There are financial risks where, as is usually the case, the loan is for a 10-year term and the insurance company is not obligated to renew the loan at the end of the term. As well, even if the loan is renewed, the interest rate can be adjusted at that time. If loan rates decline from the current levels, even while maintaining a 2% spread on the credited rate to the policy, the program may not work as effectively.

- If the policyholder runs into financial difficulties in the future and cannot service the loan interest, the policy may be fully or partially surrendered to repay the loan. This would trigger a policy disposition and any gains in the policy would be taxable at that time.

- It is possible to structure the collateral loan program so that the corporation is the owner of the insurance policy but the shareholder borrows personally, using the policy as collateral security. It is open for the CRA to assess a shareholder benefit in these circumstances unless a commercially reasonable guarantee fee is paid by the shareholder to the corporation. The same issue exists with back-end corporate leveraging strategies, discussed earlier in this chapter.

- It is possible that the CRA will argue that the interest rate is not reasonable and thereby deny a portion of the interest deduction. The interest rate can generally be justified when it is measured against other lending arrangements such as ten-year residential mortgages. However, clients and their advisors should satisfy themselves that the rate being charged is appropriate given prevailing market conditions.

(d) Other Collateral Loan Arrangements

It is also possible to implement a front end collateral loan arrangement using a loan from a separate financial institution rather than from the insurance company itself. This program may entail less tax risk, but typically involves fluctuating loan interest rates and non-guaranteed rates of return within the insurance policy. This creates greater commercial risk to the client and, unlike the fixed-rate policy loan or collateral loan programs already described, requires the client to provide the lender with other security in addition to the policy.

4. Retirement Compensation Arrangements

Basic Elements

Frequently, corporations have programs to provide income to retired executives over and above that payable out of registered pension plans and similar vehicles. These supplemental retirement programs are often necessary because statutory plans may not allow highly paid executives to maintain a level of income commensurate with that received during their working years. For example, defined benefit pension plans provide for maximum pension levels, and money purchase pension plans and registered retirement savings plans have annual contribution limits.

In many circumstances, however, these supplemental arrangements are unfunded and amount to little more than a promise to pay a certain amount in the future. If the corporation was ultimately unable to live up to these commitments, the executive would essentially be an unsecured creditor with limited prospects of collecting the amounts owing. This problem was well illustrated in the case of senior executives of Confederation Life, whose unfunded pension arrangements were found by the courts to rank behind the claims of policyholders and secured creditors.

Retirement compensation arrangements ("RCAs") are an attempt to address these problems. To paraphrase the definition contained in the Act, an RCA is a plan under which contributions are made by an employer to a custodian (or trustee) in connection with benefits to be received "by any person on, after or in contemplation of any substantial change in the services rendered by the taxpayer, the retirement of the taxpayer or the loss of

... employment of the taxpayer ...". This definition is subject to a number of specific exclusions, including registered pension plans, registered retirement savings plans and salary deferral arrangements ("SDAs"). (See discussion of SDAs below.) Insurance policies are also excluded from the definition of RCA, but are subject to a whole range of special rules which will be explained below.

The following may be seen as some of the key advantages of RCAs to both employees and employers:

- The availability of an RCA allows employers to more easily attract and retain key executives.

- A funded RCA relieves the employer of a substantial liability in the future and will not burden the employer with the same public disclosure issues as unfunded plans.

- An RCA provides greater protection to the employee against his or her creditors and (as noted above) those of the employer. In addition, the RCA affords greater protection against unfriendly takeovers and changes in the Board of Directors and senior management. In these cases, funds held within the RCA, together with the legal commitments that are an intrinsic part of these arrangements, provide a much greater level of security to the employee than an unfunded promise to pay.

- An RCA is not subject to any legal investment restrictions and may be established for one or more individuals.

Income Tax Aspects

(a) Basic Rules

The following are the basic rules for RCAs as provided in the *Income Tax Act*:

- Contributions to an RCA are subject to a refundable tax of 50%; therefore, 50 cents out of every dollar contributed must be paid to the CRA.

- Income earned within an RCA (including capital gains and dividends) is also subject to refundable tax at a rate of 50%.

- Tax is refunded at a rate of one dollar for every two dollars paid in benefits; therefore, if a $20,000 payment was made to a member of the RCA, the RCA would receive a $10,000 tax refund.

Under the Act, employers may deduct all contributions, including refundable tax, for income tax purposes. Amounts received under an RCA are fully taxable to the recipient. Deductibility of RCA contributions is subject to the general limitation contained in section 67 of the Act, which provides that an expense is deductible only to the extent that it was reasonable in the circumstances. In most cases, this section will not be of concern, particularly if proper actuarial work is done to ensure that contributions relate appropriately to the employee's compensation level and years of service.

(b) Distinguishing RCAs from SDAs

In determining whether an RCA is appropriate for a given situation, advisors should have regard to the rules governing SDAs. The SDA rules will generally apply where an employee has a right to receive an amount at a future date, where it is reasonable to consider that tax deferral is one of the main purposes for the establishment of that right, and where the deferred amount is in lieu of salary or other amounts. Where a particular arrangement is an SDA, the employee will be taxed currently on amounts accruing for his or her benefit. Benefits actually received from an SDA will be tax-free except to the extent that they exceed amounts previously taxed under these accrual rules.

In most cases, therefore, an RCA should be funded with amounts outside of the employee's usual compensation. It is for this reason that the receipt of RCA benefits will often be tied to duration of employment, and in this sense is akin to an unregistered pension plan involving no element of salary deferral.

The Impact of Tax Rates on the Market for RCAs

RCAs are essentially tax neutral vehicles for corporations that pay tax at a 50% rate. They become less attractive as tax rates decline to the extent that they are generally of little interest to corporations that pay tax at the low small business rate (approximately 15 to 17%, depending on the province) or that pay no tax due to certain tax exemptions, deductions, or loss carryforwards. However, even corporations whose income exceeds the small business limit pay tax at a rate significantly less than 50%. These rates vary according to province and other factors, but generally do not exceed 33%. Therefore, from the corporation's standpoint, income tax considerations rarely provide the motivation for establishing an RCA.

Lower personal tax rates may also discourage individuals, particularly owner/managers, from establishing an RCA. The top marginal rate on salaries is less than 50% in all provinces. As discussed in Chapter 2, the tax rate on eligible dividends is attractive in most provinces. This is relevant because the source of funds for eligible dividends and potential RCA deposits is the same, i.e., corporate income in excess of the small business limit. Absent other relevant factors, therefore, most owner/managers would be in a better position if they received a salary, bonus, or dividend rather than having their corporation make RCA deposits on their behalf.

RCA Advantages on Becoming Non-Resident

Despite the above drawbacks to RCAs in the owner/manager market, there are certain circumstances where they merit close attention. For example, where the individual expects to retire outside of Canada, there may be significant tax savings relating to the RCA benefits. When RCA benefits are paid to a non-resident of Canada, they will be subject to withholding tax (generally 15% where the individual resides in a country with which Canada has a tax treaty, and 25% in other cases). In many cases, however, the payments are not subject to tax in the country of residence. At the same time, the payments will generate a 50% refund of the tax previously paid by the employer on contributions to, and income earned by, the RCA.

There may also be some benefit in using an RCA if the owner/manager intends to move, on retirement, to a province with a lower tax rate. For example, a shareholder in a province with a top marginal tax rate in the 45% to 48% range might consider an RCA if he or she expected to live in Alberta, with its 39% tax rate, after retirement.

In the above cases, however, the individual would have to ensure that RCA deposits did not constitute salary deferral.

Another possible advantage to owner/managers is the ability to use an RCA for improved corporate financing. This is addressed below under the heading "Leveraging Against Refundable Tax".

The Use of Life Insurance as a Funding Vehicle

As previously noted, there are no restrictions under the *Income Tax Act* on the investments that may be made by an RCA. The tax deferral available within exempt life insurance policies has made them potential investments for RCAs, either alone or in conjunction with other investments. As indicated earlier in this chapter, however, life insurance as an accumulation vehicle is not as attractive as it once was.

Over time, the use of leveraging, shared ownership and other concepts have brought additional levels of creativity to these arrangements.

(a) Use of Back-End Leveraging in an RCA

One approach is a variation of the leveraging concept described previously. In this approach, the RCA purchases an exempt policy on the life of the employee using funds contributed by the employer. Once the necessary amount of cash reserves have accumulated, the RCA funds the payment of retirement benefits by using bank borrowings secured by the CSV of the insurance policy. As with the conventional back-end leveraging arrangement, principal loan payments would be advanced to the RCA for a given period of time, interest on the loan would be capitalized, and the death benefit would be used, at least in part, to repay amounts owed to the bank. Alternatively, the RCA could make interest payments, rather than capitalize the interest, using the tax refund generated on the payment of the retirement benefits. Note that no interest deduction would be available to the RCA in these circumstances, as it could not be said to be borrowing funds for the purpose of earning investment or business income.

One of the issues with this approach is that while the death benefit is received on a tax-free basis by the RCA, any proceeds in excess of the amount required to repay the outstanding loan could only be distributed on a taxable basis.

(b) Combination of Leveraging and Shared Ownership

A second enhancement is to combine leveraging with the shared ownership concept described in Chapter 4. Under this version of shared ownership, the employer would be the owner and beneficiary of the face amount of the life insurance policy and would pay a reasonable portion of the insurance premium on its own account (rather than as a contribution to the RCA). The premiums paid by the employer might, for example, be based upon equivalent term insurance rates being offered in the marketplace. The purpose of this insurance would be to compensate the employer for financial losses occasioned by the employee's death and/or to assist it in hiring and training new management personnel.

Alternatively, the employee could be the owner and beneficiary of the face amount of the policy and could name the beneficiary of his or her choice. In this case, the insurance proceeds would be used for estate liquidity purposes.

In either case, the RCA owns the CSV of the policy and pays the balance of the premiums with funds contributed by the employer. These latter deposits are treated as RCA contributions subject to the taxation rules described previously. Accumulated cash values are used to fund RCA benefits, as described below.

On the employee's retirement, the RCA would commence payment of the agreed-upon benefits. It could finance these payments in a variety of possible ways: through loans from the employer or from a financial institution, by partial surrenders of its interest in the CSV by policy loans. Loans from the employer or a financial institution could be made on the security of the CSV of the insurance policy using the leveraging strategy, with the principal and interest portions being repaid on the employee's death.

At the time of retirement, the employer could also transfer to the retiring employee ownership of the death benefit portion of the insurance contract (on the assumption that it was no longer required by the employer for "key person" purposes).

On the employee's death, if it occurred prior to any transfer of the policy's death benefit portion to the employee, the corporation would receive tax-free insurance proceeds equal to the face amount of the insurance policy. This amount, less the corporation's ACB, would be credited to the corporation's CDA (assuming it was a private corporation). These proceeds would be used for the corporation's purposes as described above. Alternatively, if the death benefit portion were owned by the employee, the proceeds would be paid tax-free to the named beneficiary.

This points out the key advantage of having the face amount of the insurance paid outside the RCA under the shared ownership arrangement. As noted above, if the policy were instead held entirely within the RCA, the proceeds would be received tax-free, but would be subject to tax on distribution to the RCA beneficiary.

The RCA would receive a tax-free death benefit equal to the CSV of the policy at the time of the employee's death. Depending upon the structure of the program, these funds could be used to repay outstanding indebtedness to the employer and/or the bank. In addition, some or all of these proceeds might be reinvested in the RCA for the benefit of other plan members.

(c) Is the Employer's Portion of the Insurance Policy Part of the RCA?

Arguably, premiums paid by the corporation under the shared ownership arrangement would not be part of the RCA and would therefore not be subject to refundable tax, nor be deductible by the corporation. Similarly, insurance proceeds received by the corporation would be outside of the RCA itself and be eligible for capital dividend account credit treatment, as described above. Planners should proceed with caution in this area, however, as the CRA may attempt to argue that the corporation's interest in the life insurance policy is "subject property" of an RCA, within the meaning of the Act, and that the receipt of the death benefit by the corporation is a form of "terminal funding", which is subject to the RCA rules.

There would appear to be a number of strong arguments to counter this position, however:

- The conventional meaning of "funding" suggests specific assets being set aside to provide funds for future needs. In the above circumstances, the necessary assets would be held within the RCA itself; no retirement benefits would be provided through the employer's interest in the insurance policy. Thus, it would not seem appropriate to consider the interest held by the employer as constituting "funding" for these purposes.

- This may be reinforced by the employer's argument that its share of the policy is being acquired for key person purposes. On the employee's death, the proceeds would be used by the corporation to satisfy its own financial needs, not to pay RCA benefits. This argument may be further reinforced if the death benefit portion of the policy is assigned to the employee upon retirement.

- The Act excludes corporate-owned life insurance from the RCA rules if it is part of an arrangement that is otherwise an RCA. Assuming the shared ownership plan can be considered as one single arrangement through which RCA benefits are already being provided by the RCA trust itself, then the acquisition of the death benefit portion of an insurance policy by the employer should be excluded from RCA treatment under this rule.

(d) Life Insurance Deemed to be Part of an RCA

In reviewing the use of corporate-owned life insurance to provide retirement funding for owner/managers, it is crucial to consider rules in the Act which can deem such a policy to be part of an RCA. In circumstances where these deeming rules apply, the RCA rules would be imposed upon the arrangement, including the requirement that refundable tax equal to the amount of life insurance premium be remitted by the corporation. The Act states that these rules apply where "by virtue of a plan or arrangement an employer is obliged to provide retirement benefits ... and acquires an interest in a life insurance policy that may reasonably be considered to be acquired to fund, in whole or in part, those benefits ...".

Private corporations acquire life insurance on their shareholders for a variety of purposes, most of which are related to the availability of a death benefit. Some common reasons for the purchase of corporate-owned life insurance are:

- to provide funds for the purchase of shares held by a deceased shareholder;

- to provide a "key person" benefit to the corporation so that it may overcome short-term financial problems caused by a shareholder's death;

- to provide funds for the payment of bank debt; and

- to provide funds which may be paid as a capital dividend to the estate of the deceased shareholder for estate liquidity purposes.

In the absence of formal documentation, it will generally be difficult for the CRA to establish that there is an obligation on the part of a corporation to provide retirement benefits to its key employees/shareholder(s). Rather, this is usually an option that may be available to the parties at some future point in time, and essentially represents a possible side benefit of a policy whose main purpose is to provide a death benefit. In this regard, it would be helpful to have evidence which documents the reason for the purchase of the life insurance. This could be in the form of correspondence from the insurance agent, details provided on the insurance application itself, or corporate minutes.

Alternative RCA Funding Methods

The Act contains no restrictions regarding the type of investments that may be used to fund an RCA. Therefore, while the unique features of life insurance have made it a popular funding mechanism, there are alternatives which may be of interest in given circumstances, and which may be used either alone or in combination with a life insured plan.

(a) Sinking Fund

Under the sinking fund method, RCA funds would be invested in a portfolio chosen by the trustee. The investments could include any one or more of stocks, bonds, GICs, segregated funds and mutual funds, all of which would be subject to annual taxation in accordance with the RCA rules. In this regard, it is important to note that all RCA income is subject to tax at a 50% rate, including dividends and the full amount of capital gains, which are normally taxed at more favourable rates.

(b) Letters of Credit

In order to minimize cash outlay, some employers have chosen to "fund" their RCAs with letters of credit issued by a bank. The terms of the letter of credit would require the bank to advance funds to the RCA trustee on the happening of certain events, such as the failure of the employer to provide retirement benefits, or its failure to obtain a replacement letter of credit before the expiry date.

For income tax purposes, the value of each letter of credit would appear to be the amount of any fee paid to the bank, plus the value of any required security initially provided by the employer. Refundable tax equal to 50% of this total would be payable. The CRA has stated that security constitutes an RCA contribution only where specific assets are involved. This would suggest that security in the form of a general security agreement, for example, would not be subject to refundable tax.

Letters of credit normally have an expiry date and must therefore be replaced as required. If the employer fails to qualify or apply for a new letter of credit, the trustee will generally be required under the trust agreement to draw upon the existing letter of credit in order to ensure that funds are made available to the RCA.

As noted, the use of a letter of credit can reduce the amount of up-front cash required to fund RCA obligations. On the other hand, it can increase cash flow problems in later years when benefits are being paid. At that time, either the employer must fund benefits out of existing cash flow, or the trustee must draw upon the letter of credit and pay the benefits with borrowed funds.

Leveraging Against Refundable Tax

Under certain leveraged RCA strategies, the refundable tax itself can be used as security for additional RCA financing. Consider the example of a private corporation that has earned $1 million over the amount for which the small business tax rate is available. A typical strategy would see the corporation pay a $1 million bonus to the shareholder in order to reduce its income to the desired level. If the shareholder were in a 46% tax bracket, for example, he or she could lend the after tax bonus ($540,000) back to the corporation as additional financing for the business.

As an alternative to this strategy, an RCA could be established for the shareholder. Rather than paying a bonus, the corporation would deposit one-half of the available funds ($500,000) into the RCA trust, and the other half would be remitted to the CRA as refundable tax. The portion invested in the RCA trust would be used to acquire a universal life policy on the life of the key executive, or to purchase other investments, as determined by the client and his or her financial advisors.

For financing purposes, the refundable tax would be an asset of the RCA and could be used as security for a bank loan to the RCA (a loan equal to 90% of the refundable tax account, or $450,000, would normally be available). When added to the collateral available in the RCA trust itself (say, an additional $450,000), this provides security for a loan of $900,000. This compares very favourably with the amount of $540,000 that would be available as a loan from the shareholder under the traditional bonus strategy described above.

Under this strategy, all of the funds borrowed by the RCA would be loaned to the employer or a related corporation. The interest rate would be marginally higher than that paid by the RCA to the bank in respect of the first loan and, assuming the borrowed funds were used for business purposes, interest paid by the employer would be tax deductible.

As noted, this strategy's main attractiveness is that, in addition to providing retirement benefits to the shareholder, it enables the corporation to receive more favourable financing than would otherwise be available. This additional financing can be used for business expansion or, in many cases, to provide funding for a third party to purchase shares.

It should also be noted that, if this strategy were employed, the assets of the RCA would be significantly encumbered and would be directly tied to the employer's financial well being. This would significantly impair the creditor protection normally available to plan members, thus defeating one of the key advantages of RCAs.

There are also income tax concerns regarding this strategy, as evidenced by certain CRA internal correspondence. In a letter to the Winnipeg Tax Services Office, the Rulings Directorate stated as follows: "Where an employer makes a payment to a third party and the funds are effectively returned to the employer, either as a loan or investment in its shares, it is questionable whether the payment was made in connection with benefits to be received on retirement. If an arrangement is not an RCA, payments made by an employer under the terms of the arrangement can not be deducted under paragraph 20(1)(*r*) of the Act. It is a question of fact whether an arrangement is an RCA or some other form of arrangement". (Document No. 9730067.)

In light of these comments, it appears that there will be income tax risks in situations where the RCA seems primarily intended as a financing vehicle.

The RCA, as evidenced by the documentation prepared by the client's lawyer, must be first and foremost a retirement plan, and have all the necessary attributes established under the Act.

Commentary on the Need for RCAs

RCAs tend to be specialized vehicles that are implemented far less often than would be expected, given their prominence in the marketing materials of many financial institutions and the frequency with which they are discussed in client meetings. The primary reasons for the relative scarcity of RCAs relate to their complexity and to the fact that there are usually income tax costs implicit in the arrangements.

Despite these problems, there are situations where RCAs merit serious consideration, most of which have been addressed above. The following is a summary of situations where RCAs should be considered:

- RCAs can provide creditor-protected "golden handcuffs" to key executives who are not major shareholders in the corporation. In such cases, the tax cost of implementing the plan is outweighed by the need to attract and retain key personnel. In the case of a private corporation, whose key executive and controlling shareholder are often the same person, a formalized arrangement like an RCA is usually unnecessary.

- RCAs can be tax-effective where benefits are to be paid at a time when the individual will be non-resident. Significant tax savings can be achieved in many circumstances.

- Even for an individual who intends to remain in Canada, RCAs may be advantageous if he or she expects to be in a lower tax bracket in retirement. This might occur because the individual expects to have lower income in retirement, or because he or she expects to move to a province, such as Alberta, where tax rates are lower.

5. Corporate Insured Annuity Arrangements

This section will consider how an insured annuity arrangement can be structured within a private corporation.

Structure

The first component of a typical corporate insured annuity arrangement involves the purchase by a corporation of an immediate annuity on the life of a key shareholder. This is generally accomplished with the payment of a lump sum amount to the life insurance company. In order to maximize income, the annuity will generally be paid for the life of the annuitant, with no guarantee period. Occasionally, the annuity will have a short guarantee period.

The second component is the purchase of an insurance policy on the key shareholder's life, using the after-tax portion of the annuity payments to pay premiums. Like the personal version discussed in Chapter 3, insurance policies with little or no cash surrender value, such as Term to 100 plans or "minimum-funded" universal life policies, are most commonly used. If desired, the face amount of the life insurance can equal the capital that was used to purchase the annuity.

These arrangements are often attractive to a corporation holding significant investment assets that are not required by the shareholder for ongoing living expenses. Most often, these assets cannot be distributed without being taxed as salary or dividends. Typically, the shareholder is in an older age bracket (at least in his or her sixties). In these circumstances, an insured annuity arrangement can provide attractive cash flow, affordable life insurance coverage and significant tax planning opportunities.

Ideally, existing corporate funds should be used for the acquisition of the annuity and life insurance policy. Funds are then borrowed to replace the capital and, where desired, can be used to reacquire any liquidated assets. Where borrowed funds are used to establish the arrangement, there is a tax risk that will be discussed below.

The investment return to the corporation must be considered on an after-tax basis, taking into account the tax treatment of the annuity payments, the costs of the insurance premium and any financing costs.

Taxation

(a) While the Shareholder is Alive

While the shareholder is alive, the corporation will receive payments under the annuity contract. Since the annuity is corporate-owned, it does not qualify as a "prescribed annuity". A non-prescribed annuity is not eligible for level taxation treatment afforded to prescribed annuities, as described previously in Chapter 3. Instead, much like a mortgage, the interest component of the payments is very high in the early years of the contract and gradually reduces over time. This, in turn, creates a higher level of taxation in the early years than would be the case with a prescribed annuity. Correspondingly, in the later years, the interest component of a non-prescribed annuity will be less than that under a prescribed annuity.

Where funds are borrowed to replace capital used to purchase the annuity, interest paid on the borrowed funds would normally be deductible. Where the funds are used in the direct purchase of the annuity, however, the amount of interest deduction is limited to the amount of interest earned in the annuity. This may apply even if the borrowed funds are not used directly to purchase the annuity. For example, a corporation could borrow money to pay a dividend to a holding company, which would then use the funds to establish the insured annuity arrangement. Although interest deductibility is generally permitted when the borrowed funds are used to pay a dividend, the CRA could argue that the real intention of the borrowing was to purchase the annuity. If the CRA succeeded in this argument, interest deductibility would be limited to the amount of annuity income.

For this reason, it is generally more attractive for the corporation to use existing capital to purchase the annuity. If the corporation borrows funds to replace this capital, and uses this amount for a business or investment purpose, full interest deductibility should be available.

It is possible for the CRA to challenge full interest deductibility on the basis that the true purpose of the borrowing was to acquire the annuity contract. However, its ability to do so was dealt a significant blow by the Supreme Court of Canada in the 2001 decision in *Singleton*. In that case, the taxpayer was a partner in a law firm who withdrew $300,000 of equity in the law firm to assist in the purchase of a personal residence. He then borrowed an almost identical amount from a bank and invested the funds back into the partnership to replace the funds taken. Mr. Singleton deducted interest paid on the borrowed funds on the grounds that the borrowed money was used to earn income from a business. The CRA denied the deductions on the basis that the true purpose of the borrowed funds was to help purchase a house.

The Court found in favour of the taxpayer, holding that the borrowed money was used directly to refinance the taxpayer's capital account. This was a direct, eligible use of the funds in respect of which interest deductibility under the Act was available. Accordingly, Mr. Singleton was entitled to deduct the interest expense.

The *Singleton* case provides a high degree of support to the deductibility of interest under a corporate insured annuity program where, as is usually the case, the borrowed funds are used directly by the corporation in the purchase of investment assets. New court cases and legislative changes must, of course, be monitored.

In most corporate insured annuities, the corporation must assign the life insurance policy as collateral for the loan. Typically, a deduction will be available for the lesser of the premium and the net cost of pure insurance. This further enhances the tax flow advantages of the strategy. See the discussion regarding the NCPI deduction in Chapter 4.

(b) On the Death of the Shareholder

Immediately before death, the shareholder is deemed to have disposed of his or her shares of the corporation for their fair market value. The value of the investment assets held by the corporation at that time would be used in calculating the value of its shares. However, for these purposes the value of the annuity (the payments from which expire on death) and of an insurance policy without cash surrender value would be nil. Therefore, to the extent that corporate assets have been used to finance the insured annuity arrangement, there would be a reduction in the value of the corporation for income tax purposes. Similarly, if the corporation borrowed funds to replace these corporate assets, the corporation's value for tax purposes is reduced by the amount of any debt owed to the bank. Any combination of these factors may result in significant tax savings to the deceased's estate.

The amount of any insurance proceeds paid to the corporation, net of the ACB of the insurance policy, would be credited to the corporation's CDA. This would allow the payment of capital dividends to the estate of the deceased shareholder (i.e., a tax-free distribution that would be unavailable without the life insurance component of the insured annuity arrangement). Funds received by the estate in this fashion could be used for the payment of bequests, income tax and other estate liabilities.

Insurance proceeds paid under this arrangement must be used to repay bank indebtedness, therefore there will not necessarily be cash available for the payment of a capital dividend. The dividend can be satisfied using other corporate investments, which might have to be liquidated for this purpose. Alternatively, the capital dividend can be satisfied using a promissory note (or notes, in the case of multiple shareholders). Such a note would essentially constitute a shareholder loan that could be repaid from time to time on a tax-free basis.

(c) Risks of Corporate Insured Annuity Arrangements

The following are some tax and commercial risks relating to corporate insured annuity arrangements:

- Although insured annuity arrangements have income tax advantages, they should only be considered where they fit into the client's overall financial and estate plan. In particular, there should be a need for life insurance to solve estate liquidity problems.

- As discussed above, corporate assets may have to be liquidated in order to obtain cash for the purchase of the insured annuity. But clients should consider the income tax consequences of liquidating assets. For example, a sale of marketable securities could create a capital gain in the hands of the corporation. Interest penalties may also be payable if, for example, GICs are cashed in prior to maturity. The impact of liquidating investments on the client's overall investment strategy should also be considered, although, as noted above, the assets can generally be reacquired using the funds borrowed from the bank.

- Returns available under the annuity contract are an important factor. Annuities are less attractive in a low interest rate environment, although some clients will accept lower rates of return for greater guarantees and security. In addition, the rate of return under the annuity will generally be fixed, whereas interest charged on the bank loan will in most cases fluctuate. Cash flow may suffer if borrowing rates increase beyond expectations.

- Insured annuity arrangements are inflexible, particularly where the annuity carries no guarantee period. If the shareholder has a change of heart and wishes to collapse the plan, the annuity will have no commuted value. In addition, assuming the life insurance has little or no cash surrender value, it will lapse if premiums are not paid. In other words, the corporation should not commit anything other than totally discretionary dollars to this type of program. In this regard, cautious investors might prefer to sacrifice a certain amount of income to obtain an annuity with a guarantee period.

- In the past, some insurance companies have relaxed their underwriting requirements on the issuance of life insurance policies where the insured was also purchasing the annuity contract from the same company. This prompted the CRA to state that, if the issuance of a life insurance policy is contingent on the purchase of an annuity contract, it will treat the two contracts as one. This would effectively result in the arrangement being treated as one non-exempt life insurance policy, thus eliminating the advantages of the program. For this reason, it is imperative that the two contracts be underwritten separately on their own merits, preferably with two different insurers.

- The income tax advantages of a corporate-insured annuity arrangement are potentially significant. If the CRA feels that a particular arrangement is abusive, it may attempt to invoke GAAR. A successful challenge under GAAR could result, as noted previously, in the annuity/life insurance combination being treated as a single, non-exempt insurance policy. It could also result in a denial of interest deductibility, the NCPI deduction, or in the CRA arguing successfully that the overall arrangement does in fact contribute to the fair market value of the shares of the corporation.

The tax and financial risks described above need to be carefully assessed by the client's advisors. The more clients are able to show that this strategy has a legitimate business or estate planning purpose, the better equipped they will be to withstand the CRA's scrutiny.

(d) Comment on Joint First-to-Die Arrangements

A corporate insured annuity arrangement can often perform better when both spouses are included in the program. Again, the clients should be at least in their sixties for optimal results. In such a case, the annuity payments would be made until the first death, and the life insurance would be on a joint first-to-die basis. The benefits of a joint first-to-die program may include the following:

- Perhaps the biggest advantage is that amounts owing to the lending institution will be repaid on the first death. This creates the possibility that the loan will be outstanding for a shorter period of time than would otherwise be the case. This, in turn, would reduce exposure to potentially damaging interest rate fluctuations.

- In joint first-to-die cases, there is generally much better cash flow than is available in a single life case. This results from the interplay between the annuity payments and the insurance premiums.

- As previously noted, there is a risk that the CRA will argue that the insured annuity program has some value in calculating the fair market value of the corporation's shares. If this challenge were successful, it could increase capital gains tax liability incurred on the shareholder's death. This risk can be reduced where the program is structured on a joint first-to-die basis. In that case, on the first death, shares of the corporation will presumably pass to the surviving spouse on a rollover basis. If so, the value of the corporation at that time is irrelevant, as the shares pass to the survivor at the deceased spouse's ACB. At the time of the survivor's death, the program will have been concluded and will no longer affect the corporation's value. Obviously, this advantage does not exist where the spouses die simultaneously.

When implemented as part of a well-balanced financial and estate plan, a corporate insured annuity arrangement can represent an attractive alternative for the well-informed client. On the other hand, it can be entirely inappropriate for others. Proper fact-finding and disclosure are necessary in order to ensure a successful implementation of the plan.

References

Income Tax Act **(Canada)**

Section 3.1 — (proposed) REOP rules

Paragraph 6(1)(*i*) and subsection 6(11) — taxation of salary deferral arrangements

Subsection 12.2(1) — accrual taxation of non-exempt life insurance policies

Subsection 15(1) — benefit conferred on shareholder

Paragraphs 20(1)(*c*) and (*d*) — interest deductibility

Paragraph 20(1)(*e*.2) — deduction for premiums on life insurance used as collateral

Section 38 — taxable capital gains and allowable capital losses

Paragraph 53(1)(*e*) — additions to ACB of partnership interest

Paragraph 53(2)(*c*) — subtractions from ACB of partnership interest

Subsection 55(2) — intercorporate dividends treated as capital gain

Subsection 83(2) — capital dividends

Subsection 84(3) — deemed dividend on redemption of shares

Subsection 89(1) — definition of "capital dividend account"

Section 98.1 — residual interest of retired partner in partnership

Section 110.6 — capital gains exemption

Subsection 112(1) — intercorporate dividends

Subsections 148(1) and (2) — taxation on disposition of life insurance policy

Subsection 148(4) — taxation on partial disposition of life insurance policy

Subsection 148(7) — non-arm's length disposition of life insurance policy

Subsection 148(9) — definitions relevant to section 148 including "adjusted cost basis", "cash surrender value", "disposition", "policy loan", "proceeds of the disposition", and "value"

Sections 207.5–207.7 — taxation of RCAs

Subsection 207.6(2) — RCA deeming rule for corporate-owned life insurance

Section 245 — general anti-avoidance rule (GAAR)

Subsection 248(1) — definitions including "retirement compensation arrangement" and "salary deferral arrangement"

Income Tax Regulations

Section 306 — exempt policies

Section 307 — accumulating funds

Section 308 — net cost of pure insurance

Interpretation Bulletins

IT-66R6 — Capital Dividends

IT-87R2 — Policyholders' Income from Life Insurance Policies

IT-242R — Retired Partners

IT-278R2 — Death of a Partner or Retired Partner

IT-309R2 — Premiums on Life Insurance Used as Collateral

IT-355R2 — Interest on Loans to Buy Life Insurance Policies and Annuity Contracts, and Interest on Policy Loans (Archived by the CRA)

IT-430R3 — Life Insurance Proceeds Received by a Corporation or Partnership

IT-533 — Interest Deductibility and Related Issues

Case Law

Canada (Attorney General) v. Confederation Life Insurance Co., (1995) 24 OR (3d), 717 (Gen.Div.)

Singleton v. The Queen, 2001 SCC 61

Ludco v. The Queen, 2001 SCC 62

Chapter 9

Charitable Giving Strategies Using Life Insurance

L ife insurance has, for many years, been an attractive method for individuals to benefit charitable institutions. A lengthy series of income tax changes since 1996 has provided increased incentives for making charitable gifts in general, and have made life insurance policies an even more attractive gifting option for prospective donors.

This chapter will review the most important rules affecting life insurance and charitable giving and will provide a number of specific examples of how life insurance can be an effective tool in the charitable-giving market.

1. Income Tax Overview (Individuals)

(a) Gifts Made During Lifetime

The *Income Tax Act* has traditionally provided income tax incentives for charitable donations. Under the Act, there is a federal tax credit equal to 17% of gifts in a year, up to $200. The credit increases to 29% for total gifts in excess of $200 (subject to the annual limit discussed below). Provincial tax rates are then applied to the federal credit with the result that the total tax credit for charitable gifts is the rough equivalent of the province's top marginal tax rate.

For many years, the maximum charitable tax credit in any given year could not exceed 20% of the donor's net income. The limit was increased to 50% of net income in 1996 and to its current level of 75% in 1997. Excess donations may be carried forward for a period of five years.

(b) Gifts Made in the Year of Death and the Preceding Year

The credit available to a taxpayer for gifts made in the year of death has undergone even more significant changes. These gifts were formerly subject to the same 20% limit as other charitable gifts, but now enjoy a limit equal to 100% of net income in the year of death. In addition, excess donations in the year of death may be carried back, subject to the same 100% limit, to the immediately preceding year. For the purposes of these rules, a gift made by an individual through his or her will is considered to be a gift made in the year of death.

As discussed below, the generous new limits which apply to a deceased taxpayer have potentially significant implications for the use of life insurance as a charitable gift.

2. Charitable Giving Strategies Using Life Insurance (Individuals)

(a) Ownership of Policy by Charity

(i) Donation of New Policy

Perhaps the best-known method of charitable giving with life insurance involves the acquisition by the charity of a new insurance policy on the life of the donor. Typically, the donor will apply for the policy and then immediately assign it to the charity. This avoids the complication of requiring the charity's signing officers to apply for the policy on its behalf. The charity will, of course, name itself as beneficiary.

Premiums paid by the donor will qualify as a charitable donation, and will be eligible for tax credits under the rules described above. In most cases, the donor is able to make premium payments directly to the insurer. Upon receiving confirmation of payment from the insurer, the charity will then issue a tax receipt to the donor.

(ii) Donation of Older Policy

The owner of an insurance policy may decide, for a variety of reasons, that such coverage is no longer required. One option in these circumstances is for the owner to gift the policy to a charity in return for a charitable donation receipt. If the policy is not "paid up", the donor could then make ongoing gifts to the charity to cover future premium payments, or the charity would assume this ongoing obligation. Future premiums paid by the donor would qualify as charitable gifts.

Until recently the CRA took the position that the "value" of the policy for charitable receipting purposes would equal the amount by which the cash surrender value of the policy exceeded any outstanding policy loans. Therefore no charitable tax credit was available where the gifted policy had nominal or no cash surrender value (as would be the case for a T100-type policy).

The CRA's assessing position did not appear to recognize the significant discrepancy that could exist between the cash surrender value of an insurance policy and its "fair market value". In fact, the CRA had already identified for other purposes of the Act that the cash surrender value of a policy was only one factor in determining its fair market value. Other factors might include the state of health of the insured, the policy's conversion features, and its current replacement value.

Given these potentially conflicting valuation principles, the CRA was recently asked to confirm its assessing practices where an in-force policy is gifted to a charity. It was also asked to confirm the calculation of the "proceeds of disposition" to the donor, which in turn would determine if there was a taxable gain from the transfer of a policy to a charity. The questions were posed at a Quebec tax conference (Conference Association de Planification Fiscale et Financièr (APFF)) in October 2007.

In responding to the valuation question, the CRA noted that recently enacted legislation (referred to as the "split receipting rules", discussed in greater detail below) contains provisions stating that the eligible amount of a charitable gift is the amount by which the fair market value of the gifted property exceeds the amount of any advantage in respect of the gift. The CRA confirmed that if a qualified valuator, presumably an independent actuary, determines that the fair market value of the policy exceeds its cash surrender value, that higher amount may be receipted by the charity.

This result should provide additional tax incentives for the gifting of in-force policies. For example, consider the case of a 70-year old male who purchased a $1 million Term to 100 policy when he was 50 years old. This policy currently has no cash surrender value. Under the prior CRA position, the charity would not have been able to provide any charitable gift receipt for the donation of that policy.

However, under their new interpretation, an actuary could be engaged to determine the fair market value of the policy. The actuary would consider the fact that the policy has been in force for 20 years and as a consequence could not be replaced without paying significantly higher premiums. The life insured's health would also be reviewed, as well as special policy terms and provisions which may make this policy more valuable than currently issued policies.

Based on this review, the actuary would determine that the policy had a fair market value equal to a discounted portion of the death benefit. Depending on the circumstances, this value could be in the hundreds of thousands of dollars, making it extremely attractive as a charitable donation. Certainly, the policyholder would be in a significantly better position by gifting the policy to charity rather than surrendering it for no proceeds. Any policyholder who is considering the surrender of a policy should consider this gifting alternative as the value of the tax credit will, in many cases, be higher than the after tax cash surrender value.

The CRA then considered the tax implications to the donor of gifting an insurance policy to a charity. Such a transfer is a disposition for tax purposes, and the difference between the proceeds of disposition and the policy's ACB is taxable to the donor. The CRA indicated that where the transfer of a policy results from a gift, the proceeds of disposition will equal the "value" of the policy at the time of the gift. For these purposes "value" is defined in the Act to equal the cash surrender value of the policy (rather than the fair market value which is used to determine the value of the gift).

As a result, where a policy is gifted to a charity, the donor/transferee will be taxed only to the extent the policy's cash surrender value exceeds the ACB of the policy. This is the case even where the donor has received a charitable receipt reflecting a much higher fair market value for the policy. In the above example, the donor would have no taxable income as the Term to 100 policy has no cash value.

All this is a very welcome development and creates new incentives for the donation of in-force insurance policies. Advisors can play a key role in alerting clients to these advantages and in turn help create significant long term funding support for charitable organizations in Canada.

(iii) Non-Exempt Policies

In some cases, it may be appropriate for the donor and charity to consider the use of a universal life policy, which is non-exempt for income tax purposes. Such a policy is subject to accrual taxation on its annual income, but this is of no concern to charities, as they are not taxable entities. In the ideal situation, a charity would be able to enjoy the usual benefits of life insurance in combination with significant investment returns and cash accessibility, all within one contract.

(iv) Loss of Control on Donation of Policy

One disadvantage of having the insurance owned by the charity is that the donor effectively loses control over the policy. This could be problematic if, for example, the donor decided that he or she wished to use the insurance for estate purposes, or that a different charity should benefit from the insurance proceeds. Since the charity owns the contract, the donor can no longer exercise any ownership rights. The donor may exercise indirect control by refusing to continue premium payments. But this is of little effect if the charity chooses to pay the premiums, or if the policy is already paid up.

There is a method of mitigating the loss of control when a policy is donated to charity. For example, many public foundations will assume ownership of a policy and will agree to direct the proceeds to a charity or charities of the donor's choice. The donor can make changes from time to time simply by providing new instructions to the public foundation. This does not change the irrevocable decision of gifting a policy to charity, but does provide flexibility as to which charity(ies) will benefit from the proceeds.

(b) Ownership of Policy by Individual

(i) Personally Owned Policy with Charity as Beneficiary

It is possible for the donor to retain ownership of the policy and name the charity as beneficiary. The donor can easily change beneficiaries in the future. Proceeds will not form part of the donor's estate for probate purposes. This arrangement can also provide significant estate planning benefits, as described below.

In 2000, the Department of Finance introduced new provisions allowing a charitable gift to be made where a charity was named as beneficiary of an individual's life insurance policy, RRSP, or RRIF. This has introduced a very attractive new element in gifting strategies using these products. The changes are effective for deaths occurring after 1998.

Death benefits paid to charities from life insurance policies, RRSPs, and RRIFs will be treated as having been made in the year of the individual's death. They will therefore benefit from the rules permitting a tax credit for charitable gifts of up to 100% of net income in the year of death and the preceding year. Such gifts will also benefit from these significant advantages:

- Proceeds are paid directly to the charity under a beneficiary designation, thereby avoiding probate. If the donor wishes to name a different charity at a later date, the beneficiary can be changed using a simple change form.

- The proceeds are not subject to the claims of estate creditors or potential litigants, or to unforeseen delays in the administration of the estate.

In order to understand the benefits of these rules, consider the simple example of an individual, Janet, who owns shares of a private corporation that holds marketable securities and other investments. Her shares have a fair market value of $1 million and an ACB of zero. The deemed disposition of the shares on Janet's death would result in a capital gain of $1 million, and a tax liability of $230,000, assuming a 46% marginal tax rate. The tax liability would likely necessitate at least a partial liquidation of the securities after her death and a distribution of the sales proceeds from her corporation to her estate. This might or might not be at a time when market conditions were favourable for selling the securities and could also entail additional income tax consequences.

A traditional strategy for Janet would be to acquire life insurance, either owned personally or by her corporation, in an amount approximating her estimated $230,000 tax liability. If she were charitably inclined, however, she could go one step further and acquire $500,000 of insurance on her life, naming her favourite charity as beneficiary. In this example, assuming Janet had no other taxable income, the $500,000 gift would generate a tax credit to offset the tax owing on the taxable portion of her capital gain (also $500,000). This would have the effect of eliminating her income tax liability in the year of death. (If the amount of the gift had exceeded that which was necessary to eliminate tax in the year of death, the excess could have been carried back against Janet's income in the preceding year.)

Under this strategy, Janet retains ownership of the life insurance policy, and therefore has complete control over its use. It also provides her with the ability to significantly reduce or eliminate income tax in the year of death, and the preceding year, while making a generous charitable gift. On the other hand, because she is the owner of the policy, she will receive no tax credit for premiums paid under the policy during her lifetime.

It is possible to achieve results similar to the above by having Janet's corporation be the owner and beneficiary of the policy. After Janet's death, the corporation can pay the proceeds to Janet's estate as a capital dividend, which would give her estate the funds needed to make the gift. See additional commentary below under the heading "Corporate Policy Used to Fund Estate Gift".

(ii) Funding Gifts to Charity Made Through the Will

It is also possible for an individual to take advantage of the higher donation limits for gifts in the year of death and the preceding year by making charitable gifts through the will. A policy owned by the donor, with his or her estate named as beneficiary, can be used to pay charitable bequests provided for in the will. Prior to the 2000 Budget changes, this was the best way to use life insurance so as to take advantage of the 100% donation limit.

The changes in 2000 all but eliminated the advantages of this strategy. Proceeds paid to the estate are subject to probate fees and to creditors of the estate. In addition, if the donor wishes to change the beneficiary, it necessitates a new will or a codicil. For these reasons, it is recommended that insurance proceeds be paid directly to the charity by way of beneficiary designation, rather than through the estate.

(c) Shared Ownership and Split Beneficiary Arrangements with Individuals and Charities

A shared ownership arrangement (which may also be called "split dollar") usually involves co-ownership of a life insurance policy by two parties. Shared ownership is considered in greater detail in Chapter 4.

Until recently, the CRA assessing practice did not allow for income tax relief where an individual entered into a shared ownership arrangement with a charity. However, this changed in 2002 when the Department of Finance introduced a wide ranging set of proposed technical amendments (the "Amendments") to the Act. Included in the Amendments were several new proposals related to charitable giving. In particular, the new rules will permit a donor to receive a charitable tax credit in certain situations where he or she has retained a benefit or advantage in connection with making the gift.

This section of the book will consider how the Amendments might provide new opportunities for the use of life insurance as a charitable giving tool.

(i) Background

As explained in the Department of Finance commentary accompanying the Amendments (the "Explanatory Notes"), under common law a gift must be a voluntary transfer of property without "any contractual obligation and with no advantage of a material character returned to the transferor". Therefore, where a prospective donor received any benefit or advantage in the course of purportedly making a gift, the presumption was that, in the legal sense, there was no gift at all. This rule was adopted for income tax purposes as well.

Under the *Civil Code of Quebec* (the "Civil Code"), however, the rules are more lenient. For example, the Civil Code would permit an individual to sell a property to a charity, at an amount less than market value, and be treated as having made a gift of the difference.

The Amendments appear to be an attempt to provide a level playing field to prospective donors in all provinces. The Amendments are effective for gifts made after December 20, 2002.

(ii) The Specific Proposals

Pursuant to the Amendments, a donor will be entitled to a charitable tax credit even where he or she (or a non-arm's length party) receives a related benefit, provided the value of the gifted property exceeds the amount of such benefit. A simple example cited in the Explanatory Notes involves a donor who owns real estate with a fair market value of $300,000 and a mortgage of $100,000, and who transfers the property to a charity that agrees to assume the mortgage. The assumption of the mortgage by the charity is an advantage to the donor that, prior to the Amendments, would have disqualified the transfer as a charitable gift for income tax purposes. Under the Amendments, there would be a gift of $200,000, i.e., the difference between the property's value and the amount of the benefit to the donor.

By the same token, the sale of a property to a charity for an amount less than fair market value will now qualify as a gift. For example, a gift of $100,000 would result where property with a fair market value of $400,000 was sold to a charity for $300,000.

There are a number of other rules contained within the Amendments, including the following:

- A gift is presumed to have been made where the advantage to the donor does not exceed 80% of the fair market value of the donated property. Where the advantage exceeds this limit, the donor must satisfy the Minister of National Revenue that there was an intention to make a gift. This would apply, for example, if a mortgage assumed by a charity on gifted real estate property were more than 80% of the property's value.

- The advantage attributable to the donor (or to a non-arm's length party) may be conferred immediately or in the future, and may be received absolutely or contingently. The time for determining the advantage, however and whenever it is to be received, is at the time the gift is made.

(iii) CRA Perspective

The CRA took the unusual and helpful step of publishing its views on the Amendments within days of the introduction of the proposals themselves. (In most circumstances, the CRA will not publish its views until new legislation is formally passed into law.)

The CRA's views, which are not legally binding but are nonetheless instructive, regarding the Amendments, may be summarized as follows:

- There must be a voluntary transfer of property with a clearly ascertainable value.

- The advantage received by the donor or non-arm's length party must be clearly identified and its value ascertainable. If the value of the advantage cannot be clearly determined, no tax receipt can be issued.

- There must be a clear intent to benefit the charity.

(iv) Shared Ownership of Life Insurance in a Charitable Giving Context

As described in Chapter 4, a shared ownership arrangement typically involves the ownership of a life insurance policy by two or more parties. In most cases, pursuant to the terms of a shared ownership agreement, one party (the "Death Benefit Owner") owns and pays premiums for the insurance component of a universal life insurance policy and designates a beneficiary to receive the policy face amount. Another party (the "Cash Value Owner") owns the savings component of the policy and makes deposits to the policy's tax-sheltered investment accounts. A death benefit equal to the CSV is paid to the beneficiary designated by the Cash Value Owner.

It has always been legally possible for a shared ownership arrangement to be established between a donor and a charity. Prior to the Amendments, however, no income tax relief was available because the donor's contractual rights under the shared ownership agreement constituted a benefit of the sort described above. As such, even where the donor assumed the charity's premium obligations under the agreement, this was not considered a gift. For this reason, insured giving strategies have generally been restricted to single ownership situations, with policies being owned, as described earlier in this chapter, by the donor, the donor's corporation, or the charity itself.

With the introduction of the Amendments, however, shared ownership arrangements between donors and charities now merit renewed consideration. Such an arrangement could be structured as follows:

- The donor would apply for a universal life policy on his or her own life (alternatively, an existing policy could be used).

- Immediately after the issuance of the policy, in accordance with a shared ownership agreement between the donor and the charity, the donor would assign the policy's life insurance component to the charity for no consideration. The agreement would stipulate that the donor retained ownership of the CSV.

- The charity would be the Death Benefit Owner and would designate itself as beneficiary of the face amount. The donor/Cash Value Owner would designate the beneficiary of his or her choice to receive the cash value portion of the proceeds.

- Under the shared ownership agreement, the donor would pay the charity's premiums for the insurance component of the policy. The amount of each premium would be determined under the agreement, but would presumably reflect either the cost of insurance under the policy or a representative Term to 100 premium.

- The donor would also make desired deposits to the CSV policy. He or she would benefit from the tax-sheltered growth within the plan and would have access to the funds through policy loans, partial withdrawals, or leveraging.

The income tax consequences would be as follows:

- In accordance with the Amendments, the assignment of the policy's insurance component to the charity would entitle the donor to a tax credit equal to the value of the gift. This of course raises the question as to what might be the value of an interest in a newly issued insurance policy without cash value. The answer is likely "nil".

- After the assignment of the policy's face amount as described above, premiums paid by the donor (not including deposits to the policy's investment accounts) would be treated as a gift and be eligible for a charitable tax credit.

The CRA considered the issue of shared ownership in a charitable giving context at the 2003 annual meeting of the Conference for Advanced Life Underwriting (CALU). Specifically, with a view to the Amendments, the CRA was invited to provide guidelines for determining whether a given arrangement qualified as a gift and how the value of the gift should be calculated.

The Department replied very generally, stating only that a shared ownership arrangement could result in a charitable gift, but that each case would have to be considered on its own merits. The CRA also stated that it had not had an opportunity to review specific shared ownership arrangements between donors and charities and that, having done so, it might be in a better position to comment. The CRA did say, however, that shared ownership arrangements appeared to fall within the spirit of the Amendments. This suggests that the Department would be favourably disposed towards the use of this strategy.

(v) Split-Beneficiary Arrangements with Charities

It is also possible to have both the donor and the charity benefit from one universal life insurance policy under a split-beneficiary arrangement. In this case, the donor would own the policy and designate the charity as beneficiary for the desired amount (typically the face amount). The donor would designate another party (such as his or her spouse) as beneficiary of the cash value portion of the policy. During the donor's lifetime, the donor/policy owner would enjoy the same access to the cash value of the policy as the Cash Value Owner in a shared ownership arrangement, but without the complexity the latter strategy typically entails. As there is only one policy owner in a split-beneficiary arrangement, no agreement is necessary.

The donor would be the sole owner of the policy, and as such would not be entitled to a tax credit for any premiums paid during lifetime. Proceeds paid to the charity on his or her death would, however, result in a charitable gift for the purposes of the donor's final tax return, with all of the tax advantages described above. The remaining proceeds would be paid tax-free to the other named beneficiary(ies).

In addition, unlike a shared ownership situation, or one where the charity is the policy owner, the donor retains control over the policy, with full rights to change the beneficiary designation at any time.

3. Charitable Giving Strategies Using Life Insurance (Corporations)

(a) Rules for Gifts by Corporations

Charitable gifts made by a corporation create a tax deduction rather than a tax credit. Therefore, as was formerly the case with individuals, the higher the corporate tax rate, the greater the tax relief to the corporate donor. For example, a $100 gift made by a corporation whose income is taxed at the small business tax rate will create a tax refund of approximately $16, depending on the province. The same gift made by a corporation taxed at the top corporate rate for business income will generate a refund of about $32.

Annual corporate donation limits are, like those which apply to individuals, 75% of income. A five-year carryforward is available for excess donations.

(b) Ownership of Policy by Charity

Like an individual, a corporation may assign a new or existing policy to a charity. The charity would name itself as owner and beneficiary. The corporation would be entitled to a tax deduction equal to the policy's fair market value, as described above. The corporation could pay the premiums under a policy owned by a charity, or the charity could assume that obligation. Premium payments by the corporation would qualify as charitable donations deductible from corporate income within the limits noted above.

(c) Ownership of Policy by Corporation

(i) Corporate Policy Used to Fund Estate Gift

Under this alternative, the corporation would be the owner and beneficiary of a policy on the life of a shareholder. On the shareholder's death the insurance proceeds would be received tax-free and the amount of those proceeds, less the ACB of the insurance policy, would be credited to the corporation's CDA. This would allow a tax-free capital dividend to be paid to the shareholder's estate. The funds could then be used to pay bequests to charities named in the deceased's will.

The income tax benefits of this strategy to the estate would be essentially identical to those that apply where the individual donor has designated a charity as beneficiary of a personally-owned policy. The amount of the proceeds would be treated as a charitable gift made in the year of death, and potentially the prior year, subject to the allowable annual limit.

An additional benefit of this strategy is that, by having the policy owned by the corporation, additional cost effectiveness may be achieved. Assuming the shareholder is in a 46% marginal tax bracket, he or she must earn a before-tax amount of $1,850 to pay a $1,000 insurance premium. On the other hand, if the corporation pays tax at an 16% rate, it needs to earn only $1,191 before tax in order to have the same amount available for premium payments.

Note that proceeds passing through the estate are potentially subject to estate creditors and probate fees.

(ii) Corporate Policy Used to Fund Corporate Gift

Alternatively, the policy described in (b) above could be used to fund a charitable gift made by the corporation after the shareholder's death. As in that example, the life insurance proceeds would be received tax-free and the amount of the proceeds, less the ACB of the policy, would be credited to the corporation's CDA. A $100,000 gift to the charity would be deductible to the corporation. There would, however, be a further benefit resulting from the payment of the life insurance proceeds. The charitable gift would not result in an erosion of the corporation's CDA. Therefore, the surviving shareholders would be able to receive tax-free capital dividends in the future equal to the amount of the CDA credit.

(d) Gift of Preferred Shares of Corporation

A shareholder of a private corporation could gift preferred shares of the corporation to a charity and obtain a tax credit for the value of the shares. For these purposes, it is necessary that the charity not be a private foundation and that the donor deal at arm's length with the charity, its directors and officers. The corporation could acquire insurance on the life of the donor which would be used to redeem the shares on the donor's death.

Under this strategy, the donor would obtain a tax credit for the charitable gift during his or her lifetime and, following the donor's death, insurance proceeds would be available to buy out the charity's interest. The charity would receive a taxable dividend on the redemption, but would pay no tax on the dividend because of its tax-exempt status. The CDA credit created by the insurance proceeds would remain for the benefit of the surviving shareholders of the corporation.

Any capital gains inherent in the preferred shares will be realized on the gift to charity. This gain will be subject to tax at normal capital gains rates (unlike the rate applicable to public corporation shares) but will be eligible for the $750,000 capital gains exemption if the shares qualify. If the donor has already utilized this exemption, capital gains may arise when the gift is made. In that case, if the donor has any shares with a high ACB, these should be used for gifting purposes so as to minimize the income tax liability.

Consider the example of Arnie, age 60, who owns all of the shares of Arnie Co. The shares have an ACB of nil and a fair market value of $2 million. Arnie would like to share some of this wealth with a charity during his lifetime. One method of accomplishing this would be to have Arnie exchange his common shares for preferred shares with a total redemption amount of $2 million. This exchange can be accomplished on a tax-deferred basis under the Act. Arnie and/or members of his family would acquire new common shares which would reflect future increases in the value of Arnie Co.

Arnie could then gift the desired number of preferred shares to a charity which is not a private foundation and with which he deals at arm's length. A gift of $100,000 of preference shares would, for example, provide Arnie with a corresponding income tax credit, resulting in immediate tax savings of approximately $46,000 (subject to the gift being within the annual limits described above). As part of the strategy, Arnie Co. would acquire a $100,000 policy on Arnie's life.

At the time of the gift, Arnie would realize a capital gain of $100,000 less the ACB of his shares. The tax payable on this capital gain, the maximum being approximately $23,000, would be more than offset by the tax savings from the charitable gift. If the shares qualified for the $750,000 capital gains exemption, and if Arnie had sufficient unclaimed exemption remaining, his capital gain could be reduced or eliminated.

During Arnie's lifetime, the charity would benefit from dividends paid on the preferred shares. On Arnie's death, the charity would receive $100,000 from Arnie Co. on the redemption of the shares. All amounts received by the charity would be tax-free.

Arnie Co. would have a CDA credit of $100,000 less the ACB of the policy at the time of Arnie's death. This credit would remain for the benefit of Arnie Co.'s other shareholders after the redemption of the shares owned by the charity.

(e) Funding Charitable Gifts Through a Shareholder Loan Account

Another strategy may be used where a corporation has a significant shareholder loan account. These accounts typically arise when the after-tax portion of bonus payments is loaned to the corporation by the shareholder. In these circumstances, the corporation could borrow money from a financial institution and use those funds to repay the shareholder loan. This repayment would be received tax-free by the shareholder and could be used to make a charitable contribution.

If required by the lending institution, the corporation could acquire insurance on the life of the shareholder as security for the loan. The lesser of the policy premium and the net cost of pure insurance would be deductible to the corporation. Interest paid by the corporation on the loan would also be tax deductible. On the shareholder's death, the life insurance proceeds, net of the policy's ACB, would be credited to the corporation's CDA. This credit would not be reduced when the proceeds were used to repay the bank debt, and thus would remain for the benefit of the surviving shareholders.

Let us assume that, for many years, Arnie Co. has been paying significant bonuses to Arnie. These payments are made to reduce corporate income each year to the highest level (currently $400,000) at which the small business tax rate is applied. On some occasions, Arnie has loaned the after-tax portion of the bonus payments to Arnie Co., so that an accumulated shareholder loan balance of $500,000 currently exists.

Arnie Co. could negotiate a bank loan, which would be used to repay the shareholder loan, in whole or in part. This amount would in turn be used by Arnie to make a charitable gift. If, for example, Arnie wished to make a $100,000 cash donation to a charity, this amount would be borrowed by Arnie Co. and then immediately paid to Arnie on account of his shareholder's loan. Assuming a borrowing rate of 6%, Arnie Co. would pay $6,000 of interest annually to the bank, all of which would be deductible. Arnie would obtain a charitable tax receipt for $100,000, which would create income tax benefits of approximately $46,000.

At the same time, Arnie Co. could acquire insurance of $100,000 on Arnie's life to secure the bank loan. Arnie Co. would be the owner and beneficiary of the policy. If the bank required this coverage as collateral security, the lesser of the premium and the net cost of pure insurance would be deductible to Arnie Co.

On Arnie's death, the amount of the life insurance proceeds less the ACB of the policy would be credited to Arnie Co.'s CDA. This credit would remain even after the proceeds were used to repay the bank loan. This would allow the payment of tax-free capital dividends to Arnie Co.'s shareholders at any time in the future.

4. Gifting Publicly-Traded Securities

(a) New Income Tax Incentives

Many individuals prefer to make substantial charitable donations while they are alive, so that they can observe and enjoy the results of their generosity. But at the same time, they may be concerned about the impact that this will have on the amount of property being left to their beneficiaries. A donor in these circumstances might choose to purchase insurance under which the estate and/or given family members could be named beneficiaries. The insurance proceeds would replace the value of any capital donated to charity during the donor's lifetime.

This strategy is a perfect compliment to the most highly publicized change in charitable giving rules in recent years. This involves the preferred treatment applicable to the gifting of publicly-traded securities to a charity. Under the previous rules, individuals would be taxed at the normal capital gains inclusion rate (currently 50%) when these properties were gifted to any charity. However, the 1997 federal Budget reduced the inclusion rate for qualifying gifts to one-half the usual rate where such gift was made to a public charity. This measure, originally intended to expire in 2001, was later extended indefinitely.

The 2006 federal Budget went one step further and eliminated capital gains tax on the gifting of publicly-traded securities to a public charity. The 2007 Budget extended the rule to gifts made to private foundations. This will undoubtedly set the stage for increasing levels of philanthropy from Canadian taxpayers.

(b) Gifting of Public Shares Owned by Private Corporations: Impact on Capital Dividend Account

These changes have deservedly attracted a lot of attention, but public commentary has generally focused on the impact these budget measures will have on individual donors. Discussions concerning the impact on corporate donors have been less prominent, even though there are significant gift planning opportunities in the corporate sector resulting from these pro-posals.

For the sake of illustration, assume that a married couple, Jessie and James, both age 65, own all the shares of a private Canadian corporation (Jessie James Inc.). Jessie James Inc. holds a portfolio of publicly-traded securities valued at $5 million. Jessie and James would like to arrange for Jessie James Inc. to gift $1 million to their favourite charity. Rather than liquidating investments, paying the applicable tax and donating the after-tax proceeds, Jessie and James arrange for the corporation to directly gift $1 million worth of its public shares. These shares have an adjusted cost base (ACB) of $200,000.

In accordance with the Budget proposals, Jessie James Inc. would not have a taxable capital gain on the gift of the shares. It would receive a charitable receipt for $1 million, which would be available as a deduction to a maximum of 75% of its net income for the year. If the gift exceeded this limit, which is likely, the excess may be carried forward and applied against the corporation's income over the next five years. As Jessie James Inc. is subject to tax at a rate approximating 50% on its investment income, tax savings resulting from the gift would be almost $500,000.

There is, however, a significant additional benefit to Jessie James Inc. and its shareholders under the above strategy. As a private corporation, Jessie James Inc. is entitled to a CDA credit on the tax-free portion of any capital gains it realizes. In this case, the entire capital gain ($800,000) is tax-free. As the proposed rules currently stand, this amount may be fully credited to Jessie James Inc.'s CDA and is eligible to be distributed to Jessie and James as tax-free capital dividends.

If Jessie James Inc. does not have sufficient liquidity to pay a capital dividend to Jessie and James in cash, consideration should be given to paying the dividend in the form of a promissory note. This will effectively convert the CDA credit to a shareholder loan that may be paid down on a tax-free basis as cash becomes available in Jessie James Inc. from time to time. This will also have the impact of reducing the value of the Jessie James Inc. shares for capital gains purposes, resulting in tax savings on the deaths of Jessie and James.

(c) Life Insurance Opportunities

There is one final planning opportunity that presents itself in this case. As mentioned above, donors who make a substantial gift to charity may be concerned about the impact of the gift on the value of their estates. Life insurance is frequently used to replace the value of the gifted property, thus preserving the estate for benefit of surviving family members. Tax savings from the gift can be used to pay premiums.

In this case, Jessie James Inc. could acquire a $1 million policy on the lives of Jessie and James with proceeds payable on the second death. Jessie James Inc. would also be the beneficiary of the policy and would pay the premiums. The proceeds would restore the value of the gifted shares but would also (net of the policy's ACB) create a further CDA credit in the corporation. In this case, the credit would be available to surviving Jessie James Inc. shareholders, presumably family members of Jessie and James.

The annual premium for this coverage would be in the range of $14,000. If the survivor of Jessie and James died in twenty years, for example, total premiums paid would equal approximately $280,000. This cost is easily absorbed by the $500,000 in tax savings enjoyed by Jessie James Inc. on the original gift.

If desired, coverage in excess of the value of the original gift could be acquired. This would take into account anticipated future growth in the value of the donated shares and would replenish the estate accordingly.

5. Charitable Giving Strategies Using Annuities

Certain charities are legally authorized to issue annuities in exchange for a lump-sum gift from a donor. Typically, the present value of the expected annuity stream is less than the amount of the payment from the donor. The difference represents a gift that is eligible for the charitable tax credit. In addition to affecting charitable strategies involving life insurance, the 2002 Amendments discussed earlier in this chapter have provided a new set of rules for charitable annuities and other gifting strategies. The Amendments are effective for gifts made after December 20, 2002.

(a) Traditional Charitable Annuities: The Former Rules

Prior to the introduction of the Amendments, there were no specific provisions of the Act governing the tax treatment of charitable annuities. Instead, the rules were found in the administrative guidelines established by the CRA in Interpretation Bulletin IT-111R2. The rules existing prior to the Amendments may be summarized as follows:

- The excess of the lump-sum contribution over the expected annuity payments were treated as a charitable gift. The expected annuity payments were calculated pursuant to a mortality table provided in the Interpretation Bulletin.

- Annuity payments received by the donor were treated as a tax-free return of capital to the extent the expected annuity payments were less than the initial donation to the charity. The expected annuity payments were based on the 1971 Individual Mortality Table.

- The Technical Notes that accompanied the Amendments considered the example of a donor with an eight-year life expectancy who provides a lump sum of $100,000 to purchase a charitable annuity, in exchange for which the charity agreed to provide an annual annuity of $10,000. In that case, the expected annuity payments are $80,000 ($10,000 multiplied by the donor's eight-year life expectancy). Under the rules in effect prior to the Amendments, the difference between the amount contributed and the expected annuity payments ($20,000) represented a charitable donation to the donor. The annuity payments themselves were treated as a tax-free return of capital.

(b) Impact of the Amendments

The objective of the Amendments was to provide a set of rules governing what is commonly known as "split receipting" of charitable gifts. Charitable annuities fit within the ambit of the Amendments because such arrangements contain both an element of gift and an element of benefit retained by the donor. As a result, Interpretation Bulletin IT-111R2 was withdrawn, and charitable annuities will now be governed by the Act rather than administrative practice.

These changes are best illustrated with reference to the same example shown above. Under the Amendments, the tax treatment of the arrangement would be determined on the basis of the costs actually incurred by the charity in funding the desired annuity payments to the donor. The example given in the Technical Notes assumes that a lump sum of $50,000 provided by the charity to an insurance company would generate the desired annual payments of $10,000. Under that assumption, the amount remaining from the original $100,000 payment (i.e., $50,000) would qualify as a charitable donation. This is in contrast to the $20,000 donation that would have resulted prior to the Amendments.

In addition, the result of the Amendments is that annuity payments received under the plan will be treated as prescribed annuities, with a level portion of each payment ($30,000 in total over the anticipated eight-year life expectancy) being taxable to the donor. This contrasts with the tax-free treatment of charitable annuity payments prior to the Amendments.

(c) Comparison

The effect of the Amendment may be summarized using the following table:

	Old Rules	*New Rules*
Tax receipt	20,000	50,000
Tax savings (45%)	9,000	22,500
Tax on annuity (45%)	0	(13,500)
Net tax savings	9,000	9,000

As the above table illustrates, using the example provided in the Technical Notes, the net tax result to the donor under both sets of rules is the same. The real difference is in the timing. Under the Amendments, there is a much larger charitable tax receipt, which results in additional income tax benefits in the first year of the arrangement. This advantage is gradually offset by the tax payable by the donor under the annuity.

Actual results will vary depending on the circumstances. For example, the amount of annuity payments offered by an insurance company will depend upon factors such as interest rates and commission rates. The health of the donor may also be relevant. If he or she is in poor health, the insurance company may agree to pay an "impaired annuity", which results in higher payments than those otherwise available. Each case should be analyzed on its own merits.

(d) Commentary: Are Charitable Annuities Still Relevant?

The Amendments provide welcome new opportunities for charitable giving generally. However, these changes make it questionable as to whether charitable annuities are of any continuing relevance as a gift planning vehicle.

In the previous example, rather than giving $100,000 to a charity in return for a stream of annuity payments, the donor could have simply donated the gift portion ($50,000) unconditionally. The donor could then have purchased an annuity, in his or her own name, with the remaining $50,000. The income tax result would be identical, but the arrangement would be considerably less complex and more flexible than a formal charitable annuity structure. The section below discusses in greater detail the options that are available for the use of annuities in a charitable giving context.

(e) Alternative Strategies

In addition to the strategies described above, there are other methods of using prescribed annuities in a charitable giving program. Consider the following:

(i) Donating Using Income from Prescribed Annuities

Rather than arranging an annuity through the charity itself, or donating a large lump-sum "up front", a donor could use all available funds to purchase a prescribed annuity from an insurance company. The annuity would be payable for the donor's lifetime, with a guarantee period as chosen by the donor (10 or 15 years would be typical).

Consider the example of Fred, a 65-year-old male donor. In his case, a $100,000 deposit would result in annuity payments of $8,044, assuming interest at the rate of 5% and a guarantee period of 10 years. Each payment would contain a taxable portion of $2,436 and tax-free capital of $5,608. An annual gift of the taxable portion would eliminate the tax payable on each annuity payment, resulting in an after-tax return of approximately $5,600 to the donor.

In addition to the income tax benefits, a prescribed annuity provides much greater flexibility to the donor than does a charitable annuity:

- it allows the donor to decide each year which charity or charities will receive the gift; and

- the amount of the gift can be varied each year.

(ii) Combining a Prescribed Annuity with Life Insurance

A variation of the above strategy would be to use the annuity payments to pay premiums under a life insurance policy payable to the charity. In this case, the donor would be taxed on the interest element of each annuity payment and would obtain no charitable tax credit during his or her lifetime. The payment of the insurance proceeds would result in a tax credit in the donor's terminal tax return and, potentially, in the prior taxation year.

This may be illustrated using the example of Freda, a 65-year-old female who purchases a life annuity for a lump-sum deposit of $100,000, with a 10-year guarantee period and interest at 6%. The taxable portion of each annual annuity payment would amount to $3,055. This amount could be used to pay the premiums on a universal life policy, with a face amount of $100,000, under which her favourite charity was named beneficiary. As described above, a charitable tax credit would result from the payment of the insurance proceeds to the charity on Freda's death.

References

Income Tax Act (Canada)

Paragraph 20(1)(e.2) — deduction for premiums on life insurance used as collateral

Subsection 83(2) — capital dividends

Subsection 89(1) — definition of "capital dividend account"

Section 110.1 — deduction for corporations for charitable gifts

Section 110.6 — capital gains exemption

Subsection 110.6(15) — impact of corporate-owned life insurance on eligibility for capital gains exemption

Subsection 118.1(3) — tax credit for individuals for charitable gifts

Subsections 118.1(5.1)–(5.3) — designation of charity as beneficiary of insurance policy, RRIF or RRSP

Subsection 148(7) — transfer of life insurance policies by corporation and between non-arm's length parties

Subsection 148(9) — definition of "value"

Subsections 248(30)–(32) — (proposed) rules regarding donors retaining benefits in charitable gifting arrangements

Income Tax Regulations

Section 304 — prescribed annuity contracts

Interpretation Bulletins

IT-66R6 — Capital Dividends

IT-111R2 — Annuities Purchased from Charitable Organizations (Archived by the CRA)

IT-244R3 — Gifts by Individuals of Life Insurance Policies as Charitable Donations

IT-309R2 — Premiums on Life Insurance Used as Collateral

IT-430R3 — Life Insurance Proceeds Received by a Corporation or Partnership

Information Circular

IC 89-3 — Policy Statement on Business Equity Valuations (see paragraphs 40 and 41 concerning the valuation of life insurance)

Chapter 10

Life Insurance and Trusts

T rusts are among the most enduring and flexible devices in our legal system. Although trusts originated centuries ago, they continue to be indispensable planning tools in a variety of situations, particularly in the field of estate planning. This chapter will consider how trusts and life insurance can sometimes work together to provide an ideal planning solution for a client.

1. Introduction to Trusts

Types of Trusts

There are two major types of trust: an *inter vivos* trust, which is a trust created during an individual's lifetime, and a testamentary trust, which is a trust created on death. Both involve the holding of property by one or more parties, called trustees, on behalf of others, called beneficiaries.

While the trustees are considered to be the legal owners of the trust property, they hold the property on behalf of the beneficiaries, and must act in accordance with the terms of the trust document. In the case of an *inter vivos* trust, the terms and conditions under which the trustees deal with the property are typically found in a trust agreement between the trustees and the settlor of the trust (i.e., the person who establishes the trust). In the case of a testamentary trust, these terms and conditions are usually found in a will.

Trust documents should clearly stipulate the various powers to be given to trustees, including investment powers. For example, absent the appropriate legal language, trustees may not have the power to purchase insurance products. In most circumstances, trust documents contain broad investment powers that give the trustees the ability to acquire any investments they deem appropriate (subject to a requirement that they act in good faith).

The Purpose of a Trust

There is a popular misconception that trusts are established primarily as tax saving vehicles. In fact, trusts were developed long before anyone thought of devising an income tax system to benefit government coffers. While these vehicles do have their tax advantages, in most cases income tax is a secondary consideration in the creation of a trust. Most often, the need for a trust will arise when an individual wishes to provide a gift to one or more beneficiaries, but wishes to control how that gift is used. The following are common situations where the need for a trust is apparent:

- The intended beneficiaries may be minors or younger adults who would not be able to manage significant amounts of money or property on their own.

- One of the individual's beneficiaries may be disabled.

- The client may be concerned about leaving property outright to a surviving spouse for fear that the survivor will remarry and ultimately pass the property to his or her new spouse. Alternatively, the survivor may have children from a previous marriage who might inherit property at the expense of the client's own family members.

In all the above circumstances, the individual can establish a trust to hold the property on behalf of the intended beneficiaries. Trust assets would be managed, and income and capital would be distributed, in accordance with directions provided in the trust agreement or will, as the case may be.

The Taxation of a Trust

An *inter vivos* trust is taxed at the top marginal tax rate on all of its undistributed income. A testamentary trust is taxed using the same graduated income tax rates that apply to individuals. However, it does not qualify for the personal tax credit and so is subject to tax on its first dollar of income.

Income actually distributed to beneficiaries, or which is allocated to them for income tax purposes, will generally be taxed in the beneficiaries' hands at their own marginal tax rate. The *Income Tax Act* provides considerable flexibility in this regard. Generally, it is possible to allocate income between the trust and the beneficiaries in a way that results in the least amount of tax.

Where trust beneficiaries are under the age of 18, the attribution rules may apply, in which case the income will usually be taxed in the hands of the person who created the trust, typically the children's parents or grandparents. The attribution rules are discussed below.

The Attribution Rules

The attribution rules are primarily designed to prevent certain types of income splitting between family members. They arise most frequently in the structuring of family trusts, family corporations, and financial arrangements between spouses. Without attempting to be exhaustive, the following are some common examples of the application of the attribution rules:

- If one spouse gives property to another, any income or loss from that property will be attributed to the former spouse. For example, if Millie gives $20,000 cash to her husband Marty, which Marty invests in a GIC, any interest earned will be attributed to Millie for tax purposes. Similarly, if Marty invests cash from the matured GIC in shares of a publicly traded company, dividends on the shares will be attributed to Millie.

- Any capital gain or loss on the subsequent sale of the property, or substituted property, will also be attributed to Millie. Therefore, if Marty sells the shares, any capital gain or loss will be attributed to Millie.

- If a parent or grandparent makes a gift or interest-free loan to a trust for children or grandchildren, interest and dividend income earned thereon must be attributed to the person making the gift or loan. On the other hand, capital gains earned on the gift or loan are not subject to attribution and may ultimately be taxed in the hands of the children. This is discussed in further detail below.

In general, the attribution rules apply only where property is gifted to the spouse or trust, as the case may be, or where there is a loan to the spouse or trust at less than the interest rate prescribed under the Act. For example, if Millie were to sell property to Marty for its fair market value, the attribution rules would not apply to income earned on that property. There is also no attribution where property passes from one spouse to the other in settlement of matrimonial claims, or where the transferring spouse is or becomes non-resident.

Similarly, if a parent loans money to a trust for his minor children, and if the trust is charged and actually pays the prescribed rate of interest each year, no attribution will arise.

There is also no attribution on reinvested income. Referring again to Millie's $20,000 gift to Marty, interest earned on the GIC will, as noted, be attributed to Millie. However, if Marty reinvests the interest, income earned from that source will not have to be attributed to Millie. The same applies to income earned and reinvested within a trust for minor children. Over time, considerable income splitting can be achieved through the reinvestment of earnings on the original gift.

"In Trust For" Accounts and Capital Gains Splitting with Children

In recent years, there has been a proliferation of "in trust for" accounts intended to take advantage of the fact that capital gains realized by minor children are not subject to the attribution rules. In a typical case, a parent will acquire units of a segregated fund or mutual fund. The forms completed when the investment is acquired state that the units are being acquired in trust for the applicant's children, who are typically minors. There is generally no formal trust agreement.

The expectation in these situations is that capital gains earned within these funds are automatically taxed to the children without any further action being taken. Unfortunately, this is not the case. A number of problems present themselves:

- The absence of formal documentation may lead the CRA to argue that no trust in fact exists, or that the parent exercises so much control over the investment that it is in effect the parent's money. In that case, all income and capital gains are taxable to the parent.

- In many provinces, mutual and segregated funds are not legal investments for trustees unless the trust document so permits. If there is no trust document, the trustees may technically be in breach of their duties. Potentially, therefore, the beneficiaries could have a right of action against the trustees if the funds are mismanaged.

- Even if the above problems can be overcome, considerable income tax compliance is necessary to ensure the desired result.

- If capital gains earned within a trust are not allocated to the beneficiaries, they should be included in the trust's income for tax purposes. Tax at the top marginal rate is payable, assuming the trust is an *inter vivos* trust.

- As a taxpayer, the trust must report the capital gains on its tax return. If the gains are "paid or payable" to beneficiaries in the year, they may be taxed in their hands. Conversely, gains that are simply reinvested, as is often the case, must be taxed within the trust.

- If gains are paid directly to the beneficiaries, the desired income tax results can be achieved, but this is usually not an attractive alternative when the beneficiaries are young children. A better option is to use the funds for the children's benefit. For example, they can be applied towards daycare fees, babysitting costs, private school tuition or the children's share of vacation expenses. It may also be possible to give the children a promissory note for their share of any capital gains that cannot be used in any other way. The children would have the legal right to demand payment of the note upon reaching the age of majority.

In most cases, "in trust for" accounts will not withstand the scrutiny of the CRA. Proper documentation and tax compliance is a must. For those without the resources to establish large trust funds and to retain legal and tax advice, alternatives such as Registered Education Savings Plans may be preferable. A discussion of such plans is beyond the scope of this book.

2. Common Uses of Life Insurance in Trusts

There are many circumstances where a client's objectives can be best achieved using a combination of a trust and life insurance. Following are some planning suggestions involving both *inter vivos* and testamentary trusts.

Inter Vivos Trusts

(a) Insurance Trust for a Grandchild

Consider the example of a grandparent who wishes to invest excess capital on behalf of his or her school-age grandchild. There is also a need for term insurance on the life of the grandchild's mother or father.

In those circumstances, a shared ownership arrangement could be structured under which ownership of an exempt universal life policy on the parent's life was shared between the parent and a trust established by the grandparent for the grandchild. The trust would own, and be the beneficiary of, the CSV of the universal life policy, while the parent would own the face amount, designating a beneficiary of his or her choice (perhaps the surviving spouse or the trust itself). Premiums would be shared in accordance with a shared ownership agreement.

The tax-deferred growth within the universal life policy would accrue for the benefit of the grandchild. This provides an advantage over traditional, taxable investments, whose income might otherwise be subject to the attribution rules. An additional advantage is that life insurance policies held by a trust are not subject to the 21-year deemed disposition rules.

The trustees would be given the discretion to access the funds, through leveraging or partial withdrawals, to fund the child's needs, such as daycare, camp fees, and tuition fees. Tax would be payable on any income realized through partial withdrawals. If the child was under the age of 18 at the time the withdrawals were made, the income would either be taxed to the trust, at the top marginal rate, or to the grandparent, at his or her marginal rate, under the income attribution rules. If the child was 18 or older, the income could be allocated to the child and taxed at his or her marginal rate.

The trust agreement would require the trustees to transfer the CSV to the child when he or she attained a stipulated age, or at any earlier time the trustees considered appropriate. This transfer would take place on a tax-deferred basis. It might be particularly advantageous if the policy were fully paid up at the time of the transfer so that the child would have no premium commitment under the shared ownership arrangement.

(b) Buy/Sell Agreements

Shareholders frequently obtain life or disability insurance on each other's lives for the purposes of funding buy/sell agreements. In a simple situation, one shareholder would own, and be the beneficiary of, insurance on the life of the other shareholder. Proceeds would be used to purchase shares held by the deceased or disabled shareholder.

This type of "criss-cross" buy/sell arrangement is subject to certain risks. For example, it relies upon each shareholder fulfilling his or her commitments to pay premiums and to maintain the coverage in good standing. In addition, when proceeds are paid, there is a risk, however remote, that the beneficiary might choose to ignore his or her obligations under the buy/sell agreement and misapply the proceeds in some fashion.

These risks can be avoided by having a trust be the owner and beneficiary of the insurance policies. The trustee would be given the responsibility of ensuring that each shareholder was making the necessary premium payments; in fact, such payments could be made to the trustee, who would then forward them to the insurance company. On a shareholder's death or disability, the proceeds would be paid to the trustee, who would then ensure that they were applied as contemplated under the buy/sell agreement.

A similar trust arrangement could be used to administer a buy/sell agreement amongst partners in a partnership.

Testamentary Trusts

(a) Insurance Trust for Minor Children or Grandchildren

Individuals who purchase life insurance policies frequently wish to provide benefits for minor children, or for individuals who suffer from disabilities and are unable to manage money. In such cases, it is not advisable to designate the intended beneficiary in the conventional way. Instead, it is recommended that trusts be established so that one or more trustees can manage the insurance proceeds on behalf of the beneficiaries. This portion of the book will review some key planning considerations in this regard, with a focus on how to establish insurance trusts using life insurance beneficiary designations contained in a separate, written declaration.

(i) Insurance Act Rules on Designating Beneficiaries

The various provincial insurance Acts contain a number of rules regarding the designation of beneficiaries under life insurance policies. For example, the *Insurance Act (Ontario)* states that an "insured may in a contract or by a *declaration* designate the insured's personal representative or a beneficiary to receive insurance money" [emphasis added]. "Declaration" means an instrument signed by the insured, including a will, in which a beneficiary designation is made.

While a declaration can presumably be made in any written instrument, the focus of this article will be an insurance trust declaration made in the insured's will.

(ii) "In Trust For" Designations

Insurance advisors and their clients usually recognize the need to establish a trust to manage insurance proceeds intended for the benefit of minor or disabled beneficiaries. On many occasions, however, this is achieved by means of a simple beneficiary designation worded something like this:

"Harry Hillman in trust for my children, Gert and Bernie". This wording is sufficient to create a trust arrangement under which Harry (who may be the children's uncle or some other family member) acts as trustee for the deceased's children. However, this designation is deficient in many respects, as discussed below:

- It does not contemplate Harry being unable to act as trustee, by reason of his death or incapacity, for example. Ordinarily, an alternate trustee, or trustees, should be named.

- It does not contemplate the possibility that Gert or Bernie may predecease the life insured.

- It does not give Harry any guidance as to how he should exercize his discretion regarding the investment and distribution of the trust funds.

- Perhaps most importantly, where the above wording is used, Gert and Bernie will be able to demand their respective shares of the trust fund upon reaching the age of majority. Most parents would not want their children to acquire a significant amount of money at such a young age.

For the above reasons, it is preferable that more formal trust provisions be created. These can be included in a beneficiary designation which, rather than appearing only on the insurance company form, appears in a declaration within the client's will.

(iii) Beneficiary Designations in a Will

A will frequently contains detailed provisions that establish testamentary trusts, using estate assets, for young or disabled beneficiaries. A typical trust might provide that, where a beneficiary is under the age of 25 at the time of testator's death, trustees be appointed to manage the inheritance on the beneficiary's behalf. The trustees could, if the will so provided, distribute income or capital to, or for the benefit of, the beneficiary before he or she reached that age. This could assist with post-secondary educational costs or the acquisition of a home, for example. But the beneficiary would be unable to assume full control over the inheritance until reaching age 25. The above is, of course, merely an example, as trusts may be designed in an almost limitless variety of ways to meet planning objectives.

A declaration contained in a will can create an insurance trust that provides the same flexibility and planning advantages. As described below, although the wording of such a declaration may be almost identical to that of a conventional testamentary trust, careful drafting is necessary to ensure that the two trusts are, in fact, separate.

The net result is that, even though the declaration appears in the will, the insurance proceeds do not form part of the deceased's estate. Instead, they form part of an insurance trust that exists separate from the estate. Therefore, as is the case with a policy containing an ordinary beneficiary designation, the proceeds are not subject to probate fees nor exposed to estate creditors. Similarly, if the only potential beneficiaries of the insurance trust are within the "preferred class" of beneficiaries specified in the relevant Insurance Act, creditor protection should be available during the lifetime of the insured. (See Chapter 11 for additional commentary regarding creditor protection.)

Notwithstanding the apparent intention of the *Insurance Act,* a recent Saskatchewan case *(Carlisle)* has created some doubt in this area. In that case, an insurance trust which seemed to contain the necessary clauses to be considered separate from the estate was nonetheless held by the Court to be part of the deceased's general estate for probate purposes. It is hoped that the *Carlisle* case will not adversely affect planning in this area as it seems to fly in the face of the intent of the legislation. The impact of this case beyond Saskatchewan's borders is also questionable. In any event, clients seeking to create a trust of this nature should obtain the necessary legal advice to ensure that their wishes are met.

(iv) Taxation Issues

A trust created by a beneficiary designation is a testamentary trust, which as mentioned above, is a trust that comes into effect on the individual's death. Income earned in a testamentary trust is subject to the same marginal tax rates as those applicable to individual taxpayers. Trust income allocated to beneficiaries is taxed to the recipients at their applicable personal tax rates.

These tax rules allow for optimal tax planning, in that trust income may be split among the trust and its beneficiaries in a way that maximizes the advantages of the marginal tax rate structure.

(v) Drafting Issues

Great care must be taken in the drafting of declarations in a will. This is necessary to ensure that the proceeds do not form part of the estate, thereby negating some of the key advantages of the process (in particular, creditor protection and avoidance of probate). The following are some important drafting tips:

- The wording should specifically state that the declaration is made pursuant to the applicable Insurance Act. It should identify the insurance policy(ies) specifically, including reference to the policy number.

- The wording should appear early in the will, before the section of the will that provides for the estate to be transferred to the executors.

- If practical, name different trustees to hold the insurance proceeds than those named to hold the deceased's estate. For example, one could have one more trustee than the other. State that the trustees are to receive the proceeds as beneficiaries of the insurance policy.

- The terms of the insurance trust may or may not be the same as testamentary trusts established in respect of the estate. If they are the same, it is not necessary to repeat the language applicable to the latter trusts. Instead, the wording of the insurance trust can state that it applies "as if" the proceeds formed part of the general estate.

(vi) Notice to Insurance Company

The insurance company must have notice where a declaration is made in a will or another document other than the usual beneficiary designation form. The latter form will be used, however, to identify the beneficiaries and the document in which the declaration is made. The designation form might identify the beneficiaries as "the trustees of the Betty Burford Insurance Trust, the terms of which are set out in a declaration contained in the last will and testament of Betty Burford dated [insert date]". A copy of the will should be included for the insurance company's files.

(vii) Additional Planning Issues

The following are some additional planning issues:

- A designation may be revoked or amended in a declaration signed by the insured. The revocation or amendment should specifically refer to the policy(ies) in question and should be filed with the insurance company.

- A beneficiary designation in a will cannot be irrevocable.

- A designation in a will is not effective against a designation made later than the date of the will.

- If a will is found to be invalid, for lack of necessary witnesses for example, this does not invalidate the insurance declaration made in the will.

- If a will is revoked, however, any designation contained in the will is also revoked. A common example would be where an individual marries. In that case, his or her existing will is automatically revoked (unless it was made in contemplation of that marriage).

(b) Disabled Beneficiaries

Parents who have a disabled child frequently look to life insurance as a means of providing funds for the child's upkeep. This insurance is often on their joint lives, with proceeds payable on the second death. Where the child is mentally disabled, or otherwise incapable of looking after his or her own needs, the need for a testamentary trust is obvious.

As with the above example, this insurance can be paid to trustees through a beneficiary designation provided in the will of each parent. Once again, probate fees and creditors can be avoided using this mechanism.

The terms of this trust will, in most cases, vary significantly from those established for non-disabled children. First, a trust for a disabled child will in all probability have to exist for the child's lifetime, because there may never be a time when the child is able to manage money. Second, the trust may have to be specially designed to ensure that the child continues to qualify for government programs and financial assistance. This usually means that the trust will have to be completely discretionary. Trustees will be given discretion to distribute income and/or capital for the benefit of the child, but only if they do not affect the child's eligibility for other benefits. To the extent that income or capital is not applied for the child's benefit, these trusts usually provide for it to be distributed to other beneficiaries (siblings, for example). These trusts are commonly known as "Henson Trusts", and are named after a court case that legitimized this planning strategy.

References

Income Tax Act (Canada)

Subsection 12.2(1) — accrual taxation of non-exempt life insurance policies

Sections 74.1–75.1 — attribution rules

Subsection 104(4) — deemed disposition rules for trusts

Subsection 104(6) — deduction of amounts paid or payable to beneficiaries by trusts

Subsection 104(14) — preferred beneficiary election

Subsection 107(2) — rollover on transfer of trust property to beneficiary

Subsection 112(1) — intercorporate dividends

Section 117 — tax rates for individuals and testamentary trusts

Section 120.4 — "kiddie tax"

Section 122 — tax rate for *inter vivos* trust

Subsections 148(1) and (2) — taxation on disposition of life insurance policy

Subsection 148(4) — taxation on partial disposition of life insurance policy

Subsection 148(7) — non-arm's length disposition of life insurance policy

Subsection 148(9) — definitions relevant to section 148 including "adjusted cost basis", "cash surrender value", "disposition", "policy loan", "proceeds of the disposition", and "value"

Section 186 — Part IV tax

Income Tax Regulations

Section 306 — exempt policies

Section 307 — accumulating funds

Section 308 — net cost of pure insurance

Interpretation Bulletins

IT-87R2 — Policyholders' Income from Life Insurance Policies

IT-269R4 — Part IV Tax on Taxable Dividends Received by a Private Corporation or a Subject Corporation

IT-286R2 — Trusts: Amounts Payable

IT-381R3 — Trusts: Capital Gains and Losses

IT-394R2 — Preferred Beneficiary Election

IT-406R2 — Tax Payable by *Inter Vivos* Trust

IT-510 — Transfers and Loans of Property made after May 22, 1985 to a Related Minor

IT-511R — Interspousal and Other Transfers and Loans of Property

Case Law

Re Carlisle Estate, 2007 SKQB 435

Chapter 11

Creditor Protection

I nsurance professionals quite properly tout the advantages enjoyed by life insurance and related products in providing creditor protection to policyholders. In the estate planning market, it is unusual for a client to purchase life insurance primarily because of its preferred status under debtor-creditor laws. More often, it is simply an attractive by-product. Considerations may be different in the investment market, however, as the creditor protection of segregated funds and annuities may be a significant factor in the client's buying decisions. In any event, the knowledgeable broker should be able to explain the basics of creditor protection so that his or her clients may better understand the products they have purchased. Debtor-creditor law is a complex mix of federal and provincial statutes and common (or "judge made") law. This chapter will not provide a comprehensive analysis of the law, but will instead give an overview of the legislative provisions that affect the status of life insurance policies and discuss recent cases of interest.

1. Relevant Legislation

(a) *Insurance Act*

Each province has an Insurance Act that in certain circumstances provides creditor protection to life insurance polices, as defined in the legislation. The legislation is virtually identical in every province except Quebec. The wording of section 196 of the *Ontario Insurance Act* (the "Ontario Act") is typical, and provides as follows:

> (1) Where a beneficiary is designated, the insurance money, from the time of the happening of the event upon which the insurance money becomes payable, is not part of the estate of the insured and is not subject to the claims of the creditors of the insured.

> (2) While a designation in favour of a spouse, child, grandchild or parent of a person whose life is insured, or any of them, is in effect, the rights and interests of the insured in the insurance money and in the contract are exempt from execution or seizure.

It is noteworthy that the term "spouse" in the Ontario Act includes a common-law spouse and a same-sex spouse. This definition may not be uniformly applicable across Canada.

The above wording needs to be read carefully so that its scope can be properly understood. The protection available under the Insurance Act is, naturally enough, applicable to the individual who owns the policy. However, creditor protection is only available if there is one of the given family relationships between the life insured and the designated beneficiary. (This is in contrast to Quebec, where creditor protection is determined based upon the relationship between the policy owner and the beneficiary.)

The protection given under these provisions is for contracts of "life insurance". The definition of life insurance in the Ontario Act, which again reflects that which generally applies across Canada, includes an undertaking by an insurer to pay a sum of money on death or disability. It also includes "an undertaking entered into by an insurer ... to provide an annuity", including an annuity in respect of which the periodic payments may be unequal in amount. As will be seen in the following discussion, a significant issue in a number of court cases has been whether certain types of insurance company RRSPs fell within this definition.

(b) *Bankruptcy and Insolvency Act*

The *Bankruptcy and Insolvency Act* (the "BIA") is federal legislation that applies uniformly across the country. Important amendments to the BIA, affecting creditor protection for registered plans, have recently been passed. As predicted in the earlier editions of the book, the main impact of these changes is to provide a more level playing field in the realm of creditor protection for registered plans offered by all types of financial institutions.

The following are highlights of these amendments, which are contained in Bill C-12:

- Creditor protection that is provided under provincial legislation, such as the *Insurance Act*, will be recognized for federal purposes.

- RRSPs and RRIFs issued by any financial institution will be creditor protected except for contributions made to such plans within 12 months prior to bankruptcy. This exception will not apply, however, if the plan is otherwise protected under provincial law. For example, registered plans issued by insurance companies may enjoy greater protection than other plans as regards deposits made within this time period.

- Unlike previous versions of this legislation, there will be no limit as to the amount that can be creditor protected within registered plans.

The amendments to the BIA have significantly reduced the advantages formerly enjoyed by the insurance industry as regards the creditor protection of registered plans. However, it does seem entirely appropriate that retirement savings enjoy this type of protection whether or not they are issued by insurance companies.

These changes will also have an impact on case law that has been considered in earlier editions of the book. The discussion that follows will consider these cases in light of the new BIA rules.

2. Case Law

The courts have, in many cases, been asked to rule on the scope of creditor protection provided under the provincial Insurance Acts, and to consider the interplay between these statutes and the federal BIA.

(a) *Ramgotra*

One of the most well-known cases was the 1996 Supreme Court of Canada decision in *The Royal Bank of Canada v. North American Life Assurance*

Company and Balvir Singh Ramgotra. This decision was welcomed in that it cleared up much of the muddy legal water surrounding the creditor-protected status of life insurance and annuity products. From the insurance industry's perspective, it was an extremely positive decision which reaffirmed the special status its products enjoy in the realm of creditor protection.

(i) The Facts

The facts of the case were relatively simple. In June 1990, Dr. Ramgotra transferred his non-insurance RRSP funds to a RRIF issued by North American Life, at which time regular payments under the RRIF began. The doctor named his wife as beneficiary under the contract. Dr. Ramgotra made an assignment into bankruptcy in February 1992, and was absolutely discharged in January 1993, at which time his only assets were his clothing, household contents, and the RRIF.

(ii) The Legal Issues

In arguing that the RRIF in question was liable to seizure, the Royal Bank relied upon the provisions of the BIA which state that a "settlement" made between one and five years prior to bankruptcy is void against a trustee in bankruptcy "if the interest of the settlor did not pass". In other words, the bank argued that, by moving his RRSP to an insurance company RRIF, Dr. Ramgotra had simply moved his own money around without transferring his proprietary interest to anyone. The result, in the bank's view, was that the RRIF remained part of his estate and was therefore subject to seizure by the trustee in bankruptcy.

Dr. Ramgotra and North American Life argued, on the other hand, that by naming his wife as a beneficiary of the RRIF, he had made a settlement under which his interest was passed to another person. Furthermore, even if the bank were correct in arguing that his interest did not pass, the acquisition of an insurance company RRIF was a bar to the bank's claim because it fell within the protected class of assets under the *Saskatchewan Insurance Act.*

(iii) The Decision

The Supreme Court found that the designation of a beneficiary did constitute the settlement of a proprietary interest, but that it was a contingent interest which might only be realized in the future. In other words, Dr. Ramgotra had not transferred any of his immediate interest in the RRIF when he named his wife beneficiary, and in fact retained complete control over the asset and the naming of future beneficiaries. Thus, the naming of the beneficiary constituted a settlement that was void as against the trustee in bankruptcy.

The Court did not stop there, however. It stated in very strong terms that, even if the settlement was void against the trustee, "the exempt status of the life-assured RRIF remains in effect under provincial law so as to block the creditors' claims". The Court made it abundantly clear that, all other legal considerations aside, the exempt status of the RRIF under provincial insurance legislation was the critical factor in its decision. No such protection would have been available to a RRIF issued by another type of financial institution.

(iv) The Implications of the BIA Changes and the Ramgotra Decision

If a case with facts similar to *Ramgotra* were to arise today, it is likely that it would be resolved quite simply under the new BIA rules. Both the original non-insurance RRSP and the RRIF issued by North American Life would enjoy creditor protection under the new legislation. No contributions were made in the 12 months prior to bankruptcy so an exemption for all plan funds would have been available.

Ramgotra may continue to be relevant in other situations, however. The decision was not based on the fact that the insurance product in question was a registered plan. Therefore, the decision should still apply where a transfer of funds is made to a non-registered insurance product in similar circumstances.

(b) *Sykes, Robson* and *Stock:* "Life Insurance Broadly Speaking"

Previous editions of the book considered the 1998 British Columbia Court of Appeal decision in the cases of *Sykes, Robson,* and *Stock.* Each of these cases involved one or more RRSPs, issued by insurance companies, under which the annuitant husband had named his wife as beneficiary. Each RRSP was an accumulation-type plan such as a deferred annuity or segregated fund.

The legal issue was whether such a product was an "undertaking to provide an annuity", in which case creditor protection under the *B.C. Insurance Act* was available (similar wording exists in most provincial legislation). The creditors argued that this protection should not be available during the accumulation phase, but only when payouts commenced.

In overturning lower court decisions, the B.C. Court of Appeal found that creditor protection was available to products of this nature (although

Mr. Sykes was unsuccessful in his appeal for other reasons). The following factors were key in this decision:

- The insurer in each case had undertaken to pay money on the happening of certain events, such as death, or at a fixed or determinable time (such as age 71). This was sufficient to allow the contracts to fall within the definition of life insurance in the B.C. Act, and the fact that each had a spousal beneficiary designation meant that creditor protection was available.

- The Court referred to case law, which suggested that the purpose of the expanded definition of life insurance was to provide creditor protection for retirement savings (in the form of annuities) identical to that available regarding conventional life insurance.

- The Court cited with particular approval the Newfoundland Court of Appeal decision in *Anthony* where, on similar facts, the debtor was successful in protecting his RRSPs from seizure by creditors. The British Columbia court stated that, given the similarity of insurance legislation across Canada, courts should be careful to ensure consistency in their decisions.

As in *Ramgotra*, because all of the plans in question were registered, the new BIA legislation would prevail if these cases were decided today. (It is interesting that the Court seemed influenced by the fact that the funds in question were all within RRSPs, even though there was no legal basis for distinguishing these from identical non-registered plans.) However, these cases could still be applicable in deciding whether non-registered annuities and segregated funds enjoy creditor protection under the *Insurance Act*. To that extent, these cases can still be viewed as positive ones for the insurance industry.

(c) *Amherst Crane*

As previously explained in Chapter 3, in *Amherst Crane* the Ontario Court of Appeal held that proceeds paid to a named beneficiary under a non-insurance RRSP was not part of the deceased's estate. This prevented the creditor from accessing the RRSP funds to satisfy its claims. The creditor failed in its attempt to have an appeal heard by the Supreme Court of Canada.

While this decision was made by an Ontario court, and involved Ontario legislation (the *Succession Law Reform Act* "*SLRA*"), it could have broad implications across Canada. If its reasoning is applied across Canada, creditor protection to the deceased will be available where his or her RRSP (and presumably RRIF) is payable on death to a named beneficiary. This will provide non-insurance financial institutions with the same level playing field provided under the BIA during an individual's lifetime. Differences in provincial law will have to be considered carefully, of course.

3. Suggested Marketing Approach for Insurance Professionals

Recent changes to the BIA should be welcomed despite the fact that they limit many advantages long held by certain insurance products. It is also important to remember that these amendments affect only registered plans and do not affect the broader creditor protection available to insurance products generally under provincial law. Existing case law is also supportive of the protection provided under the provincial Insurance Acts.

This remains a complex area of the law and brokers should resist making blanket statements to the effect that insurance products with the appropriate beneficiary designation will always be creditor-proof. In fact, the term "creditor proof" in the marketing of insurance products is best avoided in favour of the more conservative "creditor protected". In any event, where circumstances warrant, clients in serious financial difficulties who are considering a move to life insurance products should be advised in writing to seek legal advice. The reason is that the movement of assets on the eve of bankruptcy, for example, could be considered a fraudulent conveyance. In that case, the transfer could be ignored under bankruptcy law and the usual protection afforded by the insurance products would be unavailable.

From a marketing perspective, however, insurance professionals can be confident that, whatever level of creditor protection is offered by life insurance products, it is at least as good as, and in many cases better than, that provided by any other kind of financial instrument.

4. Other Creditor Protection Issues

The *Harrison* Case: Redirecting Insurance Proceeds to Financial Dependants

(a) Introduction

The 1996 Ontario court decision in *Harrison v. State Farm Mutual Automobile Insurance Co.* attracted considerable interest in the life insurance community. This level of interest was not surprising, given that the case involved a court order which in effect redirected, to other parties, proceeds under two policies that had been payable to a named beneficiary. Under one of the policies, the beneficiary designation was irrevocable.

Precedent cases cited by the Court would suggest that *Harrison* simply confirmed existing law, rather than breaking new ground. Nonetheless, the decision is an important illustration of the law of dependant's relief and provides interesting insight into how a court resolves seeming inconsistencies between separate pieces of legislation.

It is important to note that this case was decided by the Ontario Court of Justice on the basis of Ontario legislation. However, each province has legislation covering these areas of the law and it is likely that the principles stated in *Harrison* would have relevance beyond Ontario's borders.

(b) The Facts

Ronald Harrison and Nancy Frederick were married in 1978 and divorced in 1992. They had three children, David, Krista, and Michael. Under the terms of the divorce settlement, Mr. Harrison was required to pay monthly child support and to obtain insurance on his life in the amount of $150,000, naming his children as irrevocable beneficiaries of the policy.

In November 1995, Ronald and David Harrison were killed in a traffic accident. At that time, Mr. Harrison was in arrears of child support in the amount of $59,000, plus interest. He had also failed to purchase the life insurance which he had agreed to obtain for the benefit of his children. He had, however, obtained a $300,000 policy naming his common-law spouse, Bernadette Snider, as irrevocable beneficiary. Ms. Snider was also the major beneficiary under the accidental death provisions of Ronald Harrison's automobile policy (smaller death benefits were provided for his children and Ms. Snider's children).

(c) The Issue

The court application was made on behalf of Krista and Michael Harrison (the "Applicants"), the surviving children of Ronald Harrison. The applicants sought judgment against his estate for the arrears of child support and for an additional $150,000 relating to the insurance policy he had failed to obtain under the divorce settlement. The application was challenged by Ms. Snider (the "Respondent") for the reasons described below.

The only issue to be decided by the Court was whether recovery of these amounts could be made out of the insurance proceeds otherwise payable to Ms. Snider.

(d) The Legal Arguments

(i) For the Applicants

The Applicants' case was based upon the dependant's relief provisions in subsection 58(1) of the SLRA. These provisions state that "where a deceased ... has not made adequate provision for the proper support of his dependants ... [the court] may order that such provision as it considers adequate be made out of the estate of the deceased for the proper support of the dependants ...". They also relied on section 72 of the SLRA which deems certain transactions to be "testamentary dispositions" and to be part of the deceased's estate for these purposes. Included in this list of testamentary dispositions is "any amount payable under a policy of insurance effected on the life of the deceased and owned by him or her ...".

The Applicants therefore argued that the insurance proceeds payable under the policies on Mr. Harrison's life were part of his estate for the purposes of the SLRA. This made the proceeds available to satisfy their claim, even though the Respondent was named as beneficiary of both policies (in one case irrevocably).

(ii) For the Respondent

The Respondent relied upon familiar provisions of the Ontario Act in support of her case. This Act provides that "where a beneficiary is designated, the insurance money, from the time of [death] ... is not part of the estate of the insured and is not subject to the claims of the creditors of the insured". It also states (in subsection 191(1)) that an insured may "designate a beneficiary irrevocably, and in that event ... the insurance money is not subject to the control of the insured or of the insured's creditors and does not form part of the insured's estate".

(e) The Decision

As is seen from the above discussion, the Court had to decide between seemingly contradictory provisions of the SLRA and the Ontario Act. Not surprisingly, given the facts of the case, the Court opted in favour of the Applicants and ruled that the SLRA prevailed. However, its decision was based upon more than sympathy for the Applicants' circumstances. The Court also relied upon two earlier court cases which had addressed similar issues:

- In *Moores v. Hughes*, the deceased had left an estate of $40,000, but had assets of $365,000 payable outside of his estate, most of which was made up of insurance proceeds payable to his second wife. The deceased's first wife argued successfully that these other assets were part of his estate for the purposes of the SLRA and the assets were charged as security for the amount of the judgment granted by the Court. The Court justified its ruling by stating that the purpose of these statutory rules was to prevent hardship from being suffered by dependants where assets pass outside of a deceased person's estate by such means as beneficiary designations and joint ownership of property.

- In *Dunn v. Dunn Estate*, the Court considered a fact situation similar to that in Harrison. A dependant child from the deceased's prior marriage was successful in obtaining a charging order against insurance proceeds payable to the deceased's second wife. The Court held that the SLRA contained special rules which were an exception to the general rules under the Ontario Act.

Considering all of the above factors, the Court had little difficulty finding in favour of the Applicants. Mr. Harrison's estate, including the insurance proceeds in issue, was charged for the payment of arrears of support, and for the additional amount of $150,000.

(f) The Implications of the *Harrison* Decision for the Insurance Professional

The *Harrison* case, together with the other cases cited in support of the decision, should not be seen as making a significant intrusion into the *Insurance Act* provisions that protect insurance policies from creditors. Rather, as illustrated by these decisions, the SLRA is simply providing an exception to the general *Insurance Act* rules. This exception is based upon sound public policy which states that an individual who is financially dependent upon a deceased person should not be put at risk simply because the deceased arranged to have significant assets pass outside his or her "traditional" estate.

These cases also mean that care must be taken in advising a client on the creditor-protected nature of insurance policies, particularly in cases where there are dependants who may have claims against the estate. A thorough review of the client's financial obligations should be undertaken, particularly in situations where divorce and/or remarriage is involved, to ensure that adequate provision has been made for potential claimants. This is the best way to ensure that beneficiary designations are not overturned through dependants' relief applications.

5. The CRA as Creditor

In *Minister of National Revenue v. Moss,* the Court ruled that the taxpayer's insurance policies were not exempt from seizure by the CRA. The Court held that, while the BIA contains specific language preventing a trustee in bankruptcy from seizing assets protected from creditors under provincial legislation, no such provisions are contained in the *Income Tax Act.* This represents another statutory exception to the usual *Insurance Act* rules.

References

Case Law

Dunn v. Dunn Estate, (1992) 9 OR (3d), 95 (Gen.Div.)

Harrison (Litigation Guardian of) v. State Farm Mutual Automobile Insurance Co., (1997), 67ACWS (3d), 1160 (Ont. Ct. (Gen.Div.))

M.N.R. v. Anthony, (1995) 124 DLR (4th), 575 (Nfld. C.A.)

M.N.R. v. Moss, 98 DTC 6016 (F.C.T.D.)

Re Moores and Hughes et al. (1981), 136 DLR (3rd), 516 (Ont.)

Royal Bank of Canada v. North American Life Assurance Co. and Balvir Singh Ramgotra, 96 DTC 6157 (S.C.C.)

Sykes (Re); Robson v. Robson; A.R. Thomson Ltd. v. Stock, (1998) 156 DLR (4th), 105 (B.C.C.A.)

Amherst Crane Limited v. Perring, 241 D.L.R. (4th) 176 (Ont. C.A.)

Chapter 12

Living Benefits: Disability Buy-Outs and Critical Illness Insurance

T he focus of this book is the role that life insurance can play in estate planning for owner-managers and other high net-worth individuals. However, disability buy-out and critical illness policies are playing increasingly significant roles in helping these clients achieve their business and estate goals. This chapter will focus on these "living benefits" products, discuss how they can assist clients in achieving planning objectives, and consider relevant taxation issues.

1. Disability Buy-Out

Life insurance has long played a significant role in funding the purchase and sale of shares under shareholders agreements. Insurance professionals, lawyers and accountants alike recognize life insurance as a key element of business-succession strategies: Chapters 5 and 6 review many of the ways in which life insurance can be used for this purpose.

Unfortunately, lawyers, accountants, and even insurance advisors, frequently pay insufficient attention to the possibility that a shareholder will become disabled to the extent that he or she will be unable to contribute further to business operations. This is surprising, given the actuarial evidence suggesting that there is a significantly greater likelihood of disability, rather than death, before age 65. This inattention to disability issues is frequently demonstrated when shareholders agreements are reviewed. More often than not, these agreements do not deal properly with the possible consequences of a shareholder becoming disabled.

This section will provide an overview of key points relating to disability provisions that should be addressed in shareholders agreements. It will also discuss income tax issues relating to the use of disability buy-out insurance in funding the purchase and sale of shares held by a disabled shareholder.

Reviewing Disability Buy-Out Provisions in a Shareholders Agreement

Following are some key disability-related issues to look for in reviewing a shareholders agreement.

(a) Definition of "Disability"

Where shares of a disabled shareholder may (or must) be sold under the agreement, it is of crucial importance that the agreement contain a clear definition of what constitutes "disability". Too often, agreements fail to provide a suitable definition. Consider the following examples taken from actual buy-sell agreements:

EXAMPLE 1

In the event that a shareholder becomes physically disabled, the other shareholder shall have the right to purchase the shares held by the disabled party.

This clause fails on a number of counts:

- It is restricted to physical disability. As readers will know, a significant number of disability claims relate to stress and other mental conditions that would be appropriate triggers for the purchase and sale of shares.

- It does not relate the disability to the shareholder's ability to provide services to the business. To use an extreme example, a person who breaks her leg skiing may be physically disabled, but the nature of the disability is not normally one that would affect her ability to work in a business long term nor prompt the sale of her shares. However, the above clause could easily be interpreted to provide the other shareholder with an option to purchase her shares. This would not be an appropriate or reasonable result in most cases.

- The clause does not provide a waiting period, but rather implies that a buy-sell could take place immediately upon a person becoming disabled. Ideally, a waiting period of at least a year should be provided so an assessment can be made as to whether the disability is permanent and whether on a long term basis it will prevent the disabled party from performing his or her customary duties in the business.

EXAMPLE 2

A shareholder shall be considered disabled if he is unable to perform his occupation by reason of a physical or psychological condition and is unlikely to improve within six months of becoming disabled.

This clause is an improvement over Example 1, in that it at least attempts to include something more than physical disability with the definition. However, its reference to "psychological condition" seems unnecessarily limiting as there are presumably mental disabilities that fall outside that term.

The clause also attempts to provide a waiting period of sorts by referring to a condition that is "unlikely to improve" within the next six months. This is an impractical provision as in many cases it will be difficult to determine what degree of improvement to expect in the upcoming months. It also fails to consider that there may be improvement, but not enough to allow the shareholder to resume his or her active role in the business. In other words, there may be some improvement in the shareholder's condition but the need to sell the shares may remain. Clearly, it is preferable to take no such action the until end of the waiting period (at least a year) and then determine if the shareholder is still disabled.

In summary, the definition of "disabled" in a shareholders agreement should include the following:

- It should refer to both mental and physical incapacity.

- The disability should be such that it prevents the shareholder from performing his or her normal duties within the business. The agreement might require a doctor's certificate to that effect.

- It should contain a time frame or waiting period. For example, disability might arise under the agreement if the employee is unable to work for a given number of working days (say 180) within a one-year period.

Some agreements will provide that a shareholder is disabled where, for example, the individual is unable to work for a consecutive period of months (typically in the range of six to twelve). This should generally be avoided, because it takes only a brief return to work — as little as a single day — to stop the time period running and to prevent the shareholder from being treated as disabled. The definition should be structured in a way that reflects the number of days missed over an agreed-upon time frame, without requiring that the days be consecutive.

As mentioned above, disability buy-out insurance is available to provide for the funding of the purchase and sale of shares owned by the disabled shareholder. Where insurance is acquired, the definition of disability for the purposes of the shareholders agreement should match that contained in the insurance policy. This ensures that the insurance proceeds will be payable at the exact time they are needed. Many disability insurance carriers require, as a condition of issuing the insurance, that the shareholders agreement be consistent with the terms of the policy.

Income tax issues relating to disability buy-out insurance will be addressed later in this chapter.

(b) The Terms of the Purchase and Sale

Having established a proper definition of disability, the agreement should then set out the specific purchase and sale terms that apply in the event a disability does arise. The following matters should be addressed:

- The agreement should state whether the purchase and sale is to be mandatory or optional. Where disability buy-out insurance is in place, the agreement would normally require that the non-disabled shareholder, or the corporation itself, purchase the shares owned by the disabled party. Where there is no insurance, the prospective purchasers would, in most cases, be given the option to buy, rather than being required to do so. This gives them the opportunity to purchase the shares if they are able to arrange the necessary financing.

- The agreement should specify whether the shares are to be purchased by the non-disabled shareholder(s) or by the corporation. These two options have significantly different income tax consequences, as will be addressed below.

- Where all or any portion of the purchase price is not funded with disability buy-out insurance, the agreement should provide for that amount to be paid over time, typically no more than five years.

Normally, there will be an agreed-upon interest rate applied to the unpaid balance. The purchaser will, in most cases, have the right to prepay the amount owing at any time. Note that certain disability buy-out policies provide for benefits to be paid in instalments over a stipulated time period, rather than being paid in one lump sum.

Income Tax and Structuring Issues

Disability buy-out proceeds, like life insurance proceeds, are tax-free to the beneficiary. Unlike life insurance proceeds, however, where the beneficiary is a corporation, there is no credit to the corporation's capital dividend account ("CDA"). Therefore, the tax planning strategies relating to life-insured buy-outs, as discussed in Chapters 5 and 6, are in most cases irrelevant for disability buy-outs.

The income tax consequences of the various buy-out methods are best illustrated through an example. Assume that Murray and Bertha, who are not related to one another, each own 50% of the shares of an operating company known as Murber Inc. The fair market value of the Murber shares is $2 million. The adjusted cost base ("ACB") and paid-up capital ("PUC") of the shares is assumed to be nil.

(a) Criss-Cross Arrangements

Under an insured criss-cross arrangement, Murray would own a disability buy-out policy on Bertha, and vice versa. The premium would be a non-deductible expense to the shareholders and be funded with after-tax income. Depending upon the policy terms, the disability proceeds could be paid as a lump sum, on an instalment basis, or a combination of the two.

If Murray were to become disabled, for example, Bertha would purchase his shares for their fair market value under the terms of their shareholders agreement. On the sale, Murray would realize a capital gain in the amount by which the sale price ($1 million) exceeded the ACB (nil). One-half of the capital gain ($500,000) would be taxable. Assuming a marginal tax rate of 46%, Murray would incur a tax liability of $230,000, leaving him with $770,000 after tax.

Murray's tax liability would be reduced if the Murber shares qualified for the $750,000 capital gains exemption, assuming it had not been fully utilized by Murray during his lifetime. If the entire $750,000 exemption were available, it would reduce Murray's tax liability by approximately $172,500.

If any portion of the purchase price is payable over time, Murray can claim a reserve for amounts due in a later year. This would allow him to spread out his tax liability over a maximum of five years.

Bertha would have an increase in the ACB of her shares equal to the $1 million purchase price. The fair market value of her shares would increase to $2 million, leaving her with the same unrealized gain ($1 million) that she had prior to the purchase of Murray's shares.

(b) Redemption Arrangements

If the Murber Inc. shareholders agreement provided for shares to be redeemed (i.e., purchased by the corporation) on a shareholder's disability, the corporation would be the owner and beneficiary of the disability buyout policies. Murber would receive the proceeds tax-free, and would use the proceeds as funding for the payment of the redemption price.

As previously noted, proceeds from a disability buy-out policy cannot be credited to a corporation's CDA. For this reason, the proceeds may not be distributed on a tax-free basis. The tax consequences would be as follows:

- On the redemption of his shares, Murray would be deemed to receive a taxable dividend in the amount by which the redemption proceeds ($1 million) exceeded the PUC of the shares (nil). Tax on this dividend would approximate $310,000. This compares to a maximum of $230,000 payable by Murray under a criss-cross arrangement.

- Tax would be payable in full in the year the shares were redeemed, even if a portion of the proceeds were not payable until later years. This is in contrast to the previous example, where the capital gains reserve was available.

- In calculating Murray's capital gain or loss from the redemption of his shares, his proceeds of disposition ($1 million) would be reduced by the amount of any deemed dividend received on the redemption (also $1 million). This means that his deemed proceeds and his ACB would both be nil, resulting in no capital gain or loss. Therefore, even if the capital gains exemption would otherwise be available, it would be of no benefit to Murray.

- Bertha would have no increase in the ACB of her shares, but her shares would now reflect the corporation's total fair market value of $2 million. Her potential income tax exposure has therefore doubled, even though Murray has paid tax on the redemption of his shares. This creates the likelihood of double taxation when Bertha ultimately disposes of her shares.

In summary, a redemption arrangement means that Murray will incur significantly more income tax than would be payable under a criss-cross arrangement. It causes the tax-free nature of the disability proceeds to be negated, because no CDA credit is available. It provides no reserve for proceeds payable in a later year and does not allow for access to the capital gains exemption. Finally, it creates the likelihood of double taxation.

As a result, in most cases, the criss-cross method is by far the more attractive of the two options.

(c) Holding Companies

If Murray and Bertha held their Murber Inc. shares through holding companies ("Murray Co." and "Bertha Co."), this would introduce a new set of potential income tax implications, a full description of which are beyond the scope of this chapter. Some brief observations can be made, however:

- A criss-cross arrangement would involve Murray Co. being the owner and beneficiary of a disability buy-out policy on Bertha, and vice versa. On Murray's disability, Bertha Co. would use the proceeds to purchase the Murber shares owned by Murray Co. This would result in a capital gain to Murray Co.

- A redemption arrangement would create a dividend to Murray Co. on the redemption of its Murber shares, which might qualify as a tax-free intercorporate dividend. In some cases, however, the *Income Tax Act* treats an intercorporate dividend as a capital gain, with negative income tax consequences. Careful tax planning is a must.

The involvement of holding companies creates additional tax planning opportunities and pitfalls. In many such cases, it may be advisable to have a "hybrid" form of agreement under which shares owned by the disabled party's holding company can either be sold to the survivor's holding company or be redeemed by the operating company.

Possible Role of Critical Illness Insurance

In some cases, it will be desirable to combine a disability buy-out plan with critical illness. For further details, see the comments later in this chapter.

2. Critical Illness Insurance: Income Tax and Marketing Considerations

In recent years, critical illness insurance has taken an increasingly prominent position in the Canadian insurance marketplace. The growing popularity of the product, its wide array of policy features, and its use in more sophisticated planning situations have led to inevitable questions regarding the taxation of its premiums and proceeds. In this regard, product innovation is outpacing legislative change by a large margin, which means that there are far more "grey areas" than hard and fast rules in the area of critical illness taxation.

This section will review tax issues and recent developments in greater detail and will also consider the tax treatment of the refund of premium ("ROP") feature found in many contracts.

Categorizing Critical Illness Insurance for Tax Purposes

The starting point for analyzing the taxation of critical illness insurance is to determine whether it qualifies as a "life insurance policy" for the purposes of the *Income Tax Act.* If so, it would be subject to the various tax rules that apply to life insurance policies. Unfortunately, the definition of "life insurance policy" in the Act is not helpful. The Act provides only that this term includes annuity contracts and segregated fund policies. The word "includes" suggests that other types of contracts could also fall within this definition. The most obvious example of another such contract is a conventional life insurance policy.

This question becomes more complicated where the critical illness contract provides certain benefits, such as a ROP feature, that are paid on the policyholder's death.

In determining how a critical illness policy would be categorized for taxation purposes, it is important to look at common usage in the insurance industry and under insurance law. On that analysis, the likely answer is that a critical illness policy does not constitute life insurance, as its central purpose is to provide a benefit on the occurrence of an illness, rather than on death.

The following commentary assumes that critical illness policies will not be treated by the CRA as life insurance policies for purposes of the Act.

Tax Treatment of Premiums

In most cases, premiums paid under a critical illness policy will not be deductible for income tax purposes. The following commentary considers the deductibility of critical illness insurance premiums in a variety of circumstances. The commentary under this heading refers only to premiums for the base policy, not to any premium in respect of the ROP feature.

(a) Personally-Owned Policies

Critical illness premiums paid by an individual will be considered personal or living expenses and will not be deductible for income tax purposes. Neither will premiums qualify as medical expenses for the purposes of the medical expense tax credit. This credit is available for premiums paid under a private health services plan ("PHSP"). However, in order to qualify as a PHSP, a plan must be used for medical and/or hospital expenses. No such limitation exists regarding critical illness benefits and, as such, a critical illness policy will not qualify as a PHSP.

(b) Corporate Key Person Policies

A corporation might acquire a critical illness policy on a key employee or shareholder as a means of providing a financial cushion should that person become lost to the business as the result of an insured illness. This has become the most common role for individual critical illness policies in the business market, although premiums paid by the corporation would not be tax-deductible. "Grouped critical illness", as discussed below, has also become very popular in the employee benefit field.

A critical illness policy might also be used to help fund the purchase and sale of the individual's shares in the event of illness, although these policies have limitations in this regard. Critical illness insurance for buy/sell purposes is discussed in greater detail below.

(c) Collateral Security

Premium deductibility is less clear in the case of a critical illness policy being assigned as collateral for a business loan. The Act expressly contemplates a life insurance policy being assigned for this purpose, and provides a level of deductibility where certain stipulated conditions are met. No such rules exist for critical illness premiums. While there may be an argument that critical illness premiums are deductible in this situation as an expense of borrowing money, the CRA is unlikely to agree, and the *Guertin* case, previously discussed in Chapter 4, may be authority that deductibility is not available.

(d) Premiums Paid by Employer for Employees: Opportunities for "Grouped CI"

Premiums paid by an employer under an employee-owned critical illness policy, which is set up as a "stand alone" individual plan, should be deductible by the employer as a cost of doing business. The amount of the premium will be included in the employee's income as a taxable benefit, but proceeds would be tax-free to the employee. As described below, however, policies set up on a grouped basis may have more advantages.

An employer might also purchase critical illness policies on the lives of a group of employees. Each insured employee would be beneficiary of the policy on his or her life. As above, these premiums should be deductible to the employer. However, a good argument exists for this arrangement to be considered a "group sickness or accident insurance plan", in which case no taxable benefit would be incurred by the employees for premiums paid by the employer. Furthermore, the employee would not be taxed on any benefits received in the form of a lump sum. If this argument can be sustained with the CRA, this represents a significant opportunity for insurance advisors.

Different considerations apply where the employee under one of the above arrangements is also a shareholder of the corporation in question. See the discussion immediately below.

(e) Premiums Paid by Corporation for Shareholders

If a corporation provides critical illness insurance for its shareholders, or where it subsidizes the payment of premiums under policies owned by the shareholders, it is necessary to determine whether the resulting taxable benefit is one arising from the individual's status as a shareholder or, where applicable, as an employee of the corporation. A tax deduction to the corporation would be available only if the benefit was categorized as one from employment. An expense incurred by a corporation for the benefit of a shareholder is not considered a cost of doing business and is therefore not deductible.

In addition, as described above, where the critical illness coverage is provided as part of a group sickness or accident insurance plan, no taxable benefit will arise regarding premiums paid by the corporation if the benefit is one from employment. No such favourable treatment exists where this is considered a shareholder benefit.

The following are some guidelines for determining whether or not a particular benefit is an employee or shareholder benefit:

- Where a corporation provides a benefit to shareholder-employees that it does not provide to other employees, the CRA will presume that the benefit is received as a result of the individual's shareholdings.

- Where the benefit is received by all employees, or by an identifiable group of employees (e.g., the management team) irrespective of whether or not they are shareholders, a strong case exists for the benefit being one from employment.

- Where all employees are also shareholders, the payment of premiums by the corporation should qualify as a benefit from employment as long as the critical illness plans can be seen as part of a reasonable compensation package, i.e., one that would be offered to a similar group of non-shareholder executives.

In all cases, it will be a question of fact as to whether the payment of critical illness premiums in the above circumstances constitutes a shareholder or an employment benefit.

Taxation of Benefits

(a) Personally-Owned Policies

In order to subject critical illness benefits to taxation, the CRA would have to establish that the proceeds represented income from a source such as employment, property, or business. On this analysis, it is unlikely that the CRA would succeed in arguing that critical illness benefits were taxable. In fact, it is doubtful that the Department would attempt to make such an argument. It is more likely that it would adopt the same position as that which has long applied to personally-owned disability plans, i.e., that premiums paid for such plans are non-deductible personal expenses and therefore any resulting benefits should be tax-free.

(b) Corporate-Owned Policies

Similarly, critical illness benefits paid to a corporation should be tax-free on the basis that premiums are non-deductible. No credit to the corporation's CDA is available. Therefore, while a corporation might receive benefits on a tax-free basis, in most cases it would be unable to distribute the proceeds to its shareholders except in the traditional, taxable manner (salary or dividends).

Taxation of Refund of Premium

(a) Single Ownership

For an additional premium, the owner of a critical illness policy may purchase a ROP benefit. Depending upon the policy terms, the ROP might be payable if the policyholder died, or reached a certain age, without having claimed critical illness benefits. The treatment of ROP benefits is perhaps the most uncertain of all the questions concerning critical illness taxation.

Consider the following example:

> *Annika is a 45-year-old non-smoker who has a $100,000 critical illness policy under which the base annual policy premium is $966 per year and the premium for the ROP rider is $441. Her total annual premium, including a $75 policy fee, is $1,482. Her refund at age 75, if she is eligible, would be $44,460 (30 years multiplied by $1,482).*
>
> *Concern has been raised that the CRA would attempt to tax the roughly $31,000 difference between the ROP benefit ($44,460) and the amount of ROP premium paid (30 multiplied by $441 = $13,230).*

This amount could be taxed, so the argument goes, either as income from an investment contract or as a capital gain. Many arguments exist to the contrary, including the following:

- Arguably, the ROP benefit is itself insurance, as it is merely a contingent benefit, and should be tax-free in the same manner as the base policy proceeds.

- Insurance in general is not considered to be capital property, i.e., property that is subject to a capital gain or loss on disposition.

- The ROP benefit does not contain the essential attributes of an investment contract, such as the payment of interest, which would normally be associated with that type of instrument.

It is hoped that the latter arguments would prevail. Some comfort may be taken from a technical interpretation given by the CRA regarding a ROP benefit under a disability policy. In that case, the CRA stated that the benefit was simply the refund of a personal expense and was non-taxable. This opinion is, of course, not binding and does not necessarily represent departmental policy regarding disability or critical illness policies.

(b) Shared Ownership

Yet another layer of complexity is added where ownership of the base policy and ROP feature is shared between a corporation and a shareholder or employee. For example, the corporation may be owner and beneficiary of the base policy and the individual could own and pay for the ROP. It is possible that the CRA would attempt to tax, as a shareholder or employee benefit, the difference between the individual's cost and any benefits paid under the ROP. While arguments may exist that such benefits should be non-taxable (see discussion above), the CRA might argue that the "profit" made by the individual arose directly from his or her status as a shareholder or employee. If the CRA were successful in that argument, the individual would be taxable.

Commentary on Income Tax Issues

Critical illness insurance will continue to be a significant component of the Canadian market. There is good reason for confidence that critical illness benefits will be tax-free. The taxation of ROP benefits is less clear, but strong arguments also exist for treating these benefits as tax-free. The insurance industry is attempting to clarify all the rules governing the tax treatment of CI products, and is working on a submission to the federal government on this subject. Until further clarification is received, it is wise to make sure your client and advisors are aware of the current ambiguity in the tax laws. Unfortunately, the industry has been awaiting clarification for many years and through several editions of this book.

Critical Illness Insurance as Buy/Sell Funding

As already discussed, shareholders agreements typically provide for the purchase and sale of shares on a shareholder's death or disability. They may also provide for a purchase and sale of shares upon the occurrence of a critical illness.

There is a question, however, as to whether critical illness is always an appropriate "triggering event" in a shareholders agreement. For example, a shareholder may have a mild heart attack, or incur a treatable form of cancer, and have a full recovery. In such a case, critical illness benefits may be paid, but it may not be appropriate to require a sale of his or her shares at that time since the individual may be fully able to continue to work. The situation is therefore not as clear as in the case of death or permanent disability, where a purchase and sale of shares is generally appropriate.

Nonetheless, there will be circumstances where the onset of a critical illness triggers a desire on the part of the affected shareholder to sell his or her shares. In such a case, critical illness insurance could provide significant financial help to the purchasing shareholder(s).

In consideration of the above issues, a shareholders agreement could be designed to provide for the purchase and sale of shares in the event that an insured critical illness arose. The shareholder suffering the illness would have a given period of time, say six months, to decide whether or not a sale would take place. This would give the shareholder sufficient time to determine whether the illness was serious enough to warrant a sale.

Possible buy/sell structures involving critical illness insurance, and related income tax issues, mirror those involving disability buy-out. See the examples earlier in this chapter.

(a) Use of a Trust Arrangement

In a cross-purchase arrangement, it may be advantageous to hold the critical illness proceeds in a trust for the benefit of the shareholders. The shareholders would pay the critical illness premiums from their own after-tax dollars. After the onset of a critical illness, the critically ill shareholder could decide whether or not to sell the shares, as described above. If he or she decided to sell, the proceeds would be distributed to the purchaser and used to finance the purchase. If not, the proceeds could be paid to the critically ill shareholder as an "ordinary" critical illness benefit.

The advantage of the trust arrangement is that it would not require a taxable distribution of the proceeds from the corporation. The proceeds would be received and distributed tax-free by the trust. The selling shareholder would obtain capital gains treatment, which is generally preferred over the dividend treatment that applies on a share redemption. The purchasing shareholder would obtain an increase in the ACB of his or her shares.

(b) Combining Critical Illness and Disability Buy-Out

In many cases, the amount of critical illness and/or disability buy-out insurance will be relatively modest in relation to share value. For example, if two shareholders own a corporation worth $6 million, it is unlikely that the corporation would acquire $3 million of critical illness insurance on each life as funding for an optional purchase and sale. In fact, under current underwriting practices at least, it is unlikely that an insurance company would underwrite such a high level of critical illness or disability buy-out insurance. Given these considerations, where a sale did take place, the insurance proceeds would in many cases represent only a down payment of the purchase price, with the balance being payable over a period of years.

In these circumstances, it may be appropriate to combine the two types of insurance within a shareholders agreement. For example, the agreement might provide for a funded disability buy-out using one of the methods described earlier in this chapter. The agreement could also provide that, if the event that caused the disability benefit to be paid was also an insured illness under the critical illness policy, the critical illness proceeds would be used to supplement the disability buy-out proceeds.

References

Income Tax Act (Canada)

Subsection 6(1) — employee benefits

Subsection 15(1) — shareholder benefits

Paragraph 20(1)(e.2) — deduction for premiums on life insurance used as collateral

Section 38 — taxable capital gains and allowable capital losses

Subparagraph 40(1)(a)(iii) — capital gains reserve

Section 54 — paragraph (j) of definition of "proceeds of disposition" — exclusion for amount of deemed dividend on redemption of shares

Subsection 55(2) — intercorporate dividends treated as capital gain

Subsection 84(3) — deemed dividend on redemption of shares

Subsection 89(1) — definition of "capital dividend account"

Section 110.6 — capital gains exemption

Subsection 112(1) — intercorporate dividends

Subsection 138(12) — definition of "life insurance policy"

Industry Publication

Taxing Issues Surrounding Critical Illness Insurance, published by the Conference for Advanced Life Underwriting, December 2002

Case Law

The Queen v. Antoine Guertin Lteé, 1988 DTC 6126 (F.C.A.)

Chapter 13

The *Family Law Act* (Ontario)

1. The *Family Law Act* (Ontario)

With the passage of the *Family Law Act* (the "FLA") in 1986, family law became, for the first time, an important consideration in estate planning in Ontario. This chapter will review some important provisions of the FLA regarding estate planning, and will also consider some important life insurance marketing strategies that it introduced. Provincial matrimonial laws vary, of course, so the rules that apply outside of Ontario are beyond the scope of this chapter.

Some Misconceptions

One way to explain the FLA is to discuss what it does not do:

- The part of the FLA that deals with the division of matrimonial property does not apply to common-law spouses. It deals only with legally married couples of the same or opposite sex. A common-law spouse may be required to pay support to the other under certain circumstances, but the concept of "net family property", described below, does not apply to them.

261

- The FLA does not confer ownership rights on a spouse. People frequently assume that, if there is a marriage breakdown, "my spouse will get half of everything". This is not necessarily true. The FLA provides that, with certain exceptions, spouses are entitled to share equally in the value of property acquired during marriage. In simple terms, this involves a calculation of the value of property owned by each spouse as of the date of marriage, and another similar calculation at the end of the marriage (this effectively exempts from the family law "pot" the value of property owned prior to marriage). This value is referred to as "net family property", and if one spouse's total is higher than the other's, the one with the lower total is entitled to a payment, called an equalization payment, to bring the totals even. This payment can be in the form of cash or other property and is in addition to any support or alimony which might be ordered.

- The FLA does not just apply on marriage breakdown, but can also apply on death. For example, if a surviving spouse receives less from the deceased's will than would have been received as an equalization payment on marriage breakdown, the survivor has a choice. He or she can decide, within six months' time, either to accept the gifts provided under the will, or to drag the deceased's will into court and claim an equalization payment instead. (There is a life insurance solution to this situation which is described later.) Thus, the FLA is far more important from an estate planning point of view than the legislation it replaced, which dealt only with marriage breakdown.

Some Exceptions

As stated earlier, the value of property owned on the date of marriage is exempt from division under the FLA; however, there is one very important exception to this rule. If one spouse owns a home on the date of marriage, which thereafter becomes a "matrimonial home", the value of that home is included in the calculation. And as will be seen below, this is not the only situation where the matrimonial home is given special treatment.

In addition, there are a number of very important exclusions from net family property, including:

- *Gifts received from a third party during marriage* — If a spouse receives shares of a public company, for example, either under someone's will or during that person's lifetime, the shares (including increases in value) will not be included in net family property. If the same gift is received before marriage, increases in value from the date of marriage will be included in net family property.

- *Damages for personal injuries* — Damages for personal injuries, nervous shock, mental distress, or for loss of guidance, care, and companionship are excluded from net family property.

- *Income from the above if the person making the gift says that it is to be excluded* — This peculiar provision would exclude dividends paid on the above shares as long as the testator's will made statement to that effect (which wills made prior to 1986 rarely do). If the gift was made during the donor's lifetime, a written statement accompanying the gift would be necessary for this purpose.

- *Life insurance proceeds received as a consequence of the death of the life-insured* — As a general rule, the CSV of a life insurance policy owned by a spouse (at the time of separation, for example) will be included in his or her net family property like any other asset, unless it falls under one of the exceptions. (For example, if the individual received the policy after the date of marriage as a gift from a third party, it will be excluded.) The commuted value of an annuity, or the value of a segregated fund contract, would be subject to the same rules. However, proceeds payable on the death of the life insured, whether received before or during marriage, are excluded. Neither the life-insured nor the beneficiary is required to include the proceeds in net family property. This rule applies to any policy that is considered life insurance within the meaning of the *Insurance Act (Ontario)*. Thus it applies to death benefits paid under annuities, segregated funds and conventional life insurance policies.

- *Property (other than a matrimonial home) into which any of the above four items can be traced* — If, for example, a person uses life insurance proceeds, or a post-marriage gift from a third person, to buy a house for himself and his or her spouse, the value of the home will be included in net family property. The same would apply if the proceeds were used to pay down the mortgage on a matrimonial home. On the other hand, if the proceeds were deposited into an investment account in the recipient's name alone, an exclusion would be available. In this regard, it is important to note that a couple may have more than one matrimonial home (e.g., home and cottage).

- *Property excluded by domestic contract* — The FLA allows spouses to contract out of virtually all of its terms. A domestic contract can be executed before, during, or at the end of a marriage. Proper formalities are essential here, including independent legal advice, and full financial disclosure.

Some Marketing Applications

The following is a brief list of marketing opportunities presented by the FLA, some of which have been briefly referred to above:

- The exclusion of life insurance proceeds from net family property can have varied applications, bearing in mind that such proceeds will be excluded no matter when they are received (unlike other gifts, which are excluded only when received after marriage). The advantages of naming your child as beneficiary of an insurance policy are obvious. Clients in receipt of death benefits should understand the advantages of keeping them invested separately from other assets.

- The tracing provisions present interesting opportunities in buy/sell situations. If a shareholders agreement is funded with personally-owned insurance, proceeds received by the surviving shareholder would be excluded from his or her net family property, as would the shares purchased with those proceeds. (This is inapplicable in most corporate-owned situations because the insurance is received by the corporation, not by the individual shareholders.)

- The tracing rules should be considered whenever a death claim is paid to a beneficiary in Ontario, whether or not the proceeds are being used to fund a buy/sell agreement. Where appropriate, clients should be advised to seek legal advice in order to ensure that their rights under the FLA are protected.

- A marketing opportunity that predates the FLA is the use of life insurance to secure the obligations of a spouse's estate to continue support payments after the spouse's death. The purchase of insurance for these purposes is frequently court-ordered.

One final opportunity for life insurance relates to the election, noted above, that may be made by a surviving spouse within six months of the death of his or her spouse. If the survivor makes this election, he or she will receive an equalization payment rather than whatever would have been received under the deceased's will or the rules of intestacy. This could arise in a number of common planning situations: a business owner might leave shares of the family business to an adult child; someone married for the second (or third or fourth) time might leave significant assets to children from prior marriages; or a spouse might leave the survivor with an income interest in property rather than giving him or her outright ownership of the property. In all of these cases, absent a domestic contract under which the spouses agreed to some form of property distribution, the survivor might challenge the deceased's will and apply to a court for an equalization payment. The FLA provides that, where a spouse elects to receive an equalization payment, the following amounts will be credited against his or her entitlement:

- The proceeds of a life insurance policy owned by the deceased on his or her own life under which the survivor was beneficiary. Again, life insurance for these purposes is as broadly defined in the *Insurance Act (Ontario)*. This also includes group insurance on the deceased's life.

- Lump-sum payments provided under pension plans or similar plans (including RRSPs).

Insurance professionals should be alert to situations where an individual may be leaving the bulk of his or her estate to someone other than the surviving spouse. This can often be gleaned from a review of the client's will. If there is no domestic contract governing the situation, the simplest method of avoiding a dispute after the client's death may be to have the client acquire enough insurance, payable to the spouse, so that a court application would be unnecessary.

References

Family Law Act (Ontario)

Subsection 4(1) — definition of "net family property"

Subsection 4(2) — property excluded from net family property

Subsection 5(2) — equalization of net family property on death

Subsections 6(1) and (2) — election by surviving spouse to receive equalization payment

Subsection 6(6) — credit against equalization payment to surviving spouse

TOPICAL INDEX

267